BUSHIDO

THE WAY OF THE WARRIOR

BUSHIDO

THE WAY OF THE WARRIOR

A New Perspective on the Japanese Military Tradition

JOHN NEWMAN

GALLERY BOOKS
An imprint of W.H. Smith Publishers Inc.
112 Madison Avenue
New York, New York 10016

Published by Gallery Books
A Division of W H Smith Publishers Inc.
112 Madison Avenue
New York, New York 10016

Produced by
Brompton Books Corp.
15 Sherwood Place
Greenwich, CT 06830

Copyright © 1989 Brompton Books Corp.

ISBN 0-8317-1031-4

Printed in Hong Kong

10 9 8 7 6 5 4 3 2 1

Page 1: Retainers of General Takeda Shingen putting on their armor; each figure depicts a different stage of the process.

Pages 2-3: A column of spearmen and musketeers. Note that the gun muzzles are covered with fabric to protect them from rough weather.

Page 4: In peacetime samurai practised the tea ceremony in order to develop a calm mind. Before a battle it was performed to demonstrate complete self-possession.

Page 5: A method of self-defense from the formal sitting position. The samurai on the left has just attempted to use his sword but has been pulled in and paralyzed before he can make a cut.

Contents

Introduction

Below: Various family emblems which would have been worn on armor and displayed on flags in battle.

Right: Tomoe, a woman warrior of the Genji period (cAD 1000). Samurai women were expected to practise the martial arts and invariably carried a weapon.

Far right: Commodore Matthew Perry (US Navy) commanded the 'Black Ships,' as the Japanese called his fleet, which sailed to Japan in 1853 to negotiate using the island as a refueling post between San Francisco and Shanghai for the newly formed Pacific Mail Steamship Company. A long nose and fierce expression were characteristic of the Japanese Tengu Demon to which foreigners were compared.

Bushido means the Way of the Bushi, the professional warriors of Japan who arose as a distinct class in the twelfth century. Subsequently they successfully united Japan against Kublai Khan's Mongol invasion forces at the end of the thirteenth century but, from this high point, the dominance of the class was undermined by continuous inter-clan fighting, which finally ended in 1600 following the new national unification undertaken by the Tokugawa family. During most of this time, the emperor was usually little more than a figurehead, though officially revered. The Bushi (or samurai, as they came to be known) were the *de facto* ruling class and, as such, had to develop their administrative skills — they had always been literate, and indeed poetic. Under their guidance peace was successfully kept for some 250 years, with Japan largely isolated from the rest of the world. Then, in 1853, Western navies forcefully opened Japan to foreign influence. Between 1865 and 1867 there was a successful revolt against the Tokugawa shogunate led by disaffected samurai, and the Emperor Meiji was installed as the new ruler. The country was modernized, with some parliamentary institutions established along Western lines, and the samurai class abolished. The process was, however, largely carried out by ex-samurai, who proved remarkably flexible in adapting to the new situation.

Bushido, the Way of the Warrior, was supposed to be primarily concerned with the inner spirit of the samurai. The term itself is not particularly ancient; originally it was the Way of the Bow and Horse, having much in common with the Western idea of chivalry. Bushido was an attempt to inculcate the men of power with a sense of responsibility and kindness, as well as physical and moral courage. In Western Europe

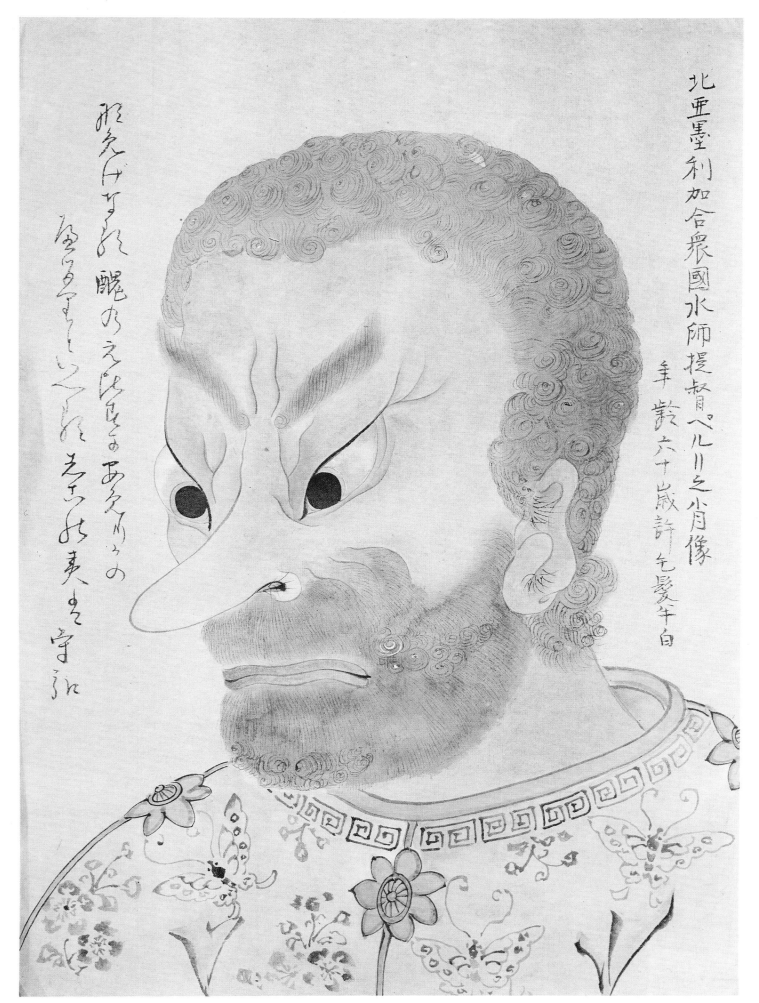

Above: The medieval Japanese were never great sailors and this European warship depicted in a Hokkei print must have made them realize their naval impotence.

chivalry left a legacy based on consideration for the weak backed by moral courage: it became part of the code of the gentleman which, in its turn, passed away, though leaving a certain general respect for courage, honesty and kindness. Bushido too has left a legacy – part of this can be seen on modern Japanese television, which every weekend at peak viewing times has hour-long historical dramas depicting heroic, posturing and sword-wielding samurai. These programs are watched by both young and old, men and women, with keen interest; they are primarily entertainments, but they have continued for so many years that there is no doubt that they have a much deeper significance.

It must be admitted that the centuries of warrior rule in Japan, despite the many brutalities and wholesale massacres that took place (all paralleled by similar events in Europe), were singularly successful in a number of fields. Japanese rulers, with the active support of the population, repeatedly showed themselves eager to learn and then improve upon what they had learnt. They acquired the basics of writing from neighboring China, but levels of literacy in Japan over the centuries have generally surpassed those of China. Nor was the provision of education solely confined to men: the outstanding position achieved by women in Japanese literature is perhaps unique in the world's history. Warriors too were among the foremost writers and poets. Remarkably, as we shall see, even Japanese peasants could quote and compose verses in the Middle Ages.

During the 250 or so years of peace from the emergence of the Tokugawa shogunate to the arrival of Commodore Perry in 1853, members of the ruling class were paid fixed salaries, which meant that many of them were relatively poor. Undoubtedly there was some corruption but officials could not in general amass huge personal fortunes or live in conspicuous luxury. This lack of venality in the administrative class promoted an austere lifestyle which prevented its members from neglecting their duties. The samurai were also patrons of the arts, which in Japan flourished in forms unknown elsewhere. When Japan was finally opened up to foreign influence in the middle of the nineteenth century, the Western nations, confronted by Japanese arts such as ivory carving in miniature, could not easily adopt their usual pose of dismissive superiority. Japanese today are aware that their history shows a by-no-means inferior record and some of them perhaps are turning to the past in search of new inspiration for a national identity.

Part of this new surge of interest in the past consists of attempts to rediscover the moral and spiritual basis of Bushido. In fact it was, at least initially, not much more than a basic code of decency and good conduct. Here are a few typical maxims from the famous *Family Instructions* (*kakun*) of Hojo Shigetoki, written for his son Nagatoki who, at the age of 18, became the shogun's deputy at Kyoto in 1247. Shigetoki's instructions consist mainly of advice on practical problems which the young officer might come up against – professional advice rather than moral teachings. The first article advocates:

Be fearful of Gods and Buddhas, and show unquestioning obedience to lord and parent.

Be fully aware of the relation of cause and effect (*karma*) and consider the result of your actions for future generations.

Be cautious in your relations with others and always avoid the company of useless people.

In all things be generous, and deserve the praise of others.

Be firm and never show cowardice.

Be diligent in the practice of the military arts.

Be honest in all dealings, showing sympathy to the poor and weak.

The last statement is about religious morality as much as the ethics of a warrior class. In his *Family Instructions*, Shigetoki lays no special emphasis on duty to a feudal superior, the claims of a parent being put upon the same level as the claims of a master in the secular sphere. There are more than 40 of these brief articles, and Shigetoki consistently stresses ways in which a young leader can make a good impression on his colleagues and the men under him. Much attention is also paid to social etiquette, no doubt because Nagatoki had to mix with members of the court at Kyoto whose standards of behavior were very severe. Questions of courage, loyalty and obedience are not gone into; they are taken for granted. Indeed, it is manners rather than morals that are discussed at great length.

Also included in the first article is advice on the treatment of social inferiors by a high-ranking warrior. As the shogun's deputy, Nagatoki would have to keep the young warriors in order. On this matter Shigetoki could speak with some authority, having spent many years in military posts both in war and peace. These are a few of his recommendations:

The men under your command must be carefully chosen.

Do not employ 'difficult' men.

If you employ men who, however loyal, are wanting in intelligence, do not trust them with important duties: rely on older, more experienced men.

If in doubt ask me, Shigetoki.

When dealing with subordinates do not differentiate between good and no-good. Use the same kind of language, give the same kind of treatment. In this way you will get the best from the worst.

Do not lose sight of the distinction between a good character and bad character, between capable and incapable.

Be fair, but do not forget the difference between men who are useful and those who are not.

Remember that the key to discipline is fair treatment in rewards and punishments.

Young soldiers and others occasionally commit small misdeeds. Make allowances for this if their conduct is usually good.

Do not be careless or negligent in the presence of subordinates, especially of older men. Therefore you must not spit, snuffle or lounge about on a chest with your legs dangling.

Preserve your dignity. If you behave rudely, they will tell their families and the gossip will spread.

There will be times when a commander has to exercise his power of deciding questions of life and death. Since human life is at stake you must give careful thought to your actions.

Never kill or wound a man in anger, however great the provocation. It would be better to get somebody else to administer the proper punishment.

Decisions made in haste before your feelings are calm can only lead to remorse. Close your eyes and reflect carefully when you have a difficult decision to make.

Remember that there must be another side to an accusation.

But the key to all that Shigetoki wrote is provided by a simple rule: 'The warrior must always bear in mind his moral duty. A good heart and the faith of a warrior are like the two wheels of a carriage.' This, then, was the very heart of Bushido, the Way of the Warrior.

Below: The first Japanese ambassador to Europe. Following the arrival of Perry, the Japanese moved on to the world stage. Close links developed with several Western European nations which provided technological expertise.

The Earliest Samurai

It is difficult to appreciate fully the importance of the great Fujiwara clan in Japanese history. The rise to power of the Fujiwara in the mid-ninth century both coincided with, and was partially responsible for, the evolution of Japan's almost unique system of government in which full sovereign power was exercised by regents on a hereditary basis on behalf of cloistered or juvenile emperors; as such it has great bearing both on later military history and the country today.

There were several branches of the Fujiwara clan, but by dint of usurpation within the clan itself, and sometimes by merciless disposal of powerful rivals in other clans, the northern branch had achieved a dominant position by the mid-ninth century. This was a time when the external threat to Japan was minimal: there were no overseas adventures, the threat from the mainland had ceased to exist in any real sense, and the main task facing the Fujiwara was the subduing of the Ainu, an indigenous tribe already driven back far to the north and east of Japan. Thus, military matters were of little apparent concern to the general population; in any case the peasants in all the provinces of Japan were forced to allow the warlords' armies to sweep across the land in pursuance of their battle aims. The court at Kyoto was in the eighth and ninth centuries a place of romance, poetry and, above all, political machinations.

In this latter sphere of court life the Fujiwara clan was paramount from the time of Yoshifusa, who married a daughter of Emperor Saga in 826 and who, after a series of palace intrigues, was able to install his nephew Michiyasu first as crown prince and then as emperor on the death of Emperor Nimmyo in 850. Yoshifusa further strengthened his position by marrying off his own daughter, Akiko, to the emperor, by whom she had a son in 850. This son was nominated as the legitimate successor some months later, against the emperor's wishes. This incident shows how powerful the Fujiwara had already become by virtue of their matrimonial links to the crown. Indeed, at this time of comparative peace, it was a relationship to the emperor by marriage which counted for more than anything else in terms of power at court. On the death of his son-in-law, Emperor Montoku, Yoshifusa had a grandson only nine years old, and had himself declared regent (*sessho*) to the child-emperor. When the child reached adulthood in 866 Yoshifusa had himself invested with the formal title of regent by imperial decree, and thus continued in power despite there being an adult male emperor on the throne. This emperor, Seiwa, was the first child-emperor of Japan and the first male to rule under non-imperial domination. In the next 200 years there were 15 emperors and their consorts were invariably Fujiwara women. Seven of the emperors were children when they ascended the throne and eight abdicated, either of their own volition or under Fujiwara pressure, when they reached majority or not long afterward. Thus every emperor at this time had a Fujiwara maternal grandfather, a Fujiwara father-in-law and, very often, at least one Fujiwara son-in-law.

It is often said that the Fujiwara regime was a more just and moral one than any other in Japanese history. There is some reason to accept this view. Certainly banishment rather than death was the favored punishment for the enemies of the Fujiwara. And, of course, the installation of Fujiwara children as emperors was a surer way of maintaining power than any military action or removal of political opponents could ever have been. It does appear from the surviving records of the time that the Fujiwara regents were motivated more by a conservative ideology of maintaining the emperor and ensuring stable government rather than by any thoughts of subduing barbarians or engaging in conquest. There was little attempt at conquest during the Fujiwara years, and the defeat of the 'barbarian' Ainu in the north was left to provincial warlords who did not figure at court and whose lack of any close ties to the emperor through marriage made them politically insignificant.

Thus was the power of the Fujiwara

Far left: A stylized *Kabuki* poster of a samurai. The sharply rising eyebrows are characteristic of a hero.

established in the land. But their domination of the court and succession was to be threatened by military action rather than by any political difficulties, which the Fujiwara had already shown themselves adept at resolving in their favor. One of the early tests for the Fujiwara came in 877 with the accession of Emperor Yozei. The clan was now under the domination of Mototsune, Yoshifusa's nephew and adopted son. Emperor Yozei was nine years old when his father Seiwa abdicated and became a monk, and even at this early age showed signs of sadistic mental disturbance. As Yozei grew older one of his favorite pastimes was forcing his subjects to climb trees so that he could shoot them down as if they were sparrows. He seems also to have found pleasure in kidnapping girls, tying them up with lute strings, throwing them into ponds and watching them drown. Mototsune was moved to take the then unprecedented step of pressurizing Yozei to abdicate at the early age of 17. Yozei's successor was middle-aged and completely under Mototsune's power. By 914 Mototsune's younger son, Tadahira, had been declared civil dictator (kampaku), with Tadahira's own two sons holding the two most senior ministerial posts at court. Thus all the great offices of state were held by a single family for the first time.

This was the high point of the Fujiwara domination of the Kyoto court, but the beginning of the end could already be seen as the first military threats were beginning to appear on the horizon. Previously the court at Kyoto had seen fit largely to ignore the plunderings and piracy that took place far from its walls in the east, south and southwest of the country. Tadahira was no exception in this, and appears to have been a man who immersed himself in palace ritual and the reading of signs and portents. But even he was forced to take steps to levy troops when word came from the south of large-scale pirate activity in the Inland Sea. In 934 another Fujiwara, Sumitomo, was sent from Kyoto at the head of an expeditionary force to subdue the pirates, but on the accomplishment of his mission, instead of returning to Kyoto, he set himself up as a pirate chief on his own account.

Sumitomo not only carried out raids and plundered merchant ships, he also took over the government house at Tosa, burnt down the Imperial Mint, and had at one time 1500 ships under his command. The Kyoto court took no action other than sending him a letter of warning, so remote were the Fujiwara courtiers from events in the rest of the country. For over five years, until 940, Kyoto had no control over the Inland Sea. Indeed the example of Sumitomo seems to have been followed by other provincial warlords who also felt that they too could set up their own fiefdoms with impunity so long as they were far enough away from Kyoto. It was not until 940 that the Kyoto authorities appointed an arresting officer (tsuibushi) to head an expedition to bring Sumitomo to heel. Even then it is likely that Sumitomo could have held out had not one of his lieutenants betrayed him. Sumitomo's fleet was burned by imperial troops, and although Sumitomo himself escaped, they pursued him to Iyo, killed him there and then brought his head back to Kyoto as a warning to other would-be rebels. The Sumitomo episode, though a victory for the imperial forces, marked the beginning of the end for the Fujiwara, although their power was to last for some time yet.

It was in 935 that the name Taira Masakado was first heard in Kyoto. Taira was the surname taken by the younger sons of emperors, who also received the revenues of Japan's eastern provinces. The princes did not usually go to the east themselves, but entrusted the work of governing the provinces to civil officials. Junior branches of these princes' families, bearing the surname Taira, amassed great lands and fortunes for themselves in the east. Taira Masakado, it would seem, had gone to Kyoto in the hope of preferment at court, but had been rebuffed by Fujiwara Tadahira and had returned to the east nursing grudges. There he had become embroiled in local feuds and in 935, with a large band of mercenaries, had attacked and killed his uncle, who was the governor of Hitachi province. This incident provoked large-scale fighting in which Masakado's forces proved superior to those of his uncles and cousins. Formal complaint was made to Kyoto, but amazingly Masakado was found to have done nothing blameworthy. It seemed that the Kyoto government was allowing individuals to make private war with anyone they pleased – an error of judgment by Tadahira which would have serious implications for the future.

Masakado went from strength to strength: he joined forces with a corrupt official of a neighboring province, burned public offices and carried off the official seals. Eventually, observing that the penalty for seizing the entire eastern (Kanto) region would be no more severe than that for taking over a single province, he proclaimed himself ruler in the east. Then declaring himself the new emperor, he sent an emissary to Kyoto to inform Fujiwara Tadahira of that fact and to command him to bow to the inevitable. Tadahira, although the holder of supreme power at court, was a typically indolent Heian court noble; it is said he had a cuckoo painted on his fan and used to imitate the bird's sound whenever he opened it; he is also reported to have laughed softly with derision when he heard of the self-styled emperor in the east.

At first Masakado was allowed to continue his depredations without hindrance; but soon houses were being burnt on the outskirts of Kyoto itself – not only by Masakado's troops but also by those of other rebellious warlords, including Fujiwara Sumitomo, who were encouraged by the lenient treatment of Masakado. It was this which finally moved the Kyoto authorities to act. They did go so far as to send an elderly general with no military experience to see what all the fuss was about, but before he could reach the east news was brought that Fujiwara Hidesato, also known as Tawara Toda, had killed Masakado himself. Hidesato had simply walked into Masakado's camp and asked to see him. Masakado was relaxing, having his hair dressed at the time. This encouraged Hidesato, who concluded that a man with so little regard for the proprieties could not be much of an opponent. Hidesato killed Masakado with an arrow and sent his head to Kyoto, thereby becoming a hero at court.

The Masakado insurrection, although crushed, permanently changed the system of the provincial government. To begin with, officials were granted permission to carry swords, a privilege they had not enjoyed since the eighth century. This produced a significant change in that the appointment of rising members of military families to governorships became more common and these provincial officials would have the beginnings of a private army in the body of their own retainers. However, the insurrection did not revitalize the Fujiwara regime in Kyoto or make it feel its own mortality. Although the seeds of its destruction were already sown, its best and brightest hour was yet to come.

Michinaga (966-1027) was perhaps the most powerful of the Fujiwara regents. According to the chronicles of the time, he had all the sensuous and aesthetic virtues expected of a Kyoto noble, and his daughters were married to emperors. But because of the increasing restiveness in the provinces, it would not have been possible for Michinaga to have retained the autocratic power he undoubtedly had in Kyoto for some 30 years if he had not made political friends of the rising stars among the military families. He chose to ally himself initially with the Minamoto clan of the Seiwa branch, that is descendants of the Emperor Seiwa's younger offspring. The Minamoto of this branch had been military governors for several generations, mainly in the north, by Michinaga's time, and it was they that Michinaga chose to overhaul Kyoto's military forces. For some time the Imperial Guard had virtually ceased to operate outside Kyoto itself, and the six companies still there were little more than a rabble, looting and extorting in the streets of the city. This left the central authorities defenseless against external threat and powerless to go into battle should the need arise. Fujiwara Michinaga was quick to see the need for a strong militia. Rather than trusting to the Imperial Guard as previous Fujiwara regents had done, he formed his own force under Minamoto command. Some branches of the Taira clan were also associated with the imperial forces, particularly Michinaga's son, Yoriyoshi. All three parties, Fujiwara, Minamoto and Taira, gained greatly from the alliance.

The wars in the north, undertaken by the Fujiwara with Minamoto and Taira help in the mid-eleventh century, were the first military adventures in which samurai played a central part. The rise of the military families meant that they could now offer material rewards to their fighting men, usually in the form of land or the income from it. Samurai fought alone. There was little understanding of united troop movements or coordinated attack at that time; individuals fought less for the commanding general of an army than for their

Right: Minamoto Yoshiie, the great-grandfather of the famous Yoritomo who founded the Kamakura *bakufu* (feudal government) in 1185.

Below: Yabusame, firing an arrow while on horseback. Archery was one of the original arts in the Way of the Warrior. Bows were made by laminating together sections of wood and bamboo.

immediate overlords – and material gain. It is now that we hear of stupendous feats of daring and self-sacrifice by individual samurai, but there were also many instances of outright treachery. Sometimes a samurai would change sides simply in order to be seen to be on the winning side and to get his share of the spoils of victory. Nonetheless, his family was vitally important to a fighting man, as it was to his masters the Fujiwara, Minamoto and Taira. It became customary in the eleventh century for a samurai to recite his lineage before going into battle, usually with the disclaimer that his own life was unimportant. While many of the heroic feats of pride and valor chronicled must be apocryphal, it

is true to say that to a samurai death was preferable to defeat or capture.

The war in the north, known to Japanese historians as the 'Early Nine Years War,' was begun in 1050 to extract taxes from Abe Yoritoki, the superintendent of the Ainu lands north of the capital, and to subdue his recalcitrant clan. Abe Yoritoki himself was killed early in the war, but his son Sadato carried on a spirited defense of his family's domains. An attack on Sadato's forces at Kawasaki in 1057 in a blizzard resulted in defeat for the Minamoto and Fujiwara generals. Stung by this, Minamoto Yoriyoshi mustered another 10,000 men from the neighboring Kiyowara clan, thus outnumbering Sadato's forces. Sadato was

killed defending his encampment at Kuriyagawa in 1062 during a furious battle in which it is said that women and children fought as bravely as the men. It was also in this battle that Minamoto Yoriyoshi's son, Yoshiie, distinguished himself so greatly that he earned the nickname *Hachiman Taro* (First-Born of the War God). During that last battle at Kuriyagawa, Yoriyoshi is said to have vowed to erect a shrine to *Hachiman*, the war god, if he was victorious. And this was the first thing Yoriyoshi did, at Tsurugaoka in 1063, even before returning to Kyoto to report on the success of the battle and display his trophies.

By the latter part of the eleventh century the Minamoto and Taira were unquestionably the two leading warrior families of Japan. Their recent role on the government side had given them court preferment, and, more importantly, had given prowess in battle the respect it had not had while the Fujiwara in Kyoto favored dalliance, intrigue and aesthetic considerations above the rough pleasures of the barrack-room. It should be noted that although the Mina-

moto and Taira continued to increase their power throughout the eleventh and twelfth centuries, they, along with the Fujiwara, controlled only a small portion of Japan. Also, for many years the clans acted independently and were often engaged in internecine feuding. This was especially true of the Taira who were particularly dominant in the eastern Kanto region. During the eleventh century Taira Tadatsune carried out a series of aggressive actions against his own relatives which resulted in widespread famine as the peasants fled the land. These depredations made it possible for the Minamoto to gain a foothold in the region.

Throughout the twelfth century there was a series of revolts and uprisings in various parts of the empire which had important effects on the respective prestige of the Minamoto and Taira clans. Taira Masamori achieved great renown and high position under Emperor Shirakawa by putting down a revolt in Izumo led by Minamoto Yoshichika, son of Minamoto Yoshiie. Masamori's branch of the clan became governors and effective rulers in Ise and Bizen. The Taira thus gained fame and fortune by service in western Japan and in the capital, although their original power base was in the east. The Minamoto on the other hand had their base close to Kyoto, but found their fame and followers in the far north, where they had built on their earlier victories.

Minamoto Yoshiie is noteworthy, apart from his valor in combat, for having been among the first to take seriously the study of military strategy. He did this by studying classical Chinese scholars. He was reportedly encouraged to do so by court members at Kyoto which was in itself a sign that the art of war was now being taken seriously. Yoshiie also instituted a system among his fighting men of allotting places according to each man's performance in the previous day's battle, which helped to instill in the fighting man a sense of the importance of honor above the preservation of life. This can be illustrated by a story about a young soldier in Yoshiie's army, who was hit in the eye by an arrow during an assault on the stockade at Kanazawa during a rebellion there. The youth broke off the shaft of the arrow and killed the man who had shot him. When a friend tried to help him pull out the arrow by putting a foot on his face, the youth swore to kill his friend for the indignity; to trample on the face of a warrior was worse by far than to be killed or blinded by an arrow.

Despite Yoshiie's many victories in the north, the court at Kyoto refused to honor him, contending that he was merely engaged in settling scores of his own. They declined to punish him for engaging in war on his own behalf, however. Yoshiie took care to reward his soldiers from his own purse, thus ensuring their loyalty in any dispute between the Minamoto and the imperial authorities. Another difficulty facing

Below: Minamoto Yoshiie was a boy of 15 when his father, Yoshiyori, took him on a campaign against the Abe family which lasted for nine years. In the earliest accounts of the campaign Yoshiie is described as a brilliant warrior who displayed 'a godlike military prowess.' The enemy allegedly trembled at his name and he was called Hachiman Taro, 'first born of the God of War.'

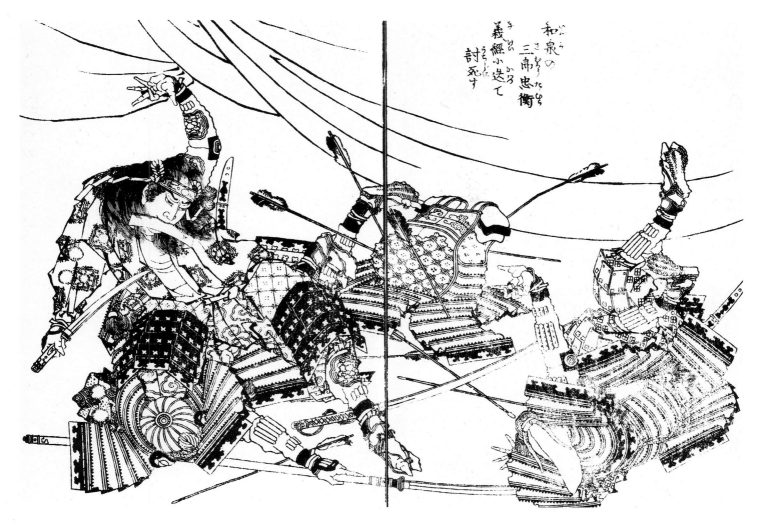

和泉の三浦忠衛
義経小送て
討死す

the Kyoto authorities was the turbulence of the monasteries. It appears that little attention was being paid by the monks to the moral precepts of Buddhism, and the greatest monasteries maintained corps of mercenaries to settle their quarrels. The court had occasion to call on both Taira and Minamoto forces from time to time to quell demonstrations by priests and monks in the streets of Kyoto – yet another factor in the two clans' rise to military prominence.

The twelfth century was a time of strife and upheaval. There were armed warriors everywhere and quarrels between the samurai of rival houses became more and more frequent while the court remained supine. Dissension came to a head in 1156 when the cloistered Emperor Toba died suddenly and a dispute arose between two of his sons, the former Emperor Sutoku and the reigning Emperor Go-Shirakawa (Shirakawa II). Rival members of the military clans, Taira, Minamoto and Fujiwara, allied themselves with one faction or the other. It was now clear that the samurai were no longer mercenaries for the Fujiwara nobles but were acting in their own right, in defense of what they saw as their own interests and those of their lords. The chief Fujiwara supporter of Sutoku was Yorinaga, and among the Minamoto allied to that faction was Tametomo, whose own older brother, Yoshitomo, was on the opposing side. Tametomo pledged to deal

personally with his brother if Yorinaga would authorize a night attack. This Yorinaga refused to do, saying it was a crude tactic suitable only for petty squabbles between samurai. Tametomo protested, but in vain, as Yoshitomo's forces launched their own night attack and scored a crushing victory despite Tametomo's fighting skills.

After the battle, known as the Hogen Incident, the leaders of the Sutoku faction were publicly executed. This was a shock to many as it was the first public execution carried out in Kyoto for 350 years, and what was most shocking of all was that Yoshitomo beheaded his own father. Tametomo avoided the death penalty but his bow arm was disabled and he was sent away to a distant province. He became a legendary figure; chronicles describe him as seven feet tall, and he is even supposed to have gone to Okinawa in the Ryukyu Islands far to the south, where he is said to have founded the line of kings of those islands. Some years later, Tametomo traveled as far as Oshima where he carried out piratical attacks and indulged in blackmail, apparently in an attempt to carve out a kingdom for himself in the east. Kanto troops were sent to crush him in 1170. They failed to take Tametomo's force by surprise, however, and Tametomo is said to have fought bravely at the head of his archers. When most of his ships had been captured or

Above: A defeated warrior commits *seppuku* (ritual disembowelment) in an illustration from the Gikei medieval epic. The first such suicide is recorded as having taken place in the twelfth century.

Following pages: The abduction of the former Emperor Go-Shirakawa (seated in the imperial chariot) in 1159 by Fujiwara no Nobuyori.

朝倉家の敗れし時く齋藤龍興主従戦死を

Above: An illustration from the Taiko-ki, showing a defeated warlord about to plunge a short sword into his stomach.

Right: The battle of Ichinotani (1184) in which Yoshitsune defeated the Taira when his mounted bowmen stormed the reputedly impassable Hideyori gap and smashed through the enemy like an avalanche of boulders.

Far right: A palace coup attempt – detail from a scroll painting.

sunk and almost all his followers killed, Tametomo disemboweled himself. This is the first clearly recorded instance of *seppuku* (more crudely known as *hara-kiri* or belly-slitting), which was to become one of the most controversial features of Japanese life.

There is some disagreement among Japanese historians as to the origins of the *seppuku* tradition. There are references in early literature, but the question is what weight is to be attached to references in early epics like the fourteenth century *Taiheiki*. There is a view that most of this material is of little more reliability than Shakespeare's reference to Brutus and other Romans falling on their swords. There are pictures of the Japanese *seppuku*, but the Japanese historian Yagiri Tomeo maintains that *seppuku* was originally not voluntary at all. He quotes an early history: 'From earliest recorded times in Japanese history, death by one's hand was always either [by] setting fire to oneself, or hanging oneself. There are no official records of anyone killing himself by cutting open the abdomen.' Nevertheless, there are accounts which purport to be from eye-witnesses, of which the suicide of Tametomo is the earliest. There are others, more extreme, in which heroes are described as cutting themselves open, scooping out a grave in the earth with their hands and lying down in it. Some historians dismiss the whole tradition as legendary exaggeration, but

most maintain that, even allowing for exaggerations, it is clear that there was a custom of voluntary self-dispatch by this means from at least the thirteenth century. A history of the period remarks that in some cases at least a cruel method of execution (not suicide) was glossed over with the euphemism 'seppuku.'

There is a well-attested, and extremely

Far left: Rebels burning the imperial palace after the forceable abduction of the former Emperor Go-Shirakawa.

Left: A scene from the Heiji *Monogatari Emaki* (scroll) showing samurai searching a cart.

Below: Another scene from the scroll showing a night attack on Sanjo palace by Minamoto (Genji) in the crucial civil war with the Taira (Heike).

Bottom: An army in flight, from the Heiji picture scroll.

Above: A late thirteenth-century scroll depicting the night attack on the Sanjo palace.

Below: Taira Kiyomori (1118-81) had many moral and intellectual weaknesses, also a sense of humor. Here he surveys his garden which seems filled with the skulls of his victims.

Far right: Taira Kiyomori, a portrait by Kuniyoshi.

Below right: Kiyomori commands the sun to stand still.

dramatic, example of a mass *seppuku* at the end of the fierce resistance of the last of the Hojo regents at Kamakura in 1331. The chronicler relates that the struggle went on in the streets: 'The shouts of warriors, whistling of arrows, sound of the feet of armed men and hoofs of chargers did not cease for five days.' On the last day the regent, Takatoki, set fire to his headquarters and withdrew to Toshoji temple, where he committed suicide with 800 of his followers.

After the Hogen Incident, the victor, Minamoto Yoshitomo, was disgruntled because his ally, Taira Kiyomori, received greater reward and honors than he did. In 1159 Yoshitomo launched a coup attempt at court in the absence of Kiyomori, and when Kiyomori rushed back to Kyoto at the head of his Taira troops, the armed struggle in the capital was drawn up along strictly clan lines. The Taira, however, took the precaution of smuggling the emperor, then aged 17, into their camp disguised as a lady in waiting. They went on to win a great military victory claiming that they had done it in the name of the emperor. Here again a precedent was being established for later conflicts in Japan: concern for the emperor's interests had to be stated if one or other side was to enjoy any advantage. Following this victory over the Minamoto leadership, Kiyomori found himself master of Japan, and very soon afterward, in 1167, attained the highest ministerial rank in the land. He soon resigned the dictatorship (the holding of the rank by a mere military man had been a shock to the of the Fujiwara nobles) but his leadership, which was to last some 20 years, was assured.

This period of Taira dominance, known

24

as the Heike period (Heike being another version of the name Taira) was chronicled some 75 years after the events described, and Japanese commentators have generally been hostile to Kiyomori. Stories are told about his ineptitude under fire. He is said once to have put his armor on backwards by mistake but justified this by saying that he was defending the emperor's house and that it would therefore be disrespectful to show the emperor the reverse of his armor.

One reason for the hostility toward Kiyomori and the period of Taira dominance generally might be the series of natural and unnatural disasters which befell the Kyoto area during that 20-year period. Among these were plots against Kiyomori by the Minamoto in which the Buddhist mercenaries of Miidera and other temples were ranged against the Taira. The main plot, led by Minamoto Yorimasa, narrowly failed, and Yorimasa committed *seppuku*. But plots and counter-plots kept Kiyomori's forces busy for most of the time, and the temples were a constant thorn in his side. Little was done to punish the temple mercenaries for their part in the Yorimasa rising. In fact the few sackings of temples that took place so incensed some of the courtiers that they refused altogether to appear at court. The worst problems faced by Kiyomori, however, were the droughts, floods and famines which plagued the Kyoto area for several years. Chronicles of that time describe heaps of corpses left on river banks and report that people pulled down their own houses for firewood to sell in the local market.

In 1181 Kiyomori died of illness and old age. He had heard not long before of a Minamoto rising in the east led by Yoritomo. Many people from Kyoto had flocked to Yoritomo's standard, in some cases because the famine was far less acute in the east and

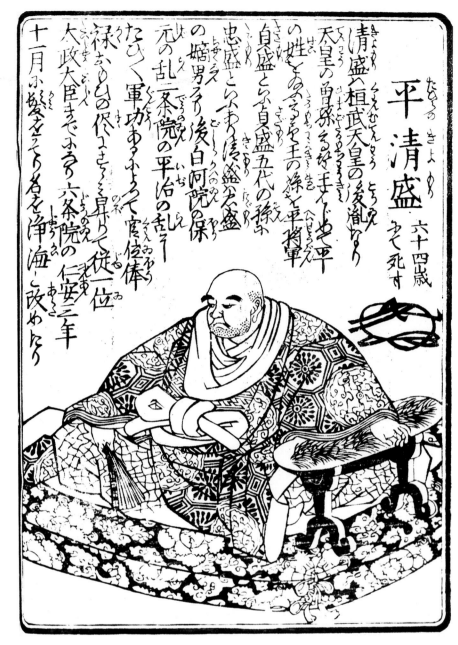

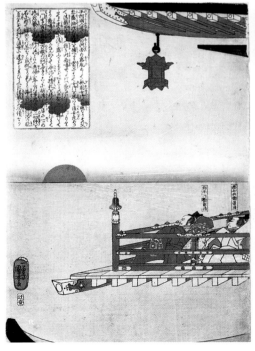

Above: The Kamakura cave where the last Hojo regent, Takatoki, together with his immediate family and about 800 retainers, committed *seppuku*.

burn down Kanetaka's house and kill him; shortly after this Yoritomo's marriage to Masako was celebrated.

In 1180 Yoritomo received warning from Kyoto that the Taira were preparing to exterminate the Minamoto. He took Hojo Tokimasa into his confidence, revealing that for several years he had been in counsel with many of the leading noblemen of Izu and Sagami, with a view to launching an uprising against the Taira. It is interesting to note that most of these noblemen were in fact of Taira descent, and that without the support of the Taira in the east, who felt

soldiers there stood a better chance of getting food for themselves and their families. Kiyomori's dying wish was that no prayers should be said or sacred books read for him; he asked only for the head of Yoritomo to be cut off and hung on his tomb. As he was dying Kiyomori must have known that the rise of Yoritomo in the east was largely the result of his own blunders. Yoritomo was one of the sons of Yoshitomo, who Kiyomori had allowed to survive in exile in the east, where the Minamoto had always had their most devoted following.

There are many romantic tales about Minamoto Yoritomo and his half-brother Yoshitsune. Yoritomo spent 20 years in exile and semi-imprisonment. He made conquests of the daughters of his jailer, Ito Sukechika, and the Taira-descended nobleman, Hojo Tokimasa. The latter, fearful for the consequences to himself of any liaison between his daughter and a Minamoto, had her betrothed to the Izu govenor, Taira Kanetaka, but the bride, Masako, disappeared on her wedding night and could not be found. Soon after Yoritomo's rising against the Taira, he also sent troops to themselves treated as rough provincials by the Kyoto nobles, it is unlikely that Yoritomo could have achieved power at all. The first sortie by Yoritomo and his men, in 1180, was a failure and he retired to Kamakura in the east. A defeat for the Taira later that year, inflicted by Yoritomo's Minamoto cousin and rival, Yoshinaka, encouraged Yoritomo to consolidate his position, and by 1183 he was in command of seven of the eight Kanto provinces. Yoritomo was jealous and suspicious of his cousin, but was not above profiting from his victories. There was considerable intrigue within the family, and the rivalry between the cousins was only partly assuaged by the betrothal of Yoshinaka's son to Yoritomo's daughter.

Yoshinaka's fortunes varied: a defeat at Echizen at the hands of Taira forces caused most of the local samurai to rally to the Taira cause, but then, in 1183, the powerful Buddhist monks of Hieizan offered Yoshinaka their support, causing the Taira to evacuate the capital in fear. The retired emperor, Shirakawa, also went over to Yoshinaka, marching back into Kyoto and immediately ordering most of the Taira nobles in the capital to be stripped of their

Below: The Battle of Yashima in February 1185 saw troops under Yoshitsune inflict a major defeat on the Taira, who fled in panic from the battlefield.

Above: Minamoto Yoritomo (1147-98), the great barbarian-subduing general. He was the first shogun, and his system of government was destined to last 700 years.

Right: A portrait of Minamoto Yoshitsune. Myth alleges that in order to avoid his brothers' murder attempts he fled to the continent of Asia and became none other than Genghis Khan.

rank and wealth. Yoshinaka, despite having marched into Kyoto in triumph, almost immediately found himself out of favor there. The cultivated nobles found him and his men uncouth and countrified, and Yoshinaka allowed his troops to run wild in the streets, perhaps out of pique at being laughed at by fashionable society.

Meanwhile, Yoritomo was still declining to come to court, as he had intelligence that the Taira were gathering for another onslaught. Yoritomo, by taking over yet more eastern provinces, aroused his cousin's jealousy once more, which was made worse by Yoshinaka's defeat at Mizushima when the troops under his personal command deserted. The retired Emperor Shirakawa was taking no small part in the intrigues, playing the cousins off against each other. In 1184 Shirakawa made Yoshinaka *Sei-i-dai-Shogun* (Barbarian-Subduing Shogun) while simultaneously sending emissaries to Yoritomo at Kamakura asking him to deal with his troublesome cousin. Yoritomo had been spending his time organizing the adminis-

tration of the eastern provinces he had captured, not forgetting to send the taxes from them to the capital. The ex-emperor's secret message was matched by a swift response from Yoritomo, who sent a force of 60,000 men to meet Yoshinaka. Yoshinaka was defeated and killed by an arrow while ignominiously galloping away through a half-frozen rice field.

Yoritomo now turned his attention to the final defeat of the Taira. In this he employed his half-brother Yoshitsune as field commander. Yoshitsune was a fighting man of legendary exploits. He had been in exile as a child, but had escaped at the age of 15 and had gone to Mutsu, where he placed himself under the protection of the lord of that province, a Fujiwara. There he had gathered around him a band of loyal volunteer-servant fighting men, including the legendary fighting monk Benkei, supposed to have been a giant of a man who liked nothing better than fighting and had once captured 1000 swords simply for the sake of the exploit alone.

Yoshitsune was 21 when he heard of his

brother Yoritomo's planned rising against the Taira, and marched to join him with 2000 volunteer samurai. The brothers inflicted a terrible defeat on the Taira at Ichi-no-Tani, a deep valley, by force of horsemanship: Yoshitsune led a band of mounted bowmen who poured down the steep valley sides, setting fire to everything, terrifying the Taira who escaped by boat if they could. A contemporary chronicler sings the praises of the Kanto mounted archers, saying that they 'know how to ride but never how to fall.' The valley at Ichi-no-Tani was supposed to have been impassable to everthing but monkeys or wild boars, so that it had not occurred to the Taira to defend the slopes leading down to the sea. The same chronicler describes the bows used by these horsemen as 'san-nin-bari' (needing the strength of three ordinary men to bend them) and records that if a father among the Kanto warriors fell in battle, his son did not retreat and vice versa; every warrior stepped over the dead and was willing to fight until his own death.

The defeat of the Taira and the loss of some of their best captains at Ichi-no-Tani was not fatal to their cause, however. Yoshitsune was now in Kyoto, whither Yoritomo sent an army from Kamakura to finish off the Taira. Yoritomo was not pleased with his brother for what he considered Yoshitsune's self-will in remaining in Kyoto. In addition the Kamakura troops sent to the Taira fortresses around the Shimonoseki straits were starving as the peasants in the area supported the Taira overlords and had fled the land rather than have to supply the Minamoto soldiers. Yoshitsune therefore proposed to go down to Shikoku with a fleet under cover of a tremendous storm which blew up in March 1185. His advisers warned against such a foolhardy scheme, but Yoshitsune had judged the Taira commanders well. The fleet made tremendous speed with the gale behind it and Yoshitsune's troops advanced on the Taira headquarters at Yashima, burning towns and villages on the way so that the terrified townsfolk fled before his army with panic-stricken tales of a great and invincible Minamoto host.

The young emperor, Antoku, was being escorted from place to place by the Taira leaders as a kind of talisman. Part of his regalia was a fan with the rising sun (hi-no-maru) on it which the Taira placed on the mast of one of their ships. When the two armies met, one of the Minamoto warriors was dared by a court lady to shoot at the fan. On Yoshitsune's instructions the warrior accepted the challenge, and shot an arrow which hit the fan, shattering the emblem into fragments. The Taira fought well in the ensuing battle, but it was an omen sufficient to dishearten them, and their fleet finally scurried away through the Inland Sea in disorder. Yoshitsune, instead of launching his troops in pursuit, was astute enough to spend some weeks in training them. The Minamoto, who had won their

Above: A screen painting of the last sea battle between the Genji and Heike clans. The souls of the defeated Heike are said to be reincarnated in the local crabs whose shells bear the markings of samurai war helmets.

Right: The Battle of Dannoura in April 1185. The hero, Yoshitune, brother of Yoritomo, is portrayed. Behind him stands his retainer, the fighting priest Benkei.

Far right: The famous general Minamoto Yoritomo fighting for the first time at the age of 13.

laurels on land subduing the north, were no sailors, and Yoshitsune recognized the need to convert the Kanto mounted archers into naval warriors.

The next sea battle took place near Dannoura, and at first the Minamoto suffered great losses. An exchange of arrows brought little result and the Minamoto, still inexperienced in naval warfare, found themselves at a disadvantage when fighting at close quarters. But Yoshitsune had thought of this possibility and had already made plans. After the Taira flight from Shikoku he had captured the son of one of the Taira commanders, treated him well and persuaded him to write to his father urging him to come over to the Minamoto. The commander's name was Taguchi Shigeyoshi. He was already suspected of treachery by the Taira commander in chief, Munemori (son of Kiyomori), but he did not have Taguchi put to death. At the crucial point of the battle Taguchi defected to the Minamoto side, turning the course of the battle decisively against the Taira. Mune-

mori was captured, but failed to commit suicide. This so enraged his brother Taira Tomomori that he promptly threw himself into the sea and drowned in order to avoid the ignominy of capture. The boy-emperor's mother and a court lady holding the emperor in her arms also flung themselves overboard, but the Minamoto troops managed to rescue them with boat hooks.

This campaign under Yoshitsune's command, which spelt final ruin for the Taira, lasted only five weeks or so but his brilliant success aroused not the praise but the suspicion of his brother Yoritomo. When Yoshitsune arrived at Kamakura he was actually forbidden entry to the city. He returned sorrowfully to Kyoto, having failed to move his brother's heart by impassioned entreaties by letter. Twelve days later Taira Munemori, his son and the last remaining son of Kiyomori were all put to death on Yoshitsune's orders, thus exterminating the house of Kiyomori – though not the Taira themselves, many of whom were now either vassals or supporters of Yoritomo.

Below: Minamoto Yoshitsune (on horseback) directing his troops against the forces of Sakurama Yoshitsura in the castle of Karasu-ura (1142).

Above: The ghosts of the Taira (Heike), appearing before the Minamoto (Genji) clan after the Battle of Dannoura, prepare to sink Yoshitsune's ship. Benkei, on the far left, is exorcising them with Buddhist incantations.

The First Shoguns

From 1186 to 1189 Yoritomo was occupied with the problem of consolidating his position. He had sent Hojo Tokimasa, his father-in-law, to Kyoto as his representative. Yoritomo had after all been proclaimed as a rebel by the imperial authorities on more than one occasion, and was determined never again to be directly exposed to the maneuverings of ex-emperors and their followers. But Yoritomo's most pressing task at this time was to hunt down and exterminate, if he could, his half-brother and victorious general, Yoshitsune.

Since he had been denied entry to Kamakura, Yoshitsune had been wandering the empire with a depleted band of loyal troops. At first he was accompanied by his lady, Shizuka, but she fell behind when the rigors of the journeying proved too much for her. Yoritomo's forces, in the person of emissaries from his Kyoto deputy, Hojo Tokimasa, caught up with Shizuka in 1186. She was pregnant by Yoshitsune at the

time, but despite that was interrogated, by all accounts most forcefully, but steadfastly refused to disclose Yoshitsune's whereabouts. Shizuka was famous as a dancer and singer, and Yoritomo's formidable wife Masako ordered her to sing and dance for them. Contemporary accounts tell us that she sang of love, regret and loyalty to the vanished Yoshitsune so movingly that Masako persuaded Yoritomo to spare her life. She was kept prisoner until her child was born. It was a boy, and Yoritomo promptly had it killed, while Shizuka herself was set free.

Yoshitsune meanwhile was still wandering, often disguised, accompanied by his loyal companion, the legendary Benkei. There is a tale that during these wanderings, he and his band were stopped by troops seeking to carry out Yoritomo's execution order. Their commander recognized Yoshitsune, although he was disguised as a servant. Benkei, however, maintained

Far left: Yoshitsune's faithful retainer Benkei, the fighting monk, as portrayed in Japanese Kabuki drama. Physically huge and enormously strong, he is said to have enjoyed nothing so much as a good fight.

Left: Yoshitsune and Benkei depicted in woodcut print. It is said that the two met one night on the Gojo bridge in Kyoto. Benkei demanded Yoshitsune's sword but the young lad defeated Benkei's great halberd by agility, finally hitting Benkei's wrist with his war-fan when he was exhausted. Accordingly, Benkei swore eternal fealty to Yoshitsune.

fiercely that this was only a humble serving man and to prove the point turned upon Yoshitsune and began to beat him unmercifully for daring to try to resemble the great warrior leader. The commander took this as positive proof that he had been mistaken; after all, a mere monk-henchman would never have dared to raise his hand to a samurai warrior. It may be that the enemy commander did recognize Yoshitsune, but was so impressed by Benkei's and Yoshitsune's willingness to reverse the traditional code of loyalty of a warrior to his lord, that he pretended to be convinced and went away. Whatever the truth of the story, it is

another example of the romance and legend which surrounded Yoshitsune during his lifetime and for centuries after his death.

Yoshitsune eventually reached the fortress of his old protector, the Fujiwara lord of Mutsu. When the news of this reached Yoritomo in Kamakura he sent orders for Yoshitsune to be captured and killed, but his Fujiwara protectors, having received no order from the imperial court at Kyoto, ignored the demand. Yoritomo then prevailed upon the imperial authorities, in the person of the ex-Emperor Shirakawa II, to insist that Mutsu carry out the order from Yoritomo. When even this looked as though

Below: Hokkei's woodcut of Benkei killing the giant carp.

it would be ignored, Yoritomo began to put pressure on the imperial court. This succeeded in spurring the Mutsu lords into action, thinking no doubt of the consequences to themselves if Yoritomo's troops arrived in Mutsu to find them harboring his enemy.

Fujiwara Yasuhira, the son of Yoshitsune's protector during his childhood exile, gathered his troops and launched a sudden and savage attack on Yoshitsune's residence at Koromogawa. Yoshitsune's troops fought bravely, but victory against such a superior force was impossible. It is said that during the battle Yoshitsune remained perfectly calm, sitting in an inner room of the house playing his flute. When told that the battle was lost, he resigned himself to the inevitable, killing his own wife and children and then committing *seppuku*. Fujiwara Yasuhira sent his head back to Yoritomo at Kamakura, and added to it the head of his own younger brother as a token of loyalty to Yoritomo's power. On receiving the head of the younger Fujiwara, Yoritomo was, according to some historians, so irritated by this act of barbarism that he prepared to send troops against the Mutsu Fujiwara to punish them for their treachery. Given the circumstances under

which Yoritomo had received the head of the younger Fujiwara, it is more likely that he had already been preparing an expedition against the Mutsu Fujiwara to take over their great wealth and lands, and that he found it preferable to pursue that campaign rather than to accept a token of loyalty from them, no matter how grisly.

Yoritomo did send troops against the Mutsu Fujiwara, and achieved a rapid and decisive victory. Fujiwara Yasuhira sent terms of surrender to Yoritomo, which were brusquely rejected. Yasuhira fled but was soon killed by one of his own entourage, who carried his head to Yoritomo. The latter, instead of rewarding the man, whose name was Kawada, had him put to death for treachery against his own lord; no doubt this was a warning to any of the samurai serving Yoritomo of what the penalty would be for treachery. The victory at Mutsu produced several advantages for Yoritomo: the rich lands of Mutsu and Dewa provided him with at least 50,000 mounted archers and the wealth from those lands, which would enable him to reward his samurai without having to approach Kyoto for favors.

It was at least partly due to Yoritomo's refusal to visit the imperial capital that his power had become so great. The court had already seen the formidable Kanto archers on the streets of Kyoto, and the longer the brains and power behind them stayed away, the more formidable he became in Kyoto eyes. In 1190 Yoritomo returned to Kyoto where he was most magnificently received and immediately endowed with ministerial rank. As propriety demanded, he at first declined the ranks offered him, and then graciously accepted them. A few days later he created an even greater impression by once more renouncing his offices, a resignation which was most graciously accepted.

Despite the great impression Yoritomo had made at court, ex-emperor Shirakawa II, who was still the real power there, held him in deep distrust. The survival of an unbroken imperial line did not seem so certain then as it appears now, and the ex-emperor had felt himself ill-used by the military chiefs of the past three decades. What Yoritomo wanted most, and this was the reason why he had made such a powerful impression at court, was the title of shogun, and this the ex-emperor declined to grant as long as he lived. This was not long, however, as Shirakawa II died in 1192. His grandson, Toba II, the titular emperor, was nominally in charge of affairs of state thereafter, but was only 13 years old and became a pawn of his ministers, who were in their turn more or less in the hands of Kamakura. So it was that, three months after the death of Shirakawa, in August 1192, two imperial commissioners arrived in Kamakura to invest Yoritomo with the title of shogun. It was a simple ceremony by Kyoto standards, in which a proxy of Yoritomo was presented with the imperial patent of

Left: Samurai hold a council of war prior to beginning a campaign.

Left: A scroll commemorating the Battle of Yashima. Yoshitsune is third from left; Benkei is mounted, fourth from left.

office, attended by warriors in full armor. Yoritomo himself remained in his Kamakura palace to preserve his dignity, emerging only later to take custody of the imperial patent.

The office of shogun was of course not a new one. But all the previous holders of the title had seen it as a kind of military commission for a specific purpose and duration, at the end of which the patent had to be returned to the emperor. This time, however, the office was given to Yoritomo permanently, and his remit was to ensure the defense and tranquillity of the entire empire. Up to 1192 there was a plethora of appeals by Yoritomo asking for imperial authority for almost every action, but his new office freed him of the need to make such appeals. As such it was highly attractive to the military class, which was now larger and more self-confident than at any time in the past. At this time army officers and soldiers were bound to obey the orders of the shogun but not necessarily those of the emperor.

Yoritomo, astute as ever, was careful not to allow his new office to go to his head. He checked most severely any attempt by his retainers and warriors to give him exalted titles. Once addressed as *kimi* (lord) Yoritomo rebuked his servant most sternly, asserting that this title belonged only to the emperor. When advised to depose the young Emperor Toba II, who appeared to be more fond of a life of pleasure than affairs of state, Yoritomo is reported to have recoiled with horror from the suggestion. Now that Yoritomo had supreme power as shogun, he needed efficient administrative machinery to exercise his power: the *bakufu* (shogunate) was divided into three sections: the Samurai-dokoro, the Kumonjo or Mandokoro, and the Monchujo.

The Samurai-dokoro was a kind of general staff. When in session in Kamakura it had responsibility not only for battle strategy and campaign planning but also acted as a promotion board and as an arbiter of proper conduct for samurai. The president (*betto*) of the Samurai-dokoro therefore had great power and influence. The first to hold that office under Yoritomo was Wada Yoshinori, who had been first to break through the Taira lines at the Battle of Dannoura. Yoritomo was notably fond of resolving disputes in person. In 1184 he set up the Monchujo as a kind of supreme court which decided all civil cases as a tribunal of last resort. Its first president was Miyoshi Yasunobu, a kind of sentimental appointment as he was the son of Yoritomo's old nurse. Yasunobu passed on the office to his son later, a general trend which became more marked in the later years of the Kamakura shogunate.

The Kumonjo was also set up in 1184, and from 1191 it was known as the Mandokoro. Its responsibilities were the general administration and decision-making of affairs of state: in short, the business of government.

Its first president was Oe Hiromoto, one of Yoritomo's trusted advisers from the early years. It had been Hiromoto who had first suggested to Yoritomo that he place constables (*shugo*) in all the provinces and deputies (*jito*) in the great feudal manors, a measure which had done a great deal to ensure the stability of Yoritomo's administration. Yoritomo recruited to the Mandokoro a great many scholars and administrators from Kyoto. These were mostly men from noble families whose line had become obscure and had little chance of brilliant careers in Kyoto, where the task of fixing official seals to documents was carried out by Fujiwara courtiers who often did not bother to read the documents concerned. They were badly needed in Kamakura which, despite the magnificent palaces and temples now built there, had been a rough military camp, whose commanders were often semi-literate.

The Kamakura shogunate was a highly efficient military government for over a century. This was due partly to the brilliant military victories achieved by Yoritomo's kinsmen, most of whom were done to death by him afterward, but was mainly due to Yoritomo's astuteness in judging others. He managed to appoint advisers whom he could trust, and he also managed to understand his opponents well enough to defeat them by anticipating their moves. His greatest skill was arguably that of knowing when to listen to advice and when to ignore it and follow his own counsel. He was also something of a showman: when it suited his purpose he would appear in the streets of Kyoto in the most magnificent pomp and surrounded by glittering bands of warriors; at other times he would remain in his Kamakura palace, a figure of mystery. He also understood that it was better to employ great warriors, who would die on the battlefield winning his victories and would then become figures of legend, than to fight and die himself.

In 1193 another half-brother of Yoritomo, Noriyori, who had also been in his confidence and instrumental in more than one of his victories, was put to death for reasons of state. He was the last of Yoritomo's immediate family and heirs to be dispatched once they had outlived their usefulness. Popular legend has it that the death of Yoshitsune had lain heavy on Yoritomo's conscience. Whether or not this was so, the tale has become woven in with the story of Yoritomo's death in 1199 at the age of 53. He had attended the opening of a new bridge over the Sagami River and on the way back was thrown from his horse and died from his injuries. The story is told that the ghost of Yoshitsune had risen from the mists of the river while Yoritomo was passing, startling him so much that he fell down in a faint from which he never recovered. Yoritomo did not truly succeed in founding a dynasty but the system of government he organized, the shogunate, did outlive him

and is the reason he is remembered today.

After Yoritomo, founder of the first warrior government in Japan, died in 1199, his widow Masako became enormously influential, so much so that she was called Amashogun, the Nun-shogun. The most powerful families in the east were the Hojo and Miura, and Masako, a Hojo by birth, lent her support to the former. At his death Yoritomo had two legitimate sons, Yoriie and Sanetomo. The elder, Yoriie, succeeded his father at the age of 17, under the title of *So-Shugo-Jito* (Lord High Constable). But his strong and politically minded mother, Masako, set up a council of 13 to conduct affairs of state in Yoriie's name. This council was headed by Masako's father, Hojo Tokimasa, and comprised four Kyoto civilian scholars and eight Kamakura military men. There was considerable dissension within the council between 1199 and 1202, when Yoriie's imperial patent of the office of shogun arrived from Kyoto. But even after Yoriie's accession the council had much to worry it: Yoriie had shown early promise as a soldier, but in his late teens devoted himself to sport and debauchery. He once, it is said, spent three months practicing a ball game from morning to night.

Yoriie's ascendancy, such as it was, did not last long. In 1203 he became so seriously ill that the question of the succession began to be discussed. Yoriie's own son was an infant, and his brother Sanetomo only 10 years old. It was finally decided that Sanetomo should be placed nominally in charge of the military administration of the 38 provinces in the west, and Ichiman, Yoriie's son, would take charge of the remaining 28 provinces. However, Ichiman's mother was the daughter of Hiki Yoshikazu, whose sister had given birth to a son by Yoritomo while still a professed nun. Hiki Yoshikazu thus saw himself as the grandfather and prospective guardian of the next shogun. He burst into Yoriie's sickroom and urged him to have Sanetomo and his supporters put to death without delay. Unknown to him, Yoriie's mother Masako was hiding behind a folding screen in the room, listening to every word. Soon afterward, Hiki was informed that Masako's father, Hojo Tokimasa, wished to see him. On arriving at Tokimasa's house, Hiki was ambushed and killed by two of Tokimasa's supporters. Hiki Yoshikazu's son, Munetomo, immediately gathered all his relatives and retainers and marched on Ichiman's palace. The infant, as well as Munetomo and most of his followers, were burned to death. Any who tried to escape from the burning building were cut down as they fled.

Yoriie, now recovered, was greatly incensed at the killing of his son. He summoned two of Hojo Tokimasa's most powerful supporters, Wada Yoshinori and Nitta Tadatsune, and ordered them to bring him the head of Hojo Tokimasa. Wada declined, despite the risks in disobeying the order of

Above: An illustration from the seventeenth century book *The Life of Yoshitsune*. In 1189 Yoshitsune found himself under attack from his half-brother Yoritomo, and after killing his wife and children, he committed suicide. His head, preserved in sake, was sent to his brother for inspection.

Following page: Todaiji temple was destroyed by the Taira clan in 1180 because of the armed monks' collaboration with the Minamoto cause. However, it was rebuilt by the Minamoto after they had won the Gempei War.

the shogun, and Nitta tried to carry out the order but lost his life in the attempt. Yoriie's mother then advised her son to shave his head and go into retirement. This Yoriie did, retiring to Shuzenji in Izu, and Sanetomo was, by general consent, made head of the Minamoto clan. By the end of 1203 Sanetomo had received the imperial patent as shogun. Sanetomo was still only 11 years old, so his grandfather, Hojo Tokimasa, was made *shikken* (regent) until Sanetomo should reach adulthood.

The dissension and lack of positive leadership which followed the death of Yoritomo had not gone unnoticed elsewhere in the empire. The Taira began to stir in the Ise region. Their two chiefs, Motomori and Moritoki, gathered warriors to the red flag of the Taira, and soon found themselves at the head of a larger force than Yoritomo had when he had won his first victories. At the news of the Taira force's first successes in Ise, Kyoto was immediately thrown into turmoil. It was now that Yoritomo's faith in Hojo Tokimasa was justified. Tokimasa placed his son-in-law Hiraga Tomomasa in command of Kyoto. Hiraga moved quickly to muster what troops remained in Kyoto and was soon able to quell the revolt and assure his own reputation in Kamakura.

It is at this time that we first hear of Hiraga's mother-in-law, Tokimasa's wife, Makiho, whispering to her husband that Hiraga should be made shogun in place of Sanetomo. Perhaps it is not unconnected that three months after the suppression of the Taira revolt Yoriie was murdered at Shuzenji by emissaries of Tokimasa. Those who were known to oppose the scheme to make Hiraga shogun began to die by violence; the fateful moment came when Sanetomo had occasion to pay a visit to Tokimasa's mansion in 1205. Makiko urged Tokimasa to take this opportunity to have the boy killed. Masako had her spies and, after being informed of the plot, appeared unexpectedly in person at Tokimasa's house and carried Sanetomo away to safety in the house of her brother, Hojo Yoshitoki, who surrounded the family with his own troops. Masako then laid evidence before the Council of Regency in Kamakura. The council at Masako's urging, obliged Hojo Tokimasa to resign the position of regent, shave his head and retire to Izu, while Kamakura troops marched on Hiraga's mansion and killed him. From this point on, Masako and her brother remained close. Their interests coincided in the preservation of Sanetomo's life and the increase of Yoshitoki's reputation. They also combined to keep Tokimasa in the background and prevent him from massing supporters who would help him in the administration of the shogunate.

There was, however, a revolt in 1204, led by Izumi Chikahira, one of Yoriie's personal adherents. The uprising was crushed and the principals judged by Wada Yoshinori, president of the Samurai-dokoro and a

Page 43: The giant bronze statue of Buddha in Kamakura was built under the patronage of Yoritomo's followers in 1252.

Left: A section of a fourteenth century scroll showing a battle scene in the Kamakura period. At this time the Taira and Minamoto were fighting for control of the court after the death of the retired emperor Toba in 1156.

Right: A detail from Takedori Monogatari (*Tale of the Bamboo*) showing fully armed archers and retainers armed with *naginata* (pole-arms). Naginata blades ranged from two to four feet in length and were mounted on shafts four to five feet long.

personal supporter of Hojo Tokimasa. Unfortunately for Wada, some of his own family were involved in the rebellion, and although the shogun agreed to spare their lives and promised their property to Wada to administer until they returned from exile, he went back on his word and assigned the property to Hojo Yoshitoki. This was too much for Wada. Resentment built up to the point that Wada's troops, led by his son, Asahina Saburo, stormed Sanetomo's palace and killed its inmates in 1213. The troops were not so successful when they turned their attention to Yoshitoki's mansion as he had sufficient support to muster troops from the surrounding manors. These poured in to aid the defense of the mansion and the battle resulted in a decisive victory for Yoshitoki and the death, either in battle or by the executioner's sword, of Wada Yoshinori and his retainers. The only survivor was Asahina Saburo, who became the hero of many romantic legends.

Yoshitoki now held supreme power in fact, if not in name, as Sanetomo was still a boy. Yoshitoki took over from Wada Yoshinori as president of the Samurai-dokoro while retaining the office of *shikken*. He and his followers systematically removed Sanetomo's rivals from his path, disposing first of Yoriie's second son by execution for his alleged part in the Izumi uprising. The youngest son of Yoriie had been placed by Masako in a monastery at Tsurugaoka, where he had taken the name Kugyo, but it seems that he was not content with a life of prayer and seclusion, and brooded on the slights endured by his branch of the family. Kugyo's chance came in 1219, when Sanetomo was given high ministerial rank and went to pay a solemn night visit to the Hachiman shrine in Kamakura to give thanks for the honor. Sanetomo refused to put on armor for the journey, against the advice of his counselors. On his way back, as Sanetomo was descending the stone staircase which led from the shrine, a figure, apparently that of a woman, rushed at him from the darkness, cried out 'Enemy of my father, receive your punishment!' cut down Sanetomo and the retainer closest to him, and then disappeared into the darkness with Sanetomo's head.

Kugyo took refuge in the mansion of the Miura family where, it is said, he devoured an enormous meal without letting go of Sanetomo's head for a moment. Kugyo sent word to the Miura clan, the most powerful in Kamakura after the Hojo, asking for support; and Miura Yoshimura sent an emissary to Kugyo. What Kugyo did not know, however, was that Yoshimura was in the pay of Yoshitoki. As soon as the emissary arrived, when Kugyo rose to greet him, he simply cut off Kugyo's head and returned with it to Hojo Yoshitoki.

For some six years after the death of Sanetomo the shogunate proceeded under the direction of Masako and Yoshitoki without a titular head. They were attempting at this time to persuade Emperor Toba II to place one of his sons in the office, but this the emperor declined to do. Toba could see that if an imperial prince was made shogun the advantages would all be on Kamakura's side. If any difference arose between Kyoto and Kamakura it would then be possible for a shogun of the imperial line to be made emperor, and Toba was determined not to allow this to happen. Masako and Yoshitoki therefore turned their attention to the great and ancient house of Fujiwara, and the infant Yoritsune was carried to Kamakura and placed in the care of Masako, receiving his patent as shogun in 1226. The Hojo aim in this was to restore the status of the shogunate in Kyoto, which had declined during the time of strife which followed the death of Yoritomo, to its former glory by attaching the interests of the court nobility to those of Kamakura.

Emperor Toba II, by now ex-emperor in favor of his son Juntoku, who also abdicated in preference to his own infant son Kanenori, had not consulted Kamakura about any of his actions since the beginning of 1221. In June of that year all the military men in Kyoto were summoned to a festival of horse-archery. They all attended, and those present naturally included the shogunate officials and troops from Kyoto. In their absence, the Kamakura deputies in Kyoto were placed under arrest. Two days later Hojo Yoshitoki was stripped of his offices and proclaimed an outlaw; three days after that, Kyoto proclaimed a state of insurrection in the east and summoned all loyal subjects of the emperor to join in seeking out and punishing the rebels. It seemed that the shogunate was about to fall through the clever maneuverings of the ex-Emperor Toba, and perhaps it would have fallen if Toba had not failed to win over the house of Miura, the only clan remotely comparable to the Hojo in power and prestige, and one with reason to resent the Hojo power. However, Miura Yoshimura, on receiving a letter from his brother in Kyoto urging him to put to death the traitor and rebel Hojo Yoshitoki, promptly showed the letter to Yoshitoki himself. At the same time, however, the imperial court was summoning the home provinces to its flag and was preparing to march on Kamakura.

When Masako heard of the situation in Kyoto, she is said to have summoned the chief Kamakura lords to her presence and challenged them, saying that if any of them had thoughts of taking sides with Kyoto they should do so now. The story goes that they all professed undying devotion, with tears in their eyes, and began a council of war. The general opinion was to defend Kamakura against all comers, but the aged Oe Hiromoto argued for an offensive, and it was his advice which prevailed. Within a week the north and east of Japan were under arms and a three-pronged attack was launched against the imperial forces under Hojo Yasutoki, son of Yoshitoki, who commanded the Tokaido division, and took possession of Kyoto within two weeks of setting out from Kamakura. The capture of Kyoto was swift because of the rapid arrival of reinforcements from the east, and the northern force, while it arrived some days later, was able to consolidate the victory by fighting its way through the provinces, large areas of which had rallied to the imperial cause.

The ex-emperor's attempt to rule the empire, then, very nearly succeeded. It is arguable that it might have done so, despite Toba's failure to gain the Miura support he had hoped for, had it not been for the skill-ful military planning of the old adviser Oe Hiromoto, now well into his seventies. If the Kamakura forces had adopted a defensive posture, as the other advisers had suggested, the emperor's troops would soon have been at the gates of Kamakura with most of the empire supporting them, and the first reversals for the Kamakura forces would undoubtedly have seen the emergence of an imperial faction within Kamakura itself. It can be seen here how ready the provincial samurai were to change sides. No doubt many of the provincial warriors who had gone over to the Kyoto side before the arrival of the northern reinforcements,

Below: A fourteenth century Japanese nobleman or priest seated on a cushion. In China at this time his counterpart would have been shown on a chair.

and who had been punished for it by the Hojo divisions, changed sides again as soon as they saw the turn events were taking.

Why were the samurai so quick to turn coat? One reason must be their sheer numbers. For a generation or more, with wars and civil strife in abundance, all the lords had need of armed and trained warriors, and battles were often bloody affairs, with great loss of life and consequent need for replacements. Many of the peasants with means at their disposal to arm themselves had taken up the military profession at this time, and had fairly rapidly established themselves within it. It was already a tradition that samurai had no right or opportunity to earn a living other than by the bearing of arms, and those who had been peasants living off the land only a generation before now found themselves in this position. Also, those of old-established warrior families had no income in peacetime other than that from their estates.

By the unwritten caste laws of the time only one son could inherit an estate so, as 10 or 12 offspring were by no means uncommon, there were likely to be great numbers of more or less hungry warriors in search of a commander. These men would be sure to welcome any civil disturbance and rally to any call to arms with alacrity. It must also be remembered that, at the time when this conflict took place, there was no actual shogun in Kamakura, the child Yoritsune being there under Masako's protection merely as shogun-designate, and so there was a kind of vacuum at the top of the shogunate, at least in the perception of the provincial houses and manors.

When the shogunate commander in chief, Hojo Yasutoki, entered Kamakura victorious, he was met by an official bearing a decree from the ex-Emperor Juntoku. This official read the decree aloud to Yasutoki; it stated that Juntoku had had no intention of destabilizing the empire; all the nuisance had been caused by self-seeking, intriguing imperial counselors, and the imperial decree was now to reinstate the office of regent, of which Hojo Yoshitoki had previously been stripped in full. Yasutoki seems to have been moved to accept this graciously, but his counselors in Kamakura prevailed upon him to exile the ex-

Emperors Toba and Juntoku to far-flung provincial palaces, and the shogunate refused to recognize the infant Emperor Kanenori, as sovereign (he died in any case only 13 years later, before reaching adulthood).

The treatment received by the court nobles implicated in the attempt to overthrow the shogunate was much harsher. Masako did intercede for two or three of them, who were spared by Yasutoki, but the remainder were either summarily executed in Kyoto, or dispatched from there to Kamakura and met with 'accidents' along the way. There was an additional bonus for those in Kamakura in the disposal of their enemies, namely the possession of the court nobles' rich estates. It was in this way that the shogunate was able to ensure the loyalty of its subjects. The newly acquired estates were generally awarded to those who had performed services, military or otherwise, for the shogunate during the recent unrest, nominally by installing their followers as *jito* (deputies). But there was a difference from previous such appointments. In the past, the appointment of

deputies had been done on an administrative basis, not of course ignoring the question of political expediency. The new appointments included a measure of proprietorial rights, not at first codified but becoming enshrined by custom and practice. The proprietors of the new estates began to pass them on to their heirs, even to daughters in some cases. Thus it can be seen that the most powerful guarantee of loyalty to the shogunate was that of self-interest. Those awarded lucrative property after helping to bring about a victory would suffer in their turn if the fortunes of the shogunate took a turn for the worse. This is how the shogunate, under the Hojo regency for the next century or so, maintained its stability in the face of a series of challenges.

It was from Kyoto that the major challenge to the shogunate had come, and it was to Kyoto that the Kamakura administration turned its attention in seeking to ensure that such a challenge was not allowed to arise again. Kyoto had always been the weak spot in Kamakura's armor, because it was there that the emperor held court, and there that the profoundly un-

Below: A saint in Hell, from the life of Sugawara Michizane (847-903), poet, statesman and patron of calligraphy, later deified as Tenjin.

military nobles were the arbiters of politics. Accordingly, Yasutoki and his uncle, Tokifusa, were installed in Kyoto, with a system of government known as the *Rokuhara* which was almost a replica of that in Kamakura. The most senior officials of the Kyoto arm of the administration were invariably members of the Hojo family, and the office was regarded as a kind of training ground for that of regent.

Both Lady Masako and Oe Hiromoto died in 1225. Masako is recorded as having been more feared and respected in Kamakura than any of the male generals and counselors of the time. These two deaths broke the link with the era of Yoritomo, and looked set to create further difficulties for the Kamakura shogunate. But in the previous year Hojo Yoshitoki had died, leaving no regent. Yoshitoki's second wife was of the Iga family, who had been implicated by the ex-emperor's machinations against Yoshitoki in 1221; her brother had been killed in Kyoto in that year. Her family began to plot to have Yoshitoki's son by her, Masamura, made regent, while her son-in-law, a court noble, would be made shogun. The Miura clan, never noted for their loyalty to the Hojo, were implicated, as the now aged Lady Masako soon discovered. It is recorded that Masako crept under cover of darkness to the Miura house, accompanied only by one old servant, and eloquently persuaded the Miura not to join the plot. This was not the last of the schemes against the Hojo administration, however. Yasutoki, who had returned from Kyoto to Kamakura as soon as his father died, spent until late 1227 crushing a series of rebellions, plots and uprisings. It was fortunate for the Hojo that these were localized events and that their perpetrators acted separately, never joining together to cause real trouble.

The Miura clan, as has been noted, was the most powerful after the Hojo. Its loyalty had been called into question from time to time, but in general the two clans remained on friendly terms, especially through intermarriage. The only real estrangement between the two arose out of jealousy. During the rule of the fourth regent, Hojo Tsunetoki (1242-46), the Adachi family had become powerful. The chief of the Miura clan, a son-in-law of Hojo Yasutoki, found that his counsel was not called for as often as that of the Adachi, and his younger brother, Mitsumura, was also aggrieved as a consequence of his close friendship with the shogun, Fujiwara Yoritsune, who had been induced to resign in 1244. This was just when Yoritsune had been implicated in the plot to kill the regent, Tokiyori. Thus the Miura came under suspicion. The Hojo response, as plots and rumors of plots thickened, was to make a surprise attack on the Miura mansion and burn it to the ground. The clan chiefs, Yasumura and Mitsumura, escaped to a neighboring temple, which they defended well, but eventually, staring into the jaws of defeat, they

both committed *seppuku*, as did 270 of their followers. The Hojo meanwhile gave orders for the slaughter of any Miura who could be found. This order was carried out with remarkable efficiency: within a few days of the suicide of their leaders, the Miura clan members were virtually exterminated and their manors and lands confiscated and distributed to Hojo supporters, to temples whose support would be useful, and in a few cases to the imperial court. There was to be a historical echo of the mass suicide some 100 years later, when the last of the Hojo regents, Takatoki (1303-33), double-crossed by some he had trusted and defeated after three days of bloody fighting in Kamakura, withdrew to a monastery and committed *seppuku* with about 800 of his own retainers.

Secrecy was a high priority for the Hojo administration. The traditional story is that when vital questions of state were to be discussed, the Council of Regency assembled in a chamber known as the Burning Room (*takibi-no-ma*) and conducted their deliberations in complete silence, by tracing characters on the ashes of the fire which was kept burning on the flat hearth (*hibachi*) there.

The shogunate's domains had spread widely by the mid-thirteenth century, and there was almost nowhere in the empire where the *bakufu* had no foothold at all. But in some areas, particularly the Nara region, there were no Kamakura deputies as the landed lords there owed allegiance neither to Kamakura nor to Kyoto. However, even in such places, a complaint or suit brought by a non-Kamakura landholder could still result in the removal from office of the nearest Kamakura official, generally for corruption.

It must be clear that the six shoguns to hold office from the death of Sanetomo were puppets in the sense that they wielded power by virtue of their regents and others and, in real terms, wielded it scarcely at all. The first two puppet shoguns were Fujiwara, in line with Kamakura's ambition to link the shogun's office with the imperial court. Toba II prevented this in 1219 but in 1252, because of the cooperation of the then emperor, Saga II, whose court was friendly to Kamakura, it became possible to install Prince Munetaka, the brother of the emperor, as shogun. Munetaka in fact tried to shake off the Hojo dominance of the shogunate when he reached adulthood in 1266, but was promptly deposed and kept virtually under house arrest in Kyoto. He was succeeded as shogun by his son, Koreyasu, an infant. Koreyasu too tried to assert his own influence when he grew up and was also relegated to Kyoto and a life of pampered confinement. Koreyasu was replaced by his cousin, Hisa-akira, the brother of the reigning Emperor Fushimi. Although Hisa-akira managed to retain his position as shogun for almost 20 years, he did it by refraining from self-assertion, but even he was forced to make way for his own son, Morikuni.

The Hojo regency, while retaining the military tradition of its origins in the Minamoto conquest of the east, did develop its own cultural tradition. There were many Kyoto officials in Kamakura, who naturally continued their cultural pastimes, but the native Kamakura tradition was more robust than that of Kyoto. Football, for instance was extremely popular among the highest in the shogunate. There is a tale of one Narimichi, who held the position of minister of state in Kamakura and had such a passion for football that he practiced it continuously for 7000 days. The Japanese game involved kicking the ball high and keeping it off the ground continuously, and Narimichi is said to have jumped from shoulder to shoulder along a row of retainers, and even on the head of a shaven priest, while kicking the ball. His touch was so light that those trodden upon said they had felt as though nothing heavier than a hawk was hopping along their backs.

The Kamakura administration added to the Kyoto-style of the arts its own practitioners, those employed to instruct the shogun and the government leaders, and all others of high birth and rank, in horsemanship, archery, swordsmanship and all the arts of the warrior. In peacetime, which is effectively what prevailed from about 1221 onward, the need for these skills diminished. However, the number of warriors was increasing, the more so as there were few battles to reduce them, and not being able to make their living in any other way, lucrative appointments in the shogun's household were coveted by the samurai. The difficulty for the rough warrior was that such appointments went only to those who also had the polite Kyoto-style accomplishments. Consequently there arose a fashion for fine clothes, beautiful houses and banquet-giving, with a corresponding need for money, even among young samurai. Thus warriors began to borrow to maintain their extravagant lifestyles, and mortgaged estates became common in Kanto. In the mid-century, the prices of commodities were fixed in an attempt to curb the inflation caused by an overheated demand for luxury goods, and in 1261 Kamakura forbade the building of houses incompatible with their owners' rank and fortune. We also hear at this time of shogunate retainers being rebuked for their neglect of the military arts; the compulsory practice of these was subsequently reintroduced. It can be argued that the Kamakura government was fighting a losing battle against what it saw as the effeminacy of Kyoto fashions.

Left: The Hojo regent Tokiyori, who completed his Zen training under the Chinese master Daikaku, censured the Bushi for their lack of attention to the military arts, especially to perfecting themselves in the Way of the Bow.

The Zen Connection

As for religion, this should not be underestimated as an influence on the Hojo regency. All its leaders were religious men, devout in their following of Buddhism. The twelfth and thirteenth centuries were times in Japan, as in Europe, when new sects and religious movements were emerging everywhere. One of the most important of these in Japan was 'New Pure Land' (*Jodo Shinshu*) under the monk Shinran. The *Jodo Shinshu* doctrine preached adherence to one Buddha, thus meshing well with the samurai code of adherence to one only lord. It was also a comparatively optimistic creed, and in a time of peace and stability, as there was for some decades from the mid-thirteenth century, it gained many followers in Japan.

Jodo Shinshu, although it flourished well in the east, had its origins in Kyoto. Much has been written about Zen and the Japanese warrior. It may be sufficient to say that Zen's emphasis on individual achievement and salvation, and on moderation in the physical appetites in order to become indifferent to one's surroundings, made it eminently suitable to the warrior caste despite, or because of, its focus on meditation and correct practice. Although it is Zen which has gone down in history as the religion of the samurai, there were many who followed *Jodo Shinshu*. Another reason for the latter's popularity was its concentration on the priesthood as part of the community rather than as a celibate and separate body. The corruption and political maneuverings of the Kyoto monasteries was unlikely to make the sects followed there attractive, at any rate to the leadership.

Another religion which had its origin in eastern Japan in the thirteenth century was the Nichiren sect (*Shu*) which has a great many adherents in modern Japan. Nichiren himself was actually born in the Kanto region, the son of a Kyoto exile. He became disgusted with the conditions and style of the Kyoto monasteries where he had studied, and on returning to Kamakura began street preaching, using drums and other musical instruments to attract custom. This was unheard of in Japan at the time, and, together with the intolerance of the creed for other religions, it caused Nichiren himself to be exiled in 1261. One aspect of the Nichiren *Shu* which is significant with hindsight was the introduction of the concept of the state and nationality in connection with religion. Nichiren insisted that truth and morality were the foundation of the peace and prosperity of a nation. His own defiance of government was because of that authority's refusal to outlaw what he saw as heretical sects, including Zen.

A further reason for the power of religion under the Hojo was the regents' devoutness and respect for the priesthood. In Kyoto the priests and monks were seen as troublemakers in government eyes, and from time to time had conducted armed uprisings, but in Kamakura the legitimate interests of the priesthood, in the view of the leadership, were carefully fostered, while abuses were kept in check with all the considerable power the *bakufu* could muster. This encouraged priests and monks from elsewhere to come to Kamakura and place themselves at the disposal of the regents with all the advice they could offer. However, devout though the Hojo may have been, they appear to have seen the role of religion as primarily political. They did not hesitate to send shogunate troops against the Hieizan and Miidera temples of Kyoto and Nara when their priests conducted armed forays against each other in the middle of the century. It is arguable that it was only in these inter-temple skirmishes that the Kamakura troops had any difficulty in maintaining order in the empire for several generations. So the Hojo respect for Buddhism may have contributed to an indigenous, warrior-caste culture in Kamakura, but it was a double-edged sword.

Why then was Buddhism so attractive to warriors? Buddhism was founded in India in about the sixth century BC. By an analysis, undertaken in deep meditation, of human experience, Buddha discovered life to consist of suffering; suffering caused by clinging to the notion and experience of a self. In his final enlightenment, sitting for

Left: To some the rock garden (*Ryoanji*) in Kyoto represents tiger cubs crossing a stream. Even under the snow the shape of the rocks is still visible and the garden retains its effect.

seven days in meditation under a sacred tree, Buddha freed himself from identification with the imaginary personal self. Of the nature of freedom and enlightenment itself, called Nirvana, he did not speak directly, but later on it became rather tentatively defined in terms of omniscience and the so-called Buddha nature of bliss and freedom. In Buddha's time it was necessary to become a monk to attain Nirvana. The most a layman could hope for was to lead a virtuous life, a road leading to rebirth in more favorable circumstances, when he could become a monk and so attain the Buddha's enlightenment. This form of Buddhism, the original form, traveled south and southeast to southern India, Ceylon, Thailand, and still farther east. But the original Buddhism in India developed into what was called Mahayana, the self-styled 'Great Vehicle,' as distinct from the so-called 'Lesser Vehicle' of the southern school. Mahayana opened the way for laymen to become fully enlightened. This Mahayana form of Buddhism went to central Asia and to China and produced its own scriptures in Sanskrit which were wonderfully translated into Chinese with the cooperation of the Indian monks who took them to China.

From the fifth century AD, Zen, which was one of the original forms of Buddhism, based mainly on pure meditation without reliance on any particular scripture, was taken to China by a succession of Indian teachers, of whom the most famous was Bodhidharma in the following century. In China he met the Emperor Liang Wu Chi who was noted for his good works. To the emperor's dismay, Bodhidharma told him that merit could not be accumulated through good deeds. When the emperor failed to accept this, Bodhidharma went to a remote monastery, where he is said to have spent nine years meditating in front of a cave wall. He is considered to have been the twenty-eighth patriarch in the direct line from Gautama Buddha.

There is a legend of the origin of Zen which does give a fairly good idea of what it is, although it is undoubtedly a much later Chinese invention. It says that when the Buddha was at a great assembly of disciples and laymen, he was presented with some golden flowers. He took one of the flowers, held it up and twirled it in his fingers without saying a word. Everybody was disconcerted except his chief disciple Kasyapa, who smiled. The Buddha then said: 'The eye of the Buddha teaching, the true vision, has been conveyed and received by Kasyapa.' It is said that by similar methods, that is to say, without direct speech but as a spontaneous springing up as a result of long practice of meditation, Zen arouses this vision and experience of freedom and enlightenment.

One of the features of the Zen transmission is that it is a 'separate transmission outside the scriptures.' In China it develop-

Below: The frontispiece to the world's earliest printed book, the Chinese translation of the *Diamond-cutter Sutra*. The sobriquet Diamond-cutter implies that the text is so hard to understand that it would cut a diamond.

ed in various ways and although there are always warnings that the final experience, the living experience of Zen, is not expressible in words, more and more it came to be referred to in phrases like 'The Buddha Nature,' and 'The Buddha Life,' and finally even as 'The Great Life of the Universe.' By the time it took root in Japan in the twelfth century, it could be expressed something like this: there is a great 'Life of the Universe,' 'The Buddha Nature,' which is a spontaneous flow of blessedness, but the knot of the human personality makes a little vortex or check in the flow. By giving up one's identification with the idea of a permanent body-mind complex, one's actions become the actions of 'The Buddha Nature' not the actions of any limited individual, and there is no check. One of the examples given is that it is like a rope which runs smoothly and easily over a pulley. If, however, there is a knot in the rope, then every time it passes over the pulley there is a little bump and check. In the same way the idea of a permanent personal self, with feelings and identifications, makes a knot in the flow of 'The Buddha Nature' through the individual; it makes a sort of bump and distorts the natural action of the Buddha life. To remove this 'bump' is the essence of Zen.

A very well attested result of the Zen practice was freedom from the fear of death and most of the sufferings of human life. The ability to transcend pain, to a greater or lesser extent, was a great feature of the famous Zen figures. It was this pair of factors, freedom from the fear of death and from the check of pain, which appealed, very strongly, to Japanese warriors. The fact that Zen Buddhism took root in Japan in the twelfth century, mainly through the warrior class, was partly due to historical accident. During that century the effective government of Japan passed to a series of regents at Kamakura, which was not the capital of Japan. The capital was in Kyoto, with a figurehead government and a figurehead emperor. The great traditional Buddhist sects were based in Kyoto, and the regents of Kamakura, partly to offset the religious prestige of Kyoto, strongly patronized the new Zen Buddhism with its independence of scriptural learning. This was not solely a political policy; many of the regents were in fact devout Zen Buddhists. For instance, Tokiyori did practice Zen vigorously: he passed through some of the Zen riddles like the one about the twirling of the flowers, the traditional origin of the religion.

Japan at this time was increasingly under the threat of the great shadow of the Mongols, who had conquered China and were now looking toward Japan. Kublai Khan in fact mounted two invasions of Japan, both of which failed through a combination of great bravery by the defenders and also extraordinary storms. The defense of Japan was organized from Kamakura,

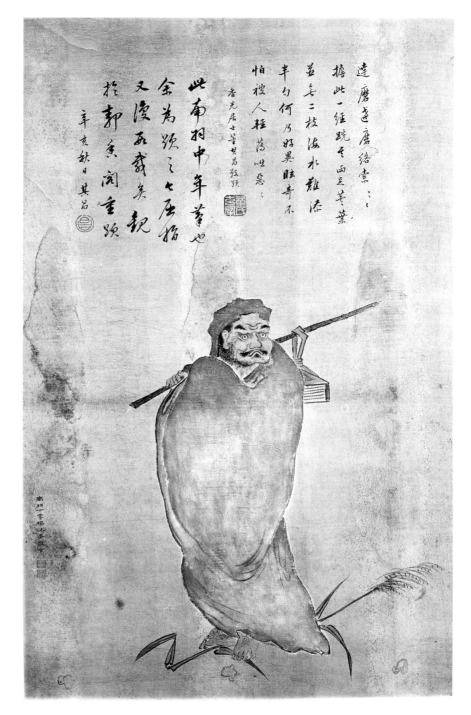

and the actual Mongol invasions were repelled by Japanese forces under the young regent Tokimune, who was a famous Zen enthusiast. There are some records of Tokimune's early interviews with his teacher.

In Zen discourse the pupil is expected to express realization, and understand that realization is not simply a matter of words. From the way the words, or perhaps actions, are expressed, the Zen teacher can tell whether there is genuine realization or what could be a parrot quotation of some famous phrase. Some of the interviews between Tokimune and his Chinese teacher Bukko can be regarded as typical of the Zen interviews between warriors and their priest-teachers. Here is one such interview:

Tokimune: Of all the ills in life, fear is the worst. How can I get free of it?

Above: A picture of Bodhidharma who founded Zen in China. He had a famous interview with Emperor Liang Wu-Tei, who was baffled by his philosophy. Bodhidharma then went into isolation, crossing a great river by treading on the reeds that came floating past. The prominent nose and wide eyes were attributed by the Chinese to the Indians.

Bukko: You must shut off where fear comes from.

Tokimune: Where does it come from?

Bukko: It comes from Tokimune.

Tokimune: Tokimune hates fear so much. How can you say it comes from Tokimune?

Bukko: Try and see. Abandon Tokimune and come tomorrow. Your courage will be so great it will fill the whole world.

Tokimune: How do I abandon Tokimune?

Bukko: You must simply cut off all thinking.

Tokimune: What is the way to cut off all thinking?

Bukko: Plunge yourself into meditation and wait for the body and mind to become serene.

Tokimune: But duties in the world leave me so little time. What can I do?

Bukko: Going, sitting, staying and lying, whatever you have to do, that itself is the best place of practice for training. This life in the world is the place to learn profound meditation.

The teacher Bukko further gave Tokimune five rules:

1. Try hard to keep your mind set at the Field of the Elixir (*tanden*, this is a point one inch below the navel). Keep yourself always calm like pure water; do not be anxious about things.

2. Do not clutch after any outer thing, remain in the state, 'I alone am the honored one' (this was the declaration of the Buddha at birth — it was also a Zen riddle).

Far left: A wooden statue of Hojo Tokiyori, the regent for the shogun between 1246 and 1256. Tokiyori is wearing the informal court dress of a Heian aristocrat.

Below: Hojo Tokimune (1251-84). Bukko, his Zen teacher said 'Tokimune had been a Bodhisattva, ruling for 20 years without showing joy or anger. When the victory came he showed no elation. He sought for the truth of Zen and found it.'

Above: After his defeat of the Mongols, Tokimune built the great monastery of Enkakuji and installed in it the representation of 'Jizo of a Thousand Forms' (seen here).

3. Do not labor to check thinking, but neither is thinking to be left unchecked. Just see to it that no thought is born.
4. Always keep a spirit of daring, a daring spirit that would not hesitate to tread on a sword blade.
5. If your vision is narrow, your courage also will be narrow. Always try to keep your thoughts universal.

The application of Bukko's injunction 'See that no thought is born, even when active' would be something like this: 'Don't have any extra thought.' For instance, if one had to take something and put it down somewhere, simply take it and put it down. Do not think 'Why am I doing this? What am I going to get out of this? How do I look? Ought I to be doing this anyway – it is a menial job. Will anyone notice me?' All those thoughts are abandoned. Simply pick it up and put it down. So we see that the answers to Zen problems were not given necessarily in any particular words: the state from which they were given was the vital thing. The warrior class under leaders like Tokimune was to meet its greatest challenge so far when there came the threat of invasion by the Mongol hordes from across the sea.

Contact between Japan and China, once so frequent and culturally fruitful for Japan (though many of the Japanese cultural imports usually ascribed to China came in fact from Korea), had ceased on an official level by the tenth century. There were still Chinese merchants in Japan, as well as doctors and scholars. In particular, Buddhist scholars from Japan had usually spent long years studying in China before achieving the eminence usually represented by Japanese historians as uniquely Japanese. The harbors of Japan, especially those in Kyushu, were often visited by Chinese merchant ships. However, these visits were not frequent enough for goods from China to become commonplace, it seems. There are records of the Kyoto imperial court issuing decrees and making regulations to deal with the near riots which sometimes resulted from competition to secure the goods from a Chinese ship. Taira Kiyomori had put considerable effort into harbor improvements, largely with the aim of increasing trade with China. So Chinese commercial and cultural influence never really disappeared from Japan throughout the whole period of the rise and fall of the Taira, Minamoto and Hojo. Some of the Japanese attitudes to foreign influence in general and Chinese influence in particular can be seen, for instance, in Taira Kiyomori's son, Shigemori, who refused to see a Chinese doctor when he was ill for sentimentally patriotic reasons. There being no Japanese doctor available with the expertise to heal him, he died.

While Japan was declining to send official ambassadors to China, the Mongol hordes were advancing into China and Korea from Central Asia. By 1264 the Mongol capital had been transferred to Peking, and it seems to have been only the Mongols' dislike of sea travel and naval warfare that kept them from Japan. Although records are scanty, of all the shoguns it seems to have been Sanetomo who had the most contact with China. In 1215 he had the idea of going to China in person, and a Chinese shipwright spent almost a year at Kamakura supervising the construction of a suitable vessel. The project was a failure, though, and the half-built ship was left to rot. Tea was another Chinese import into Japan which was first recorded in the time of Sanetomo. It is thought to have been brought to Japan in the ninth century, but when the monk Eisai returned from China in 1191, bringing tea plants with him, the drink was unheard of in Japan. Eisai is said to have cured Sanetomo of a sake hangover by giving him numerous cups of tea, which caused the leaf to be held in the highest regard as restorative of a warrior's vigor. For at least a century after this any warrior who achieved something extraordinary received a tiny jar of the precious leaf and would ceremoniously partake of it.

In 1259 Kublai Khan became emperor of China under Mongol domination. By this time the Koryo kingdom in what is now Korea had become a vassal of the Mongols after a bitter but futile struggle. It is said that it was a Korean, Cho I, who gave Kublai Khan the idea of securing Japan. Whether or not this is true, a mission was in fact sent to Japan, with a Koryo envoy accompanying the Mongols, but was driven back by a storm. It was only in 1268 that the Mongol envoys were able to hand over to *bakufu* representatives a dispatch, planned to have been sent by the first mission, asking for contact between Japan and the Mongol Empire and not failing to point out that such contact existed with Koryo and that it took the form of a lord-vassal relationship.

The shogunate took this very seriously indeed. In the past, envoys or dispatches had often been ignored or simply returned home because the government did not like the tone they took. But this time Kamakura, when the dispatch arrived through a series of couriers, felt unable to discuss its contents. It was deemed so weighty a matter that it was sent straight to the imperial court at Kyoto. The court, then about to celebrate Emperor Saga II's fiftieth birthday with great style and ceremony, drafted a conciliatory reply and sent it on to Kamakura for approval. Only then did the *bakufu* meet, and its decision was to send the envoy home without reply, having detained him for five or six months.

In May that year the Mongol invasion set sail for Japan. When the news came, Tokimune, clad in armor, went to see the teacher, saying, 'The great thing has come.' The teacher replied, 'Can you somehow avoid it?' Tokimune calmly stamped his feet, shook his whole body and gave a tremendous shout. The teacher said 'A real lion-cub; a real lion's roar. Dash straight ahead and do not look round.' After his defeat of the Mongols, Tokimune built the great monastery of Enkakuji at Kamakura and installed in it a representation of 'Jizo of a Thousand Forms.' Bukko became the first abbot. Tokimune organized a great service for the souls of the dead of both sides. Soon afterward he himself died at the age of 33, and in the funeral oration, Bukko said he had been a Bodhisattva: 'For nearly

Below: A Chinese drawing of a Mongol. After subduing the Chinese, the Mongols made several unsuccessful attempts to invade the Japanese mainland.

Right: A woodblock *Kabuki* print of a warrior. The downturned corners of the mouth imply strength at the navel.

20 years he ruled without showing joy or anger. When the victory came he showed no elation. He sought for the truth of Zen and found it.'

It was at this time, in the mid-century, that there was a series of major natural disasters, signs, and portents such as comets and floods. Also at this time the monk Nichiren was preaching in the streets of Kamakura, and was appealing not just to the individual but to the national consciousness. He urged the people to repent of their sins, or they would suffer not only civil war but also foreign invasion. The samurai by this time were more likely to respond to Nichiren's call for the creation of a national spirit, largely because of Yoritomo's reforms. Before the time of Yoritomo the samurai had owed loyalty only to their own lord or clan chief, now they were under the domination of Kamakura. Also, the defeat of Emperor Toba's attempted coup against the Kamakura administration had left the passions of the court nobles attuned only to love and poetry, Kyoto having abandoned any pretence at military ambition. So the military were in control, and a nationalist spirit was abroad in the land, just when a threat appeared from abroad for the first time in more than a century.

The Mongol mission to Japan had failed. Kublai Khan therefore instructed his Korean vassals to begin preparing an expeditionary force. The Korean king protested at first, but was soon prevailed upon by his overlords, and in 1273 the Mongol advance guard arrived in Korea. It was unable to proceed at first because of famine there, which meant that supplies could not be forwarded to the men from China until the next rice harvest. Mongol envoys were still being sent to Japan, but were still being ignored there; on hearing of the deportation of the latest envoy by Hojo Tokimune, the Mongol force at last put to sea.

Late in 1274 the Mongol force reached the island of Tsushima, which was held by a grandson of Taira Tomomori. He defended the island with a force of only 200 men and was defeated quickly, losing his own life in

Below: Mongol troops attacking the Japanese with bows. Note the difference in dress, warship design and weapons as depicted by the Japanese.

the battle. Other harbors were taken in the next few days, including those on the islands of Iki, Hakata, Imatsu and Akasaka. By the time the Mongol fleet entered Hakosaki harbor the first dispatches were reaching Kamakura with intelligence of the defeats at Tsushima and Iki. Hojo Tokimune immediately sent out a general call to arms, but this had been anticipated by the Kyushu chiefs generally, who had already turned out in force and were slaughtering as many of the landing force as they could.

Once they began fighting the Mongols on land, the Japanese troops had advantages and one particular disadvantage. The advantages lay in that they knew the terrain while the Mongols did not; and, secondly, a great many of the Mongols' troops were actually Koreans, who were held in no great respect by the Japanese, partly because they had already been beaten by the Mongols on their own soil, and partly because the Korean troops included what the Japanese called 'butchers and slaves.' The main disadvantage of the Japanese was that the Mongols had artillery, that is to say 'rockets' shot from bows, and accurate crossbows and catapults. The Japanese had of course been unbeatable as mounted archers under the Minamoto, but long years of peace had dulled their skills, and the Japanese archers in any case were from Kyushu rather than from Kanto where the tradition of mounted archery had been best maintained.

Although records of this period are poor, it seems that the Mongols beat back the defense force but did not defeat it, only making the Japanese retreat behind specially constructed dikes. At the end of the day's fighting the Mongols appear to have decided that a night camped on open ground was too risky – they had already learned to fear Japanese night attacks – and so they re-embarked, setting fire to the coastal villages as they did so. Almost as soon as the fires had begun and the Mongol troops were on board ship, there was a great downpour which must have extinguished some of the flames, and a tremendous wind which simply blew the Mongol ships back out to sea through the harbor mouth. Only one ship ran aground on its way out but it was found later that the Mongol losses had been over 13,000. When the Mongol generals reported the outcome of the battle to their emperor later, they seem to have said, not that their force had been too small to conquer Japan, but that the great wind and rain had defeated them.

Another mission was sent to Japan by Kublai Khan in 1275, ordering the emperor to appear in Peking to make obeisance. The Japanese response to this was to kill the envoys outside Kamakura and expose their heads to the public. At the same time, a general maritime conscription order was issued, and work was proceeding at great pace on the fortification of the western harbors. There were also, it is interesting to

Above: A scroll showing the aftermath of one Mongol invasion, with Japanese samurai viewing the heads of the vanquished.

note, *bakufu* dispatches urging that those lords who had failed to respond to the call-to-arms at the time of the invasion in 1274 should be dealt with. This suggests that patriotism was not always as strong in Japan as it appears from outside, especially when immediate self-interest was threatened.

It has already been said that the Hojo had become followers of the Zen sect of Buddhism. They therefore had among their advisers some monks who were Chinese and had no love for the Mongols, who had after all conquered their own country some time before. They were quick to warn the regents of the likelihood of another invasion, having seen a similar course of events in China. Kublai Khan, meanwhile, delayed for some time before sending a second invasion force. He still needed huge armies to keep Korea and southern China subjugated and had no fleet as such, only vast quantities of small boats, some holding no more than 10 or 15 warriors. It was not until 1279 that Kublai Khan again summoned the Korean king to Peking to discuss equipping another fleet against Japan — even though he was still sending missions telling the Japanese that now he had subdued southern China completely it was in Japan's best interests to enter into a lord-vassal relationship with his empire. The only notice the Kamakura government took of this was to have the unfortunate envoys publicly executed.

The Koreans had equipped their fleet for the Mongols by the spring of 1281, and set out expecting reinforcements from the north. It seems from Korean accounts that the Japanese did suffer reverses at first; certainly large numbers of Chinese troops were landed at Hizen harbor in June 1281. It is most likely that the invaders did land during the early summer of 1281 but did not advance far as the Japanese defenders kept them in check. Also the invaders were mostly Chinese who until a short time before had been fighting the Mongols themselves. The Japanese began to harry the Mongol fleet by darting out against them in what have been described as 'mosquito attacks.' The Japanese ships picked off and set fire to individual enemy vessels, while the defenders held the harbors despite heavy losses. In any event, the fighting went on for six or seven weeks.

There are varying accounts of what happened next. On 15 August 1281 it seems that a great storm arose from the west, causing the sea to run very strongly inshore. The invading fleet made for the shelter of local anchorages, but the wind was so strong that the ships were blown together into a narrow harbor mouth (probably Imari in northern Hizen), where they were smashed to pieces to the extent that one could walk from one point of land to the other on the mass of wreckage.

The great wind (*kamikaze*) which repelled the second Mongol invasion and thus

preserved Japan from foreign incursion has gone down in Japan's history as somehow bound up with the exclusiveness of the nation: the elements themselves took Japan's side against a foreign threat. However, a large number of the Chinese troops survived the naval disaster and encamped on the island of Takashima at the entrance to Imari Gulf. There was a land battle and the Chinese were routed. There were other Chinese troops who made landings at various points along the coast, but they too were put to the sword by the inhabitants of the islands where they landed, if not by the Japanese armies themselves. It is said that 3000 prisoners were taken and conveyed to Hakata, where all but three were killed. These three were spared only for the purpose of carrying back to China the news of the failure of the invasion. According to Chinese accounts, of those who landed along the coast at least 10,000 were made slaves by the Japanese.

Despite the failure of the invasion, Kublai Khan wanted to prepare another invasion force almost immediately. He had, however, to use troops other than Mongols, as it was difficult to persuade them to board ships at all, let alone solve the logistical difficulties of transporting fully trained soldiers from northern China. As he had before, Kublai Khan proposed to use Korean and Chinese troops. But the Koryo kingdom in Korea had no resources to manage the invasion itself, and the Chinese ministers under

Kublai Khan protested so strongly that the expedition had to be postponed. By 1286 Kublai Khan was preoccupied with revolt elsewhere in his empire, so the threatened invasion never really took place.

Mongol soldiers never did march on the capital, although after the fall of Tsushima there were rumors that the Mongols were already doing so which caused widespread panic in the provinces of the Kyoto region. So bad did the situation become that the transport of rice and other supplies to the army in Kyushu was temporarily suspended. For at least 20 years after the second invasion and the great wind, troops were kept in Kyushu because of persistent fears of Mongol invasion. Kublai Khan died in 1294 and it was after his death that talk of another invasion of Japan finally ended. Kublai Khan's successor, Timur, began to send envoys to Japan again, but this time he sent priests, having noted that when the last mission, in 1284, had been massacred as the others had been, only the priest accompanying it had been spared. The arrival of these priests – one was even naturalized after 1299 – did something to allay the fears of the nation, but the Hojo regency was now showing weaknesses which could not be easily remedied.

Until that time, all wars fought in Japan had been civil wars, and the victors received their reward by confiscating the possessions of the vanquished. But in repelling the invader nothing was gained in material

Above: A scene showing samurai in full armor during the Mongol invasion which was eventually destroyed by the *kamikaze* (great wind).

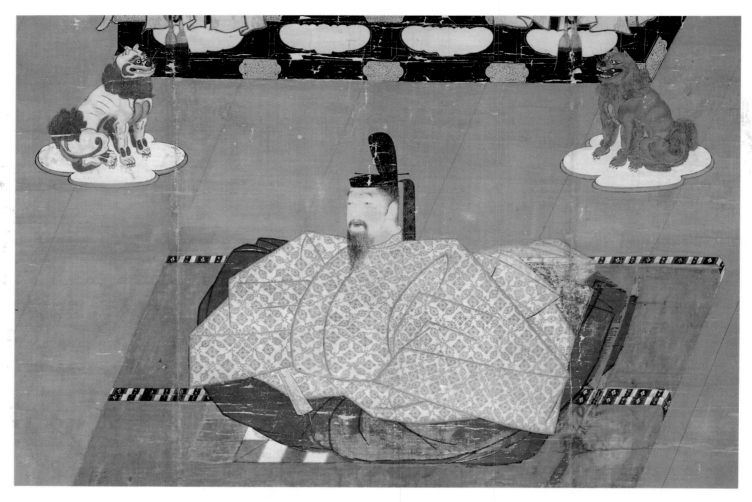

Above: Emperor Godaigo holding court in Daitoku-ji temple, Kyoto.

Right: A suit of twelfth century Japanese armor traditionally associated with Minamoto Yoshitsune.

form. For the warriors of Kyushu, men who had borne the brunt of the fighting, there were severe difficulties. However, the priests had done well. In many cases they had received grants for their temples, or had formerly confiscated land returned to them — this was sometimes at the expense of the military in the region, who had received grants of land in recompense for hard-fought service to the government. In 1275, an arm of the Kamakura government had been installed in Kyushu. Kamakura's refusal to act as arbiter when questions of recompense and reward were referred to the Kyushu government (*tandai*) had caused some discontent with the Kamakura *bakufu*; those administering the Kyushu *tandai*, Hojo or not, also began to abuse their positions in order to amass wealth.

The regent Hojo Tokimune died in 1284 and was succeeded by his son Sadatoki. Around this time there were severe punishments, including executions, meted out to those involved in plots against the Hojo in Kamakura. Not all of these plots were hatched by other clans, although the entire Adachi clan was exterminated around 1285 for treachery. Early in the fourteenth century there were a number of killings within the Hojo family as part of the struggle for high place and influence. Sadatoki died in 1311, having become a monk eight years before. He left instructions that his son Takatoki was to become regent when he grew up (Morotoki, usually thought of as

the last of the Hojo regents, had died a few months before Sadatoki). The named future regent, Takatoki, was under the tutelage of one Nagasaki Enki. Under Takatoki's nominal regency, which began in 1316, there was widespread corruption among his retainers and the high officials of Kamakura, which did nothing to lessen discontent with the rule of the Hojo spreading through the empire.

One of the chief virtues of the Hojo regency had been its legislature and judiciary. Judgment between parties in dispute had never before been prolonged or visibly corrupt under the Hojo. But a sign of the leadership's decline could clearly be seen with the plethora of new lawsuits and regulations, the interpretation of which often took years rather than days as had been the case earlier in the Hojo period. One reason for the mass of new regulations to order the lives of the subjects at the end of the thirteenth century was the increasingly chaotic economic situation. Many of the samurai class were so heavily in debt that the entire income from their estates went to mortgage holders, a great many of whom were simply peasant farmers who had managed to save some money. The samurai in Kamakura felt obliged to keep up the extravagant and fashionable standards originally brought to Kamakura by the Kyoto nobles.

The samurai often said that they were so heavily in debt because of the demands of national defense, but given the absence of

wars for a long period before the attempted Mongol invasions, the total cost of the fine clothes and expensive banquets consumed by the samurai class in Kamakura must have far outweighed the defense budget of the shogunate. In 1297 the Kamakura government resorted to the desperate measure of an 'act of good government' (*tokusei*) which canceled all mortgages and prohibited lawsuits for the recovery of debt interest. Unfortunately, the law only served to make the poorest samurai poorer, because it made it more difficult for needy borrowers to raise money. For the richest, too, there were always ways around the regulations. It seemed that the only way to save the economy would be through warfare – and civil wars were profitable as the spoils were there for the taking in land and goods, not in the non-convertible currency of dead foreign soldiers and wrecked ships.

Nagasaki Enki was succeeded in the powerful position of tutor to the regent by his son, Nagasaki Takasuke, in 1319. At this time there was a successional dispute in the Ando clan, a member of which had, for the past century or so, held the position of *bakufu* lieutenant in what is now Hokkaido to deal with the Ainu. There seems to have been considerable bribery of officials by both sides in this dispute, and Takasuke was remarkably impartial in his acceptance of gifts. The judgment in the Ando dispute, when it came at last, was so ambiguous, as it had to be in order not to offend any of the donors, that it could not possibly satisfy anyone. The parties therefore decided to settle the matter by force of arms. So the shogunate was forced to send troops to Mutsu, where battles were raging, to put down the unrest. There, Ando Goro, who looked like winning his fight against his kinsmen, went into battle against the Hojo and won. The affair was kept strictly secret by the Hojo in Kamakura, but the news gradually filtered out and the court nobles at Kyoto were delighted that the arrogant military rulers had been clearly shown not to be invincible.

There was some confusion over the imperial succession in the latter part of the thirteenth and early fourteenth centuries. The will of Emperor Saga II had provided for the crown to alternate between the lines of descent of his two sons, with predictably chaotic results. The number of ex-emperors grew, as the practice of early abdication of the throne in favor of an infant remained in force, and because all of these former rulers had to be supported financially, with consequent competition for funds and support for the management of their estates. The fact that there were two imperial lines after 1247, the so-called senior and junior lines, meant that there were two powerful and opposing factions in court circles. Only in 1319 did an emperor, Daigo II, accede to the throne after reaching maturity and remain there without abdicating. Daigo II incidentally had a son who became abbot of the powerful Hieizan temple, whose priests were notoriously warlike. This meant that he could call upon a large military force should the need arise. For the first time in centuries an emperor not only had a real sense of his own power, being old enough to exert it, but also had the means to wield that power.

Meanwhile, in Kamakura the situation had deteriorated under the influence of Nagasaki Takasuke. The regent, Hojo Taka-toki, was devoted to concubines and dog-fighting. He seems to have resented Taka-suke's power over him and it is recorded that he planned to have Takasuke murdered in 1330, blaming his own follow-ers when the plot was discovered. Emperor Daigo II was greatly satisfied at this evi-dence of dissension and disorder in Kama-kura, and laid his plans accordingly.

Daigo II came from the junior imperial line and in 1331 the *bakufu* decided to transfer the throne to the prince of the senior line under Emperor Saga's will. When Daigo heard this he escaped to the temple of Mount Kasagi, taking the im-perial seal with him. The *bakufu* sent an enormous force of soldiers after him to re-capture the seal, although they went first to the wrong temple in search of him, think-ing he was with his son at Hieizan. At the end of the battle the temple had fallen and Daigo was a prisoner. He was sent into exile in 1332. Meanwhile the empire faced a series of insurrections. The Hojo were hard put to maintain the cohesion of their domains while they held an emperor who, though in exile, had supporters in many regions and was determined to take power away from the Hojo and rule in his own right. The shogunate had after all always ruled in the name of the emperor.

In the early summer of 1333, an expedi-tion was sent from Kyoto against Daigo's supporters by the Hojo. It was commanded by Ashikaga Takauji, who was not himself a Hojo but of Minamoto descent. Two weeks after leaving the capital, Ashikaga suddenly changed sides and declared for the Emperor Daigo. The Hojo troops in the Kyoto arm of the *bakufu* gave battle, but the flower of the Kamakura troops were fight-ing under Ashikaga and the Hojo leader-ship was forced to flee Kyoto, taking the emperor of the senior line they had declared as titular sovereign, Kogon, as well as two ex-emperors, with them. At the same time, Kamakura itself and the Kanto region in general were in open revolt against the Hojo. There were many landless warrior leaders there who had lost their fortunes and presumably could see no advantage in a Hojo victory, while an imperialist victory would lead to the large-scale confiscation of manors with commensurate rewards for them.

Kamakura placed every available man under arms. Some chronicles say as many as 100,000 soldiers took up arms in defense of Hojo power. However, the provincial

chieftains began deserting to the enemy in droves, as did some from Kamakura itself, and by July 1333 the *bakufu* forces were fighting in the streets of Kamakura, which fell on the 4th or 5th of July. Hojo Takatoki and several hundred of his kinsmen and supporters committed *seppuku*, although Takatoki's son Tokiyuki escaped with his life. The pro-Hojo provincial leaders to the west who had been besieging Chihaya for months, did not know which way to turn, but when they heard that Kamakura had fallen, they surrendered to the emissaries of Ashikaga Takauji. Fifteen of their com-manders were later beheaded at night.

The Hojo fell so suddenly that, although the supporters of the Emperor Daigo found themselves victorious and in possession of most of the empire within a few short months, there was a power vacuum at the top. Kamakura itself had been virtually re-duced to ashes. There was only one cer-tainty: there would be a new regime.

After the fall of the Hojos in 1333 Japan was rent by fighting between various war lords and clan leaders. Kamakura Zen con-tinued, but gradually became seen merely as a means of overcoming the fear of death, without much attempt being made to achieve the spiritual realizations of which fearlessness was supposed to be a side effect. The wider and more fundamental realizations of Zen became to some extent shelved, as did some of its strict moral prin-ciples. In the recently discovered records of Warrior Zen called *Shonan-katto-roku*, a sect centered around the traditions of the Kamakura temples, the incidents which be-came *koans* (riddles) are mostly from the fourteenth century. There are some very early ones for the previous century, a few in the fifteenth century, and only two defi-nitely from the sixteenth.

There are a number of accounts in dif-ferent sources of how, in 1341, Master Toden of Kenchoji temple told a blustering samurai: 'The word loyalty is written with a character made up of two components: center and heart. So it means the lord (heart) in the center of the man. There must be no warring passions. But when this old priest looks at the samurai today, there are some whose heart-center leans toward fame and money, and others where it is toward wine and lust.'

In the Rinzai branch of Zen in China, the shout developed as an expression of free-dom, fearlessness and realization. It could not be imitated; it had to be a spontaneous expression of illumination and freedom, one sometimes produced in surprising cir-cumstances. This was taken up by the teachers of the Japanese warrior class, as we have seen with Tokimune. For instance, an early master, Ganto used to say, 'When I go, I will go with a great shout.' Later his monastery in China was overrun by brigands and all the monks ran away, ex-cept the master, who remained sitting in the meditation posture. When one of the

Left: A very unusual picture of an interview on the *koan* in the fourteenth century between the feudal lord Kuroda and a Zen master.

Left: Tokugawa Iemitsu, the third general of the Tokugawa Shogunate (1600-1867). During this time Japan enjoyed almost 250 years of uninterrupted peace.

Right: Fudo Myo-o, known as the Buddhist Divinity of Unshakeable Wisdom.

Right: A painting by Hakuin of Hotei, one of the Seven Deities of Fortune, depicting 'a Santa Claus with "prosperity" in his huge sack.'

Far right: A rendition of the priest Kensu showing the influence of Chinese Taoist saints, some of whom are also represented in the act of fishing.

other monks had run away, indicating that the practice of Zen did not necessarily give complete fearlessness and independence to all. But there are many of these incidents recorded and in some instances it unquestionably did.

Another famous example of the Zen shout occurred when a rebel general came to the monastery. Again the monks ran way leaving the master sitting there alone. The general strode in and demanded that the master should bow to him, which he refused to do; he simply remained seated. The general shouted, 'Don't you know you are looking at a man who can run you through without blinking?' The Zen master replied in a strong voice, 'And you are looking at a man who can be run through without blinking.' The general stared at him, made a bow, and went away.

The Japanese were not above testing the fearlessness and independence of Zen practitioners. After the importation of firearms at the end of the sixteenth century, a Chinese master happened to be visiting Japan where he was the honored guest of one of the local lords who, however, decided to test his realization. The lord arranged that the master's tea-bowl should be filled right to the brim at a meal. Although the master noticed this, he said nothing and lifted the bowl steadily to his lips. As he was about to drink, the lord gave a concealed signal and a gun was discharged in the next room. The master's hand did not shake and he quietly drank his tea without spilling a drop. The local lord was impressed and said, 'Weren't you a bit surprised when that gun went off?' The Zen master replied, 'Guns are the province of warriors, like you. That is nothing to do with a Zen priest like me.' The lord bowed his head in acquiescence and admiration, and they went on with the meal. Then, when the lord was about to sip tea from his cup, the master suddenly let out a tremendous Zen shout. The lord was very startled and the tea spilt. He turned to the master and said, 'Why did you do that? Look, the tea's all over my clothes.' To which the master answered, 'Why were you startled like that? The Zen shout has nothing to do with warriors like you, it's the business of Zen priests like me. Why did you react to my shout?'

Zen followers are expected to be able to demonstrate calm fearlessness. In one case, there were two sects who had a dispute on Zen doctrine. The Obaku, who had their headquarters in a range of mountains, put up a challenge on a noticeboard in front of their monastery which read, 'This place is the death of the Soto sect.' The Soto heard of this and their abbot assembled the monks and asked for a volunteer, but did not say for what reason. All the monks stepped forward but the abbot selected a young one named Sogyo, who then set out for the Obaku monastery. To get there he had to cross a high bridge over a stream that ran near the monastery. The Obaku

brigands came up and demanded food, the master told him that there was none. The brigand leveled his spear and ran him through, but as he was run through, the master gave a great shout which, it was said, was heard for a mile. However, the monks had heard that he was coming and paid a couple of roughs to wait at the bridge for Sogyo. When he appeared they held him upside down over the stream which was far below, and growled at him, 'What do you say now?' Sogyo replied:

'Snow and ice on the mountain peak,
The rushing torrent in the valley.'

The Obaku monks were very impressed with this and signaled the two roughs not to drop Sogyo but to put him down on the bridge. Thus he passed over, not at all upset, and entered the monastery. There, as the obligatory present, he laid his muddy sandals at the feet of the abbot. Then there was an exchange of views in which the Obaku abbot failed to outwit Sogyo, which left him rather disconcerted. Sogyo then walked out and broke the noticeboard. The strength of his fearlessness is the essential part of the story. Sogyo was calm in his fearlessness: he did not say on the bridge, 'Oh, you can drop me. I don't care.' But he was able to recite the poem. This calm response to a dangerous situation was greatly esteemed and imitated by many Japanese warriors.

Another famous test of Zen arranged by Japan's warriors was in the time of the third shogun, Iemitsu, who was a great patron of both Zen and Bushido, and kept several fencing masters at his court. Particularly in favor was Takuan, from whom many took lessons in meditation and Zen. A tiger had been imported from Korea and brought in its cage to Iemitsu. It was hungry, and the shogun turned to Takuan, saying, 'Has Zen anything else to show?' The Zen master ran down to the cage, his sleeves flying in the wind, he jumped in and faced the tiger. The master then spat on his palm and held it out to the tiger, which sniffed and then licked his hand. The master lightly touched its head, then turned and softly jumped out of the cage. 'After all,' marveled the shogun, 'our way of the sword cannot compete with Zen.'

Zen practice as it developed in China tended to bring the practitioner to a crisis. For instance, the Japanese master Hakuin's crisis developed round an account which he had read of the death of the Chinese master Ganto several centuries before at the hands of a brigand demanding food. Hakuin was profoundly affected by this story. He thought, 'Even the great Ganto could not save himself from the brigand. How can a poor creature like myself be saved from life-and-death?' He spent several months locked in struggle with this riddle which had risen spontaneously in his mind. At the end of that time, he suddenly found enlightenment bursting out from within him: 'Why, I myself am Ganto, with not a hair harmed during all these centuries!'

As this sort of riddle, called a *koan*, developed in the Rinzai branch of Zen, it was found that some pupils were taking a long

Previous pages: A Buddhist priest's *kesa* (mantle) consisting of tapestry depicting the western paradise. The item dates from the eighteenth or nineteenth century.

Below: Zen master Daikaku shortly before his death.

time to arrive at a really practical, radical *koan*. Incidents in the past which had affected the lives of great masters began to be set as riddles to test pupils, so that their awareness could crystallize more quickly around this center provided for them by the teacher. For instance, the teacher may ask: 'What is your true face, which you had before your father and mother were even born?' A modern teacher has said of this: 'If you have really gone through this, then when you are suddenly given only three weeks to live, the true face will blaze in you, and those three weeks will be three weeks in the Pure Land paradise.'

Each *koan* has a definite answer given in a definite form. It has been compared to the problems in mathematics set in school. The principle is explained, but the pupils only half-understand it. They are set a problem with a definite answer which they do not know, but by solving the problem they come to understand the principle thoroughly.

However, if they come to know the right answer in advance, perhaps from a peep at the teacher's book, they will not have really wrestled with the problem. Though they supply the right answer now, they will not necessarily be able to solve similar problems in future. This is one disadvantage of the *koan* system of preset riddles: some of the answers inevitably leak out and pupils will not really explore the *koan*, because all their efforts are directed toward what they know to be the right answer. So the teachers developed certain tests to check whether the student really understands his own answer. If his answer is a mere guess, or inference, or learnt from somewhere else, the tests will reveal that it is not fully understood.

The tests can be almost infinite. If a pupil is asked a question at school to which he does not know the answer, sometimes a friend at the next desk will scribble the answer in large letters. With a sideways glance, the pupil may be able to read it, and then supply an answer. But an alert schoolmaster will not pass this as he can tell from the voice whether the answer comes from knowledge or not. 'What is the velocity of light?' The pupil reads his neighbor's scribble and says confidently: '186,000, sir.' From a good pupil, the master would perhaps accept this, but with this one he probes further: 'Yes, but yards, kilometers, miles?' The pupil has just time to read the neighbor's 'm,' and says 'miles.' Now the master asks: 'Yes, but an hour, a second, a minute, a day, a fortnight?' and everything collapses.

It has long been known that some of the Kamakura leaders like Tokiyori passed through some classical *koans* under the Chinese masters who were coming across to Japan. For instance, the regent Tokiyori is recorded as having solved the 'Face' *koan*. It is also known that some of the samurai at Kamakura became *nyudo* (*nyu* – entering, *do* – way), that is lay practitioners of Zen who shaved their heads and took a Buddhist name, but without actually leaving their families or their military occupation. However, it has sometimes been doubted how much of the Zen training they could actually have undertaken, because the classical Zen *koan* riddles usually required some knowledge of their Chinese background, and none of the Zen classics had been translated into Japanese. Nevertheless, although the Kamakura samurai may have been ill-tutored by the refined standards of Kyoto, the capital, they were certainly not illiterate. Their accomplishments, however, could hardly be expected to extend to Chinese. Of the stream of Chinese Zen masters who came across from the mainland, from Daikaku, who with Tokiyori's support founded Kenchoji temple, to Bukko, the teacher of Tokimune who founded the equally great Enkakuji, few mastered Japanese.

Recently however some early temple

records, dating as far back as 1253, have surfaced which record interviews between Chinese Zen masters and their (mostly Kamakura) samurai pupils. These make it clear that hundreds of warriors had Zen interviews with the Chinese masters and their Japanese successors, and that the teachers did not make use of the classical Chinese *koan* riddles, but rather invented new ones relevant to the daily lives of the samurai pupils. This was called *shikin* (here-and-now) Zen, and some of these incidents were recorded and later became new *koans*, set to test samurai *nyudo* (laymen). The early records contain some remarkable details. For instance, if an interpreter happened not to be present, the Chinese master's words would be taken down phonetically by a Japanese scribe who did not understand them; some of these utterances were preserved in the original form, as well as in the subsequent translations. There were sometimes comical misunderstandings of Chinese colloquialisms, which were completely misunderstood by the Japanese. In one *koan*

the Chinese colloquial phrase for the *tanden*, the center of courage and energy, which translates literally as the 'thing below the navel,' is comically misunderstood.

The collection of 100 of these on-the-spot Zen *koans* called *Shonan-katto-roku* has recently been translated into English. Ten of the 100 center on women, pupils and teachers. There was no prejudice against women in Zen; if they could stand the training they were on the same level as the men. The form of the *koans* in *Shonan-katto-roku* is that each incident is described, and then a number of questions are asked which have to be answered by the pupil one by one, but not necessarily in words. Here are a few examples:

No 1: Daikaku's one-word sutra

At the beginning of the Kencho era (1249), 'Old Buddha' Daikaku was invited by Shogun Tokiyori to spread Zen in the east of Japan. Some priests and laymen of other sects were not at all pleased at this, and out of jealousy spread it around that the

Below: A courtesan tempting Bodhidharma, as rendered by Kunimaru, says to Bodhidharma while he is in meditation, 'O-Daruma San Just look for a moment In this world of ours are beautiful things Moon, snow, flowers, love and wine.'

teacher was a spy sent to Japan by the Mongols; gradually more and more people began to believe it. At the time the Mongols were in fact sending emissaries to Japan, and the shogun's government, misled by the campaign of rumors, transferred the teacher to Koshu. He was not the least disturbed, but gladly followed the karma which led him away.

Some officials there, who were firm believers in repetition of the formula of the Lotus, or in recitation of the name of Amida, one day came to him and said: 'The heart sutra which is read in the Zen tradition is long and difficult to read, whereas Nichiren teaches the formula of the Lotus which has only seven syllables, and Ippen teaches repetition of the name of Amida, which is only six. The Zen sutra is much longer, and it is difficult to get through it.' The teacher listened to all this and said: 'What would a follower of Zen want with a long text? If you want to recite the Zen sutra, do it with one word. It is the six and seven word ones which are too long.'

Master Setsuo used to present his pupils with this story as the riddle of Daikaku's one-word sutra. He would say to them: 'The golden-faced teacher [Buddha], it is said, in all his 49 years of preaching never uttered a single word. But our "Old Buddha" declares one word to lead the people to salvation. What is that word, say! What is that one word? If you cannot find it, your whole life will be spent entangled in creepers in a dark cave. If you can say it, with that leap of realization you will pervade heaven and earth.' Those who were set this riddle over the years tried the words 'heart,' 'Buddha,' 'dharma,' 'God,' and 'mantra,' but none of them were correct. 'When the pearly sweat

Below: A figurine of the seated Buddha Amida Nyorai, carved in wood, lacquer and gilt, from the Kamakura period of the thirteenth century.

runs down the body, coming and going for the interviews with the teacher, the one word will be met directly.'

No 2: Wielding the spear with hands empty

Nanjo Masatomo, a master of the spear, was at Kenchoji to worship and afterward spoke with priest Gio about using a spear on horseback. Gio said, 'Your honor is indeed well versed in the art of the spear. But until you have known the state of wielding the spear with empty hands, you will not penetrate to the ultimate secret of the art.' Nanjo said, 'What do you mean?' The teacher said, 'No spear in the hands, no hands on the spear.' The spear master did not understand. The teacher said further, 'If you don't understand, your art of the spear is a little affair of the hands alone.'

No 3: Tokimune's thing below the navel

When Tokimune received the news that the Mongol armada was poised to attack Japan, he went in full armor to see Bukko his teacher and said, 'The great thing has come.' The teacher replied, 'Can you somehow avoid it?' Tokimune calmly stamped his feet, shook his whole body and gave a tremendous shout of Katzu! The teacher said, 'A real lion cub; a real lion roar. Dash straight forward and don't look around!' Gio, a priest who witnessed the event, said, 'The general has got something great below his navel, so the shout too is great.'

The Field of the Elixir (tanden, the energy-center an inch below the navel) of Taoist doctrine was called in the Szechuan dialect Shii-ku-ii-mo, the thing under the navel. Gio was a priest from Szechuan who had come with Daikaku to Kenchoji in Japan, and in praising the greatness of Hojo Tokimune's tanden energy, he used this Szechuan phrase, but like many remarks of the Chinese priests, it was transcribed into Chinese characters and the Japanese, not knowing the colloquial Szechuan phrase, took it in a literal sense.

One of the regent's ministers, Masanori, when he came to know what Gio had said, asked him indignantly: 'When did Your Reverence see the size of what our lord has below his navel?!' The priest said: 'Before the general was born, I saw it.' The courtier did not understand. The priest said: 'If you do not understand the greatness of what is below the general's navel, then see through to before you yourself were born, the greatness of the thing below the navel. How would that thing become greater or less by the honor or contempt of high or low?' The courtier was still more bewildered. The priest gave a Katzu shout and said: 'Such is the voice of it, of that thing.'

At these words the courtier had an insight and said: 'This petty official today has been fortunate enough to receive a Katzu from you. I have known the greatness of the thing below our lord's navel.' The priest said: 'What is its length and breadth, say!'

The courtier said: 'Its length pierces the three worlds; its breadth pervades all 10 directions.' The priest said: 'Let the noble officer present a Katzu of that greatness to show the proof.' The courtier was not able to open his mouth.

TESTS
1. What is the meaning of dashing straight ahead?
2. Say directly, what is the general's dashing straight forward?
3. Leaving the general's dashing straight forward, what is your dashing straight forward, here and now? Speak!
4. Leaving your dashing straight forward, what is the dashing straight forward of all the Buddhas and beings of the three worlds?
5. Leaving the dashing straight forward of the Buddhas and beings, what is the dashing straight forward of heaven and earth and the 10,000 phenomena?
6. Leaving for the moment the thing below the navel of the Taoists, what is the thing below the navel in our tradition? Say!
7. Say something about the thing below the navel before our father and mother were born.
8. When the light of life has failed, then say something of that thing below the navel.
9. Leaving the general's Katzu — when you yourself are threatened by an enemy from somewhere, what great deed will you perform? Say!
10. Give a Katzu for the courtier to prove it.

According to the records in Gosan-nyu-doshu in Kamakura the samurai there were set this *koan* and wrestled with it, and even after 'seeing the nature' they were never passed through it for at least five or six years. It is said that 'dash straight forward' in the first test was often taken to mean 'swiftly' or else 'sincerely,' and that they were never passed.

No 4: Meditation of the energy-sea
A retired landowner named Sadashige of Awafune trained at Kenchoji under Nan-zan, the twentieth master. Once he was away for a time and when he returned the teacher said, 'You have been ill, sir, and for some time you have not come to the Zen sitting here. Have you now been able to purify and calm your *kikai* [energy-sea]?' Sadash-ige said, 'Following your holy instruction I have meditated on the *kikai* and been able to attain purity and calm.' The teacher said, 'Bring out what you have understood of the meditation and say something on it.'

1. This my *kikai tanden*, breast, belly, (down to the) soles of my feet, (is) alto-gether my original face.

TEST
What nostrils would there be on that face?

2. This my *kikai tanden* (is) altogether my true home.

TEST
What news would there be from the true home?

3. This my *kikai tanden* (is) altogether this my lotus paradise of conscious-ness only.

TEST
What pomp would there be in the lotus paradise?

4. This my *kikai tanden* (is) altogether the Amida of my own body.

TEST
What sermon would that Amida be preach-ing?

No 5: Heaven and earth broken up
Tadamasa, a senior retainer of Hojo Taka-toki the regent, had the Buddhist name Anzan (quiet mountain). He was a keen Zen follower and for 23 years came and went to the meditation hall for laymen at Kenchoji. When the fighting broke out everywhere in 1331, he was wounded in one engagement, but in spite of the pain galloped to Kenchoji to see Sozan, the twenty-seventh teacher

Below: The guardian figure at the Great South Gate of Todaiji temple. Generally, there are two figures at the gates of a temple, displayed as a pair. One figure has its mouth open and the other closed. One is saying 'Aaaa' and the other 'Hum.'

Far right: The seated figure of Fudo Myo – 'the Divinity of Unshakeable Wisdom.'

there. A tea ceremony was going on at Kenchoji, and the teacher seeing the man in armor come in, quickly put a teacup in front of him and said, 'How is this?' The warrior at once crushed it under his foot and said, 'Heaven and earth broken up altogether.'

The teacher said, 'When heaven and earth are broken up, how is it with you?' Anzan stood with his hands crossed over his breast. The teacher hit him, and he involuntarily cried out from the pain of his wounds. The teacher said, 'Heaven and earth not quite broken up yet.' The drum sounded from the camp across the mountain, and Tadamasa galloped quickly back. The next evening he came again, covered with blood, to see the teacher. The teacher came out and said again: 'When heaven and earth are broken up, how is it with you?' Anzan, supporting himself on his blood-stained sword, gave a great Katzu and died standing in front of the teacher.

TEST
When heaven and earth are broken up, how is it with you? (note: In the *Bukedoshinshu*, the version is: When the elements of the body are dispersed, where are you?)

No 6: The Great Katzu of Master Toden
Yorimasa was a swaggering and aggressive samurai (in the Nirayama manuscript of *Bukedoshinshu* and in some other accounts the name is given as Yorihara). In the spring of 1341 he was transferred from Kofu to Kamakura, where he visited Master Toden, the forty-fifth teacher at Kenchoji, to ask about Zen.

The teacher said, 'It is to manifest directly the Great Action in the 100 concerns of life. When it is loyalty as a samurai, it is the loyalty of Zen. "Loyalty" is written with the Chinese character made up of "center" and "heart", so it means the lord in the center of the man. There must be no wrong passions. But when this old priest looks at the samurai today, there are some whose heart-center leans toward fame and money, and others where it is toward wine and lust, and with others it is inclined toward power and bravado. They are all on those slopes, and cannot have a centered heart; how could they have loyalty to the state? If you, Sir, wish to practice Zen, first of all practice loyalty and do not slip into wrong desires.' The warrior said, 'Our loyalty is direct Great Action on the battlefield. What need have we for sermons from a priest?' The teacher replied, 'You, Sir, are a hero in strife, I am a gentleman of peace – we can have nothing to say to each other.' The warrior then drew his sword and said, 'Loyalty is in the hero's sword, and if you do not know this, you should not talk of loyalty.' The teacher replied, 'This old priest has the treasure sword of the Diamond King, and if you do not know it, you should not talk of the source of loyalty.' The samurai said, 'Loyalty of your Diamond Sword – what is

the use of that sort of thing in actual fighting?' The teacher jumped forward and gave one Katzu shout, giving the samurai such a shock that he lost consciousness. After some time the teacher shouted again and the samurai at once recovered. The teacher said, 'Loyalty in the hero's sword, where is it? Speak!' The samurai was over-awed; he apologized and took his departure. (In the account in the sixth volume of *Gosannyudoshu* it is added that Yorihara wept and presented his sword in token of repentance.)

TEST
Right now before you is that samurai. Try a shout that the teacher may see the proof.

No 7: The Kannon at Hase
Miura Nobuto, naval commander at Hase, had practiced Zen for a long time. He happened to mention to the teacher Hakudo, when he met him on the occasion of a ceremony of confession and absolution at Hokokuji temple, that the Kannon at Hase was a great figure over 10 feet high. The teacher said, 'What is the difference in weight between Your Honor and Kannon?' The commander said, 'The weight is the same.' The teacher: 'Your Honor is just over five feet tall. How can your weight be the same as Kannon over 10 feet?' The commander: 'The weighing was done before I was born.' The teacher: 'I'm not asking about before you were born. What is it now?' The commander: 'By the power of meditation on Kannon, the weight comes out the same.'

TEST
1. How can the weights be compared before birth?
2. What really is this saying that with his present body of just over five feet his weight is the same as the 10-foot Kannon?
3. What is this about the power of meditation of Kannon?

No 8: The Great Katzu of Master Torin
The Tokeiji nunnery at Kamakura was known as the Divorce Temple, because if a woman of the samurai class who was unhappy in marriage entered there and stayed three years, the marriage link was dissolved, by an imperial rescript given by Emperor Gofukakusa at the request of the Hojo regent Sadatoki. Later a period of one year's residence was made sufficient, by a ruling of the Ashikaga government, for the temple regulations regarding divorce to come into effect.

In the third year of Enbun (1358), Ashikaga Motouji sent a man to decoy Nitta Yoshioki to Yakuchiwatashi in Musashi, and kill him there. Motouji's wife Akijo, herself born into the Nitta clan, was overwhelmed with grief at the treacherous murder of Yoshioki, and requested to be allowed to become a nun to pray for his soul. But this was not acceded to.

Above: The Great Jizo. The Jizo is 16 feet in height and breadth, and weighs over 800lbs. The doors of the Buddha-hall made an opening of only eight feet. How did the monk carry the Jizo out through that opening?

Apprehending that there might now be some danger to herself also, she made a hurried escape from the palace and hid herself in Tokeiji. When she had been there a year, Kanemitsu, a minister of the governor, came to know of it, and arrived determined to take her away by force. The nun Eko, who had a senior position at Tokeiji, at once sent across to Enkakuji to ask the abbot to come. This was Torin, the thirty-second master there, and when he came he greeted Kanemitsu, and explained the regulations for the temple under which it would be forbidden to arrest Akijo, who would have right of sanctuary. Kanemitsu became angry and drew his sword to threaten the abbot with it. The latter remonstrated with him against the use of violence but he refused to listen.

Torin on the instant gave a great Katzu shout, and Kanemitsu fell unconscious. After a little while, the abbot shouted again and Kanemitsu revived. The teacher then said: 'The rule that after three years here, the marriage bond is severed was laid down in an imperial rescript of the Emperor Gofukakusa, and the regulation that even one year would be sufficient was an ordinance of General Ashikaga Takauji. These decrees have never been broken, and for a minister of the governor here to violate the sanctuary would be no light offense.' As he continued speaking, Kanemitsu found himself unable to reply; he fell into a convulsion and died.

TEST

Right now before you is a ruffian with drawn sword threatening your life. Try whether you can kill and revive him with a Katzu. Show the proof.

Those two *koans* involving a Katzu to kill and revive were very difficult to pass. There are other *koans* in the *Shonan-katto-roku* where a Katzu is used to strike down, but there are only three where this is to be followed by a second Katzu to bring back to consciousness.

At the time when Kamakura Zen flourished, there had to be a teacher who could demonstrate in actual practice in this way in order to handle the warrior students of Zen. To pass this *koan* the pupil had to apply the striking and reviving Katzu shouts to some bird or dog and so on outside the interview room. These days when Zen is enfeebled, there is not one in a hundred who could do so. It is said that Yamaoka Tesshu took these tests under the hammer of Master Geno of Chotokuji, and later perfected them under Master Ryutaku. Katsu Kaishu, again, took them at Kotokuji under Master Kisatei, and is reported to have had a hard time with them. But since the Meiji restoration we hardly hear of any who have done so, which bespeaks weakness of samurai power and an enfeeblement of Zen.

No 9: The paper sword

In 1331 when Nitta Yoshisada was fighting against Hojo Sadatoki, a chief retainer of the Hojo family, named Sakurada Sadakuni, was slain. His wife Sawa wished to pray for the dead man; she cut off her hair and entered Tokeiji as the nun Shotaku. For many years she devoted herself to Zen under Daisen, the seventeenth master of Enkakuji, and in the end she became the third teacher of Tokeiji. In the winter training week of December 1338 she was returning from her evening interview with the teacher at Enkakuji, when on the way a man armed with a sword saw her and was attracted by her beauty. He threatened her with the sword and came to rape her. The nun took out a piece of paper and rolled it up, then thrust it like a sword at the man's eyes. He became unable to strike and was completely overawed by her spiritual strength. He turned to run and the nun gave a Katzu shout, hitting him with the paper sword. He fell and then fled.

TEST

Show the paper sword is the heart sword, and prove its actual effect now. The manifestation of the paper sword as a real sword is from the cultivation of the *kikai tanden* (the elixir field in the energy sea), and originally in Kamakura Zen all the teachers gave this test. Oishi Yoshina (of the 47 *ronin*) took this *koan* under Master Bankei, and Araki Matauemon under Takuan at Nanshuji.

When Araki encountered Yagyu Tajima-no-kami, the latter was a teacher of fencing to the shogun, and it was the rule that any samurai who wished to meet him had to leave behind both swords in the waiting room. Informed of this Araki took off his weapons. When he came before Yagyu, the latter wished to test his spirit, and suddenly challenged him to a duel, drawing his own weapon. According to the old accounts Araki snatched up a piece of paper, rolled it up and was able to meet Yagyu with it as a sword. There is a widespread tradition in the Zen world about this contest, and it is accepted that Araki was able to manifest the paper as a sword by virtue of having taken this Kamakura *koan* of the paper sword under Master Takuan in his interview room.

No 10: The night interview of Nun Myotei

Myotei was a widow and a woman well known for her strength of character. She trained for some years under Kimon, the hundred and fiftieth master of Enkakuji; on a chance visit to the temple she had had an experience while listening to a sermon by him on the Diamond Sutra. In the year 1568 she took part in the winter training week. This is the most severe training week of the year; it is at the beginning of December, when according to tradition the Buddha meditated six days and nights, then looked at the morning star and attained full realization. There is almost continuous meditation broken only by interviews with the teacher, sutra chanting, meals and tea; this goes on for a week, with very little or no sleep according to the temple. On the morning after the last night's meditation and interviews the participants look together at the morning star.

Before one of the night interviews she took off her robes and came in without anything on at all. She lay down before the teacher, who picked up his iron *nyo-i* (ceremonial stick) and thrust it out towards her thighs, saying, 'What trick is this?' The nun said, ' I present the gate by which all the Buddhas of the three realms come into the world.' The teacher said, 'Unless the Buddhas of the three realms go in, they cannot come out. Let the gate be entered here and now,' and he sat astride the nun. She demanded, 'He who should enter, what Buddha is that?' The teacher said, 'What is to be from the beginning has no "should" about it.' The nun said, 'He who does not give his name is a barbarian brigand, who is not allowed to enter.' The teacher said, 'Maitreya Buddha, who has to be born to save the people after the death of Shakyamuni Buddha, enters the gate.' The nun made as if to speak and the teacher quickly covered her mouth. He pressed the iron stick between her thighs saying, 'Maitreya Buddha enters the gate. Give birth this instant!' The nun hesitated and the teacher said, 'This is no true womb; how could this give birth to Maitreya?' The nun went out

and at the interview the next morning the teacher said, 'Have you given birth to Maitreya?' The nun cried with great force, 'He was born quietly last night.' She caught hold of the teacher and put her hands round the top of his head saying, 'I invite the Buddha to take the top of this head as the Lion Throne. Let him graciously preach a sermon from it.' The teacher said, 'The way one alone, not two, not three.' The nun said, 'In their abilities, the beings differ in 10,000 ways. How should you stick to one way?' The teacher said, 'One general at the head of 10,000 men enters the capital.'

TEST
1. What is the real meaning of Myotei's coming naked for the night interview?
2. The nun hesitated about giving birth to Maitreya. Say something for her.
3. What does the one general and the 10,000 soldiers mean? What is it directly? Now say!

No 11: Benzaiten of Enoshima

Doi Yorimune came up to Mizugaoka and visited Mugaku (Bukko), a general of the Zen sect, and asked about the worship of Benzaiten (goddess of prosperity) of Enoshima Island. He recalled how on the fifth day of the fourth month of the second year of Yowa (1182), the Minamoto general Yoritomo had been strolling on the beach at Namigoe on the way to Enoshima, and there had met the holy man Bungaku who was a devotee of Benzaiten. He said he would pray for the general's success in arms, and arrangements were made for sacrificial ceremonies, and the erection of a stone *torii*. This was, he added, really with the motive of exorcizing the curse pronounced by Fujiwara Hidehara (on the Minamotos). He concluded: 'I have brought a picture of the blessing being conferred by Benzaiten.' The teacher said: 'The Benzaiten prayed to Benzaiten for the military glory of the Minamoto general, and to avert the curse of the other general of those days – is that a male divinity or a female?' Doi said: 'Whether Benzaiten is a god or a goddess, I do not know. I only know that the form of the picture here is a goddess.' The teacher said: 'So you go by the form. I suppose you would think that a woman warrior dressed in man's clothes would be a man?' Doi said: 'Well then, is Benzaiten a male dressed as a female?'

The teacher replied: 'Do you worship Benzaiten as a god or do you worship Benzaiten as a goddess?' Doi said: 'The reason I worship is nothing to do with whether it is a god or a goddess. I just pray for my welfare.' The teacher at once caught hold of Doi and rubbed his face, first against the grain of the beard, and then with the grain. Doi did not understand what he meant. The teacher said: 'This fellow! He has never believed in Benzaiten at all. Why does he come here wanting to get approval from me?'

Below: A monk reading the Scriptures. He has characteristic attributes of a saint: a protuberance on the forehead and very long earlobes.

TEST
1. Is Benzaiten a god or a goddess? Say!
2. What did Bukko mean by rubbing Doi's face with the grain and against the grain? Say!

This incident became a *koan* in Kamakura Zen when Issan, the seventh of Enkakuji, gave it to Suko, a mountain hermit.

No 12: The Sermon of the Nun Shido

At the winter training week of 1304 at En-kakuji, Master Tokei ('Peach-tree Valley') gave his formal approval (*inka*) as a teacher to the nun Shido, the founder of Tokeiji. The head monk did not approve of the *inka* being granted, and asked a question to test her:

'In our line, one who receives the *inka* gives a discourse on the Rinzairoku classic. Can the nun teacher really brandish the staff of the Dharma in the Dharma-seat?'

She faced him, drew out the 10-inch knife carried by all women of the warrior class and held it up: 'Certainly a Zen teacher of the line of the patriarch should go up on the high seat and speak on the book. But I am a woman of the warrior line and I should declare our teaching when really face to face with a drawn sword. What book should I need?' The head monk said, 'Before father and mother were born, with what then will you declare our teaching?' The nun closed her eyes for some time. Then she said, 'Do you understand?'

The monk said in verse:
'A wine-gourd has been tipped right up in Peach-tree Valley:
Drunken eyes see 10 miles of flowers.'

TEST
1. Before father and mother were born, what was the sermon? Say!
2. What is the meaning of the poem made by the head monk?
3. Are its two lines praise or criticism?

No 13: Painting the nature

Ekichu, the seventh master of Jufukuji, was famous as a painter. One day Nobu-mitsu came to see him and ask whether he could paint the fragrance described in the famous line 'After walking through flowers, the horse's hoof is fragrant.' The teacher drew a horse's hoof and a butterfly flutter-ing round it attracted by the fragrance.

Then Nobumitsu quoted the line 'Spring breeze over the river bank' and asked for a picture of the breeze. The teacher drew a branch of willow waving. Nobumitsu cited the famous Zen phrase, 'A finger direct to the human heart, see the nature to be Buddha.' He asked for a picture of the heart. The teacher picked up the brush and immediately flicked a spot of ink on to Nobumitsu's face.

The warrior was surprised and annoyed, and the teacher rapidly sketched the angry face. Then Nobumitsu asked for a picture of the 'nature' as in the phrase 'see the nature.' The teacher broke the brush and said, 'That's the picture.' Nobumitsu did not understand and the teacher remarked, 'If you haven't got that seeing eye, you can't see it.' Nobumitsu said, 'Take another brush and paint the picture of the nature.' The teacher replied: 'Show me your nature and I will paint it.' Nobumitsu had no words.

TEST
1. How would you show the nature?
2. Come, see your nature and bring the proof of it.
3. Say something for Nobumitsu.

No 14: Victory in the midst of 100 enemies

To the priest Yozan came for an interview a samurai named Ryozan, who practiced Zen. The teacher said: 'You are going into the bath-tub, stark naked without a stitch on. Now a hundred enemies in armor, with bows and swords, appear all around you. How will you meet them? Will you crawl before them and beg for mercy? Will you show your warrior birth by dying in combat against them or does a man of the Way get some special holy grace?' Ryozan said, 'Let me win without surrendering and without fighting.'

TEST
Caught in the midst of the hundred enemies, how will you manage to win with-out surrendering and without fighting?

Right: Zen religious sessions last some 40 minutes, followed by a brief period to stretch and another session.

Below, far right: The warning stick hits hard on the shoulder muscles. The recipient is prepared by receiving a warning tap first.

Below: The warning stick is used in Zen temples in China and Japan to awaken the inattentive.

No 15: The very first Jizo

Sakawa Koresada, a direct retainer of the Uesugi family, entered the main hall at Kenchoji and prayed to the Jizo of a Thousand Forms there. Then he asked the attendant monk in charge of the hall: 'Of these thousand forms of Jizo, which is the very first Jizo?' The attendant said, 'In the breast of the retainer before me are a thousand thoughts and ten thousand imaginings; which of these is the very first one?' The samurai was silent. The attendant said again, 'of the thousand forms of Jizo, the very first Jizo is the Buddha-lord who is always using those thousand forms.' The warrior said, 'Who is this Buddha-lord?' The attendant suddenly caught him and twisted his nose. The samurai immediately had a realization.

TEST

1. Which is the very first Jizo out of the thousand-formed Jizo?
2. Which is the very first out of the thousand thoughts and 10,000 imaginings?
3. What did Koresada realize when his nose was twisted?

No 16: The diamond realm

In 1313, on the evening of the seventh day of Rohatsu (December training week), Suketaka Nyudo, a Zen layman training there, crept into the Buddha hall at Kenchoji and stole the delicacies from the altar to make

up for the poor food. However, the monk in charge of the hall happened to come back, and caught him. He said to him: 'According to the Rohatsu rules, this week is the strictest time of the whole year. For you to steal the food from the Buddha hall at a time like this is no small crime. But I will put a question to you, and if you can answer, I will let you off.' Suketaka replied, 'Out with it then.' The monk said, 'What is it, your taking food like this? The other answered, 'The universal body (*dharma-kaya*) eats the cakes, the cakes eat the *dharma-kaya*.' The monk said, 'is the difference between you and the universal body large or small?' Suketaka said, 'The taste of the salt in the water: the transparent glue which holds the color of the paints.' The monk said. 'What is that supposed to mean?' Suketaka said, 'A gust of wind – the more you try to paint it the more you fail.' The monk said, 'Let's try to paint it.' The samurai then said, 'The diamond realm.' The monk said, 'The diamond realm – what's that?' Suketaka replied, 'Going into the fire it does not burn: going into the water, it does not drown.' The monk of the hall said, 'Let us try a test on you.' He took a bundle of incense sticks (at that period it would be 200 sticks), set them alight and put them on the other's head. The warrior leapt up and ran out toward the training hall; he tripped and fell into the big Sleeping Dragon well at the bottom of the steps. The monk put the lid on the well and cried, 'Just now you were saying that in fire it does not burn, and in water it does not drown. Now say quick, what is the diamond realm!' Suketaka could find no reply.

TEST
1. Say something of your own on the diamond realm in the fire.
2. Say something of your own on the diamond realm in the water.
3. Say something of your own on the diamond realm on the edge of a sword.
4. Say something of your own on the diamond realm in the wineshop and in the brothel.
5. Say something on the diamond realm on the thirtieth day of Rohatsu (after death).
6. Say something on the diamond realm in the screams of hell.
7. That thieving man said, 'The *dharma*-body eats the cakes; the cakes eat the *dharma*-body.' What should these words really mean?
8. Again he said, 'A gust of wind – the more you try to paint it the more you fail.' What is the essential principle of this?

No 17: The verse facing death
In the eighth month of the second year of Te Yu, priest Mugaku (Zen master Bukko) when facing death by the sword of a Mongol soldier spoke the verse:
In heaven and earth no crack to hide;

Joy to know the man is void and the things too are void.
Splendid the great Mongolian long sword, Its lightning flash cuts the spring breeze.

TEST
1. Which line contains the essence of all four lines?
2. Men and things are right before us now; how can one make them out to be void?
3. What does the phrase about the lightning flash mean?

No 18: The gate by which all the Buddhas come into the world
Originally Enkakuji was a place forbidden to women, with the exception that unmarried women of a samurai family who were training at Zen were allowed to come and go through the gate. After 1334 a rule was made that unless a woman had attained to 'seeing the nature' she was not allowed to go to the Great Light Hall. In time it became the custom that the keeper of the gate, when a woman applied to go through, would present a test question. According to one tradition from that time, five tests were in use at the gate of Enkakuji.

TEST
1. The gate has many thresholds: even Buddhas and patriarchs cannot get through.
2. The strong iron door is hardly to be opened. Let one of mighty power tear off its hinges.
3. Vast outstretched in all directions – no door, no gate. How will you recognize the gate?
4. 84,000 gates open at the same time. He who had the eye, let him see.
5. What is it this gate by which all the Buddhas come into the world?

A pupil of Ninpo, the nun teacher at Tokeiji, was Yoshihime (daughter of General Kanazawa Sada), who was ugly and also exceptionally strong. Her nickname was 'devil-girl'. She wished to have Zen interviews with Old Buddha Seisetsu, and went across to Enkakuji up to the gate. But the gate-keeper monk barred her way with a shout: 'What is it, the gate through which the Buddhas come into the world?' Yoshihime got hold of his head and forced it between her legs saying: 'Look, look!' The monk said: 'In the middle, there is a fragrance of wind and dew.' Yoshihime said: 'This monk! He's not fit to keep the gate; he ought to be looking after the garden.' The gate-keeper ran into the temple and reported this to the master's attendant, who said, 'Let us go down and test this, and see if we can give a twist in there.' At the gate, he tested her with the question: 'What is it, the gate through which the Buddhas come into the world?' Yoshihime again got hold of the head and held it between her legs, saying: 'Look, look!' The attendant said: 'The Buddhas of the three worlds come giving light.'

Yoshihime said: 'This monk is one with the eye; he saw the 84,000 gates thrown open all together.'

TEST
1. Say a password for Yoshihime to enter the gate.
2. Sweep aside the iron door that bars you.
3. Vast outstretched in all directions: how is that state?
4. How do you see the 84,000 gates? Say!
5. What is it, the gate through which the Buddhas come into the world?
6. What is this 'fragrance of wind and dew'?
7. I do not ask you about the Buddhas of the three worlds giving light, but how do you give light right now?

(Note: Those who do not know Kamakura Zen may give a derisive smile at the gate-keeper's reply: 'In the middle there is a fragrance of wind and dew,' and for them I add a few words. The two legs represent the opposites of being and non-being, form and emptiness, ultimate and provisional truth, and so on. The fragrance of wind and dew is the experience of the Middle Way apart from these opposites. Nevertheless the gate-keeper's response was a very pedestrian one from the Zen point of view, and Yoshihime did not assent to it.)

No 19: Daibai's shari-pearls
Sakuma Suketake of Okura (in the Kamakura region), a student of Zen, was known in the world as Demon Sakuma. For many years he was in active service in the army, but finally his left hand and right leg were disabled by wounds so that he could no longer take part in warfare.

He entered the monk's training hall at Enkakuji and practiced hard at Zen for over 10 years, being given the name lay brother Daibai. In the winter of 1394 there was a great snowfall during the Rohatsu week, and following the precedent of Tanka's Buddha burning, he found in the Jizo hall outside the mountain gate a Buddha-image whose wood was rotting away, and was setting light to it against the freezing cold when the lay brother in charge of the Houn-kaku hall at the mountain gate shouted at him to stop.

Daibai said: 'What is wrong with burning a wooden Buddha whose ashes will have no shari-pearls?' The other was a huge man of great strength, and he pushed Daibai towards the fire saying: 'Your ashes certainly will have no shari-pearls, so let us burn you.' Daibai shouted in a fury: 'How would you know whether my ashes have pearls or not? If you want to know about my ashes, I will show you!' and he jumped into the now blazing fire, gave a great Katzu shout and died standing. His body was consumed by the flames, and when the fire had died out, there were eight shari-pearls shining there.

TEST
1. The test says: Have your ashes shari-pearls? Say how many, and bring proof.
2. Putting aside for the moment dying in the fire, die standing here and now on the tatami mats, and bring the proof.

(In much later times there were cases where a live charcoal was put into the pupil's hand at the interview, and to pass this *koan* he had to remain calm, to make the demonstration of Daibai's death standing in the fire. But this kind of thing is a degeneration of Zen. It cannot compare with the traditional Zen, when the pupil standing before the teacher gave one Katzu and passed into samadhi. The *koan* cannot be passed without a keen Zen spirit and practice for some years.)

Below: On formal occasions the Japanese Zen priest may sit on a chair.

The Warrior Generals

The struggle for mastery among the various factions of the warrior class over the centuries, fueled by the Zen spiritual discipline, is revealing in itself of the nature of Bushido. One of the more important aspects of that nature was the military leader who was an example to his men both spiritually and personally, aside from his prowess on the battlefield. The traditional generals are typified by Takeda Shingen (1521-73) and Uesugi Kenshin (1530-78). The latter was a sort of Galahad, a saint among Japan's generals, and here is a short extract from some of his writings:

'The great evil that a general must avoid is only evil passions. Looking around today, there are few generals free of such desires. When a general has them, then his soldiers insofar as they are aware of it, give him up and become masterless samurai or join some other clan [kuni] or country. When it happens that soldiers are doing this and deserting, the first cause is that their own clan has become weak in the "Way of the Bowman." When one thinks this over, a human being will distance himself from desires, and evil will go away of itself. That is the true Way and if one keeps to it he will be most secure. If he throws away his hankerings and keeps to what is right, high and low will all be in harmony.'

Kenshin's life and actions give an impression of great purity. For instance, he took part in one great battle believing it to be his duty but refused to take any land as plunder, although this was the normal custom of the age. It was said of him that his politics and his wars were like some artist engaged in producing a masterpiece. Then there was a famous encounter between Shingen and Kenshin, in which Kenshin rode into Shingen's camp and aimed a blow at him with a sword shouting, 'What do you say at this moment?' Shingen managed to snatch up an iron war-fan, parry the blow and shout in reply, 'A snowflake on a red-hot furnace.' At which Kenshin turned and dashed off again on his horse. There was an historic rivalry but also a chivalrous respect between these two, and when Shingen ran short of salt, Kenshin was generous enough

to send supplies of it to his enemy. Takeda Shingen was noted for the fact that he did not have a main castle. He used to say, 'My castle is in the hearts of my people' and in fact he was highly regarded and respected in his domain.

Although firearms were entering Japan by the end of the sixteenth century these two traditionalists never made use of them.

It was somehow regarded as unsporting or perhaps they were like chess players who did not want an additional new piece on the board. In any case they did not use them. It was three generals who came just after this era who introduced firearms and transformed a clan-dominated society into one that gave expression to a new feeling of nationalism. The three 'heroes' who were to unify Japan were Oda Nobunaga (1534-82), Toyotomi Hideyoshi (1537-98) and Tokugawa Ieyasu (1543-1616).

The first, Nobunaga, dealt ruthlessly with his enemies and deserves his reputation as a brutal warlord. There are a number of accounts of his men slaughtering whole populations. One case, reported in *Shin-cho-Ko-Ki* (the chronicle of Nobunaga's deeds), occurred at Nagashima in Ise, where 20,000 followers of the Jodo Shin sect were burnt alive. No considerations of humanity prevented Nobunaga from ordering the slaughter of the women and children who survived among the ashes of the monasteries and temples. The two following examples will give a succinct idea of Nobunaga's autocratic rule.

From 1561 onward, Nobunaga repeatedly invaded Mino, an area situated in the west of Japan. After its conquest in 1567 he began to use in his seal a slogan expressing

a further far-reaching ambition: 'Tenka Fubu' (The realm subjected to the military). Then, following his reconquest of Echizen, Nobunaga appointed a general (Shibata Katsute, 1522-83) governor of the province. Shibata's authority was restricted, however, by a set of regulations (*Okite Jojo*), one of which said: 'You must resolve to do everything I say . . . You shall revere me and shall bear me no evil thought behind my back.'

However his ruthlessness should not hide the fact that he also masterminded a number of genuine accomplishments, both cultural and institutional. Nobunaga was an enthusiastic supporter of the arts, and his patronage was a powerful stimulus to the development of the brilliant culture of the Azuchi-Momoyama period (1568-1600).

Before Nobunaga, Japan was politically fragmented, but at the time of his violent death, the realm (*tenka*) united under his rule comprised over a third of the sixteenth century empire. The system of government he left behind was the foundation for the work of the two generals who followed him. In a Japanese school reading primer, there used to be a story about Hideyoshi concerning a dispute which arose as to whether untrained men could be taught more quickly to be effective with a sword or with a spear. A sword master claimed that the sword would always be better, but Hideyoshi disagreed. A test was arranged in which the sword master and Hideyoshi would each be given 10 men to train for three weeks, and then there would be a contest. The sword master spent the three weeks training his men in parrying a spear thrust and how to cut and thrust in return, but Hideyoshi gave only the most elementary instruction in spear technique. His training was of a different kind, which he kept secret.

When the time came, the 10 men with swords were lined up against the 10 men with spears. The swordsmen advanced steadily in a line, but the spearmen suddenly broke away, divided, and ran to both ends of the opposing line. Then each party of five advanced with their spear points leveled. The swordsmen were bewildered; they had no formation of their own to defeat attacks from both sides. Each, individually, was unable to break through, so the spearmen scored points off all of them. This story was supposed to illustrate Hideyoshi's capacity for organization. Similarly Hideyoshi's instructions for the Korea invasion were supposed to have been that, after defeating the enemy and forcing him to leave the battlefield and retreat, one should not pursue and massacre him, but follow his retreat at a safe distance. Thus the enemy will carry his baggage and food. When he has reached a main city, he should be overtaken and dispatched, having fulfilled his role as 'transport.' This was known as 'organizing the enemy.'

Ieyasu was Nobunaga's devoted ally and a warrior chieftain who outwitted most of his contemporaries and survived Japan's sixteenth century wars of reunification to set up the Tokugawa shogunate. In his book *The Maker of Modern Japan* A L Sadler describes him as 'calm, capable, and entirely fearless, and with a conscientious objection to revealing any brilliance.'

So these three generals, each in their own way, contributed to bringing peace to Japan after a century of civil war. It has been said that Nobunaga quarried the stones, that Hideyoshi shaped them, and that Ieyasu set them into place. Each had their own methods. Their characters can also be assessed by the replies each gave to a poem. The tradition is that the first and last lines were given and then you had to complete the second line. It should be remembered that when they were given the poem all three of these renowned warrior-lords were still quite young.

The first line of the poem was: 'Nakazumba' (if it won't sing); the last line, 'Uguisu' (nightingale). Then they had to compose the middle line. Nobunaga added this middle line: 'If it won't sing I'll kill it, the nightingale.' Hideyoshi, who was originally a commoner and fought his way to the top by great natural ability, combined with extremely hard work and vision, completed the poem in this way: 'If it won't sing, I'll find a way to make it sing, the nightingale.' The last to answer was Ieyasu, the calm, patient general who finally succeeded in uniting the whole country under his dynasty. His completion of the poem was: 'If it won't sing, I'll wait until it does, the nightingale.'

How then did the archetype of the victorious general appear in Japan during these centuries?

The Emperor Daigo II arrived in Kyoto about three months after his escape from his island prison. The nobles there now felt themselves to be in the ascendant at last. They believed that the new status quo was essentially the same as that which had existed in the tenth century, one in which the major role of the empire's people and their lands was to supply the needs of the civilian nobles and officials in Kyoto. At that time the Fujiwara nobles in the capital had had their own Samurai-dokoro, attached to

their mansions: military men who protected their houses from thieves and brigands, and acted as a kind of low-paid police force. Now that there had been a clean break with the military government, the Kyoto nobles thought that their day had returned: they would no longer have to go cap in hand for favors to the upstart samurai at Kamakura.

The government set up by Emperor Daigo II was composed entirely of court nobles, with the exception of the commander who had given the imperialist forces their victory, Ashikaga Takauji, but he was a counselor who had no voice in government decision-making. One very important but unofficial voice in government was that of Lady Renshi, a Fujiwara who was the emperor's favorite consort. She was often in dispute with Prince Morinaga, the emperor's son born 11 years before her own connection with him had begun. Morinaga had ambitions to become shogun, but there were many, especially old Kamakura hands, who favored Ashikaga Takauji for that office. Lady Renshi and her stepson continued to plot together. Their separate interests could only be preserved if they remained on the same side, that is the side of the Emperor Daigo, at least for the time being.

The restored government's first task was to subdue and organize the provinces, now that the great Hojo estates had been confiscated. But the task of allocating those estates proved more onerous than Daigo's civilian courtiers had anticipated. The empire was full of landowners with mortgaged estates or with no estates at all. Many of them had taken neither side in the battles which had brought down the Hojo. The committees set up by Kyoto, and composed of court nobles, were simply not equal to the task of controlling the intrigues of the military lords, and before long there were a number of military men and particularly former Kamakura shogunate officials among the members of those committees. Another difficulty for the would-be civilian government in Kyoto was the intransigence of the samurai in many parts of the country. Guerrilla bands sprang up among the landless Hojo and their vassals, and there was fighting as far north as Mutsu and as far south as southern Kyushu.

So far there had been no rising in the Kanto; but the Kyoto government still had to make up its mind what to do with Kamakura itself. The problem was solved in this way: many of the restive Kamakura warriors were given financial inducements to settle in the north, particularly in the Mutsu region. In 1334 Emperor Daigo sent his tenth son, Narinaga, to the Kanto region not as shogun but as imperial governor (*kozuke taishu*). Narinaga was placed in the care of the brother of Ashikaga Takauji, Tadayoshi, the governor of Sagami. This governorship, always a Kyoto appointment, had traditionally been held

by the Hojo, so it now looked as if the shogunate was being restored in a slightly different form, with the Ashikaga as regents, a move which could not have been distasteful to the erstwhile Hojo followers in the Kanto.

But the government in Kyoto was less than competent and not well respected. The various claimants to estates and preferment from around the empire had begun to send armed bands to the capital to press their claims, and these were now virtually in possession of the city of Kyoto. There was also intrigue among the Kyoto nobles themselves, resulting in more than one banishment and exile; and there were revolts by branches of the defeated Hojo clan itself.

In 1335 there was a quarrel between Ashikaga Takauji and his former ally, the powerful Nitta clan. Takauji had been in Kyoto for some time, but had removed himself to Kamakura and built a palace on the site of the old shogun's palace. Takauji's brother Tadayoshi began to send out circulars, many of which survive to this day, calling on Ashikaga supporters to assemble troops to punish Nitta. As Nitta's governorship of Kozuke was an imperial appointment, Kyoto found it had to do something. A force was sent to 'subdue the east,' with the emperor's second son receiving the appointment of 'shogun of the east,' and battle ensued once more between the Kyoto emperor's forces, supporting Nitta, and the Kanto forces supporting the Ashikaga. Partisan troops converged on the capital from all over the empire, and there was fierce and confused fighting everywhere, but by the summer of 1336 the Ashikaga brothers were once more in a position to march on Kyoto.

The Ashikaga had studied Yoshitsune's great victory at Dannoura most carefully as a model. Accordingly they equipped a fleet for the Inland Sea. The imperialist troops were ill-trained and exhausted, having been fighting and traveling hard continuously for months. They also lacked strategists of real talent. So, in July 1336, huge numbers of Ashikaga troops disembarked where the city of Kobe now stands and immediately surrounded the imperialist troops. One of the commanders in the imperialist ranks, perhaps the man best-loved by legend from this time, was Kusunoki, said to have been recommended to the Emperor Daigo in a dream connected with the characters with which his name was written. He fought bravely, encouraging his men in a hopeless battle. At last, gravely wounded, he committed *seppuku*, while Nitta managed to escape to Kyoto. The battle was decisive and the Ashikaga troops were soon in Kyoto, while the remnants of the imperial forces took refuge in the Hieizan monastery, but even the formidably warlike priests could not hold out for ever, and in November 1336 Emperor Daigo proposed terms of peace.

Two months before this a rival emperor had been set up by the Ashikaga. This was

Left: Ashikaga Takauji destroyed the Kamakura regime. The Ashikaga period (1336-1573) was to some extent a time of political instability, social unrest and general warfare in Japan, and it has been said that Takauji was one of the vilest and most traitorous individuals in Japanese history.

Above: The last stand of the Kusunoki clan whose leader, Kusunoki Masashige, became a folk hero during the fourteenth century civil wars. Kusunoki represents the traditional Japanese epitome of imperial loyalty. Centuries later, the spot where he committed *seppuku* became the site of one of Japan's most hallowed shrines, especially for samurai pilgrims. He was a Zen follower.

Komyo, then aged 14. A palace was ready for him at Yoshino and a rival court set up there. So now there were two emperors and two imperial courts. The ensuing conflicts became known as the wars between the northern and southern courts. What was really going on, however, was a whole series of private wars. There are maps and chronicles of their progress, but in fact the situation changed so fast, and allegiances altered so rapidly, that it is difficult to say that any of these serve as a true representation of the position at the time. Hardly any of the great clans remained steadfast in their support of one side or the other. Many of the military groupings fought simply to extend their own domains; and these would often change sides because of jealousy or petty disputes, and still more often because it seemed that the spoils would be greater on the other side. The only certain thing was that passive neutrality was out of the question. Accordingly, some of the clans, such as the Ito in Hyuga and the Utsunomiya in Shimotsuke, so arranged matters that different branches of a single clan would declare for opposing sides and conduct a kind of mock-battle on a long-term basis. Casualties in these battles were extremely rare, and when recruiting agents appeared the chief of the clan branch could say convincingly that he was too hard pressed at home to send troops elsewhere. Then, in the event of a decisive victory, the spoils would go not to an enemy but to friends and relatives.

Ashikaga Takauji had received his patent of office as shogun in 1338 from the northern court, although he had been acting as shogun in all but name since 1335. He had originally intended to make his seat at Kamakura, and to restore the shogunate by following the precepts of Yoritomo. Political considerations made it imperative to re-

main in Kyoto, however, so he installed his eight-year-old son Yoshiakira in Kamakura, establishing the Kamakura administrative machinery under guardians, meanwhile setting up his own *bakufu* at Muromachi in Kyoto, where it remained. The main difference between this *bakufu* and the old one at Kamakura under the Hojo was that there were no regents: Takauji ruled not only in name but also in fact. Takauji's chief commander was one Ko Moronao.

By 1348 the southerners were on the offensive, and in 1348 their troops set fire to the outskirts of Kyoto, where there was also plague and famine. This stirred the Ashikaga troops under Ko Moronao into action. The northerners' army was the stronger and, after making a two-pronged attack, Ko Moronao was able to drive the southerners back to their base at Yoshino, and eventually to capture and burn down the palace there. Just when victory seemed assured for the northerners, Ko Moronao suddenly turned his troops and returned to Kyoto. There was great dissension in the Ashikaga camp, as Ko Moronao had managed to offend many of the lords on the northern side. Takauji had disagreed with his brother Tadayoshi, who had been sent into a monastery, though not without attaching to himself the support of some powerful factions on the Ashikaga side. There ensued a fierce battle for Kyoto between Ashikaga Tadayoshi's troops and those of Ko Moronao, in which Tadayoshi's party was ultimately victorious.

So it was that the early victories of the Ashikaga northern court were thrown away by dissension in their own ranks. Takauji and Tadayoshi were reconciled in due course, but never fully trusted each other, and Tadayoshi's military following caused fear and consernation in Kyoto. Soon the intriguing was such that Tadayoshi once more retired from Kyoto to Tsuruga. In the meantime, to the chagrin of many on Tadayoshi's side, Takauji had secretly made peace with the southern court, and had actually arranged for the abdication of the northern emperor, Suko. On hearing this, many of the northern captains followed Tadayoshi east to Tsuruga and Kamakura. Takauji marched east in pursuit of his brother, but on arriving at Kamakura, where he expected a fight, found that there was to be no battle and that his brother was dead, generally believed to have taken poison to save himself from falling into the hands of Takauji's troops. Takauji stayed in Kamakura for two years (1352-53), during which time there was more fierce and confused fighting in northern and eastern Japan. Takauji also seems to have forgotten that he had made peace with the southern court, as he was soon using the calendar adopted by the northern court.

Up to 1358, the year of Takauji's death, Kyoto was occupied and reoccupied several times by a number of factions. When Takauji had made peace with the southern court, envoys had arrived there from Emperor Suko with the sacred emblems of 'His Imperial Majesty' (that is, the fabricated ones). Southern troops were soon driven out by Ashikaga partisans. By this time, however, all three ex-emperors of the northern line had been removed from the capital and were in the hands of the southerners. Takauji's son, Yoshiakira, in charge of Kyoto, therefore had great difficulty in setting up an emperor, as there was no predecessor from whom to inherit the throne, and no real sacred emblem with which to be invested.

The battles continued around Kyoto for years. The southern court had been considerably more united than the northern up to around the time of the death of Takauji in the north, but factions then began to emerge there too. The southern court only retained its existence because of large-scale defections to it by northern adherents as a result of fallings-out among the Ashikaga factions. There was still a shogun in Kyoto after Takauji's death. This was Yoshiakira, Takauji's son. He ruled for ten years (1358-68) but over an administration divided everywhere except in the east. Many of his followers deserted to the southern side, and his many attempts to reunite Japan under one emperor failed. The nearest Yoshiakira got to a reconciliation between the two courts was in 1366-67, but here too the negotiations failed.

As the northerners were strong and united in the Kanto, so the southerners retained their power for longest in Kyushu. In 1371 the southerners' power was unquestioned on that island; and it took another ten years or more for the Ashikaga to re-establish their supremacy there.

When Yoshiakira died in 1368, he left provision for his ten-year-old son Yoshimitsu to succeed him as shogun. Yoshimitsu's tutor was Hosokawa Yoriyuki, and it is to his credit that the northern administration climbed slowly back throughout the 1370s to re-establish the rule of law and thus indirectly the unity and discipline which enabled the Ashikaga eventually to conquer the south. But Hosokawa Yoriyuki was not popular. At the court in Kyoto there were so many intrigues against him that finally, in 1379, he set fire to his own mansion and retired to his estates in Shikoku to express his disgust. The shogun, Yoshimitsu, remembered his old tutor, however. In 1391 the shogun was having trouble with the Yamana clan: they had subdued Kishu and Izumi provinces in the shogun's name, but then refused to give them up, treating them as their own. By this time Kyushu had been subdued by the northern court, and the southern court was still in existence only by virtue of the northern court's consent. Yoshimitsu naturally took any such insubordination far more seriously than he would have done ten or 15 years earlier, when insurrections were the norm rather than the exception. The shogun therefore determined to recall Yoriyuki and take his advice in any struggle which might ensue.

In January 1392 the chief of the Yamana clan mobilized an army against the shogun and attacked Kyoto. The attack failed after desperate fighting, and ended the prestige of the Yamana clan. The clan chief had to retire and the family as a whole was stripped of its offices. This victory was good for the morale of the Muromachi shogunate, and soon afterward the last fortress of the southern court, Chihaya castle, was captured and almost all its defenders laid down their arms. Yoshimitsu was thus finally in a position to open negotiations with the southern court. In 1392 a deputation of six southern court nobles arrived in Kyoto and handed over the imperial sacred emblems to the representatives of the northern court. The northern emperor, Komatsu II, was then acknowledged sole sovereign, and the southern nobles' goodwill assured by guaranteeing them estates and support.

The effect of these long and wearying battles was of course to reduce the esteem in which the imperial court was held throughout the empire. That there was disrespect toward the imperial land holdings can be seen by the Yamana's arrogating imperial manors to themselves in 1392. There were also some southern military men who never accepted the northern line, and who withdrew to their estates to await the moment when a southern emperor could be placed upon the throne. Also, the Muromachi *bakufu* had gained governmental and legislative influence over the empire away from the court itself, but at the same time it had lost the influence over the provinces that the Kamakura shogunate had always retained. The process of decentralization had gone ahead so strongly as a re-

Far left: A print of a warrior showing the head characteristically thrust forward.

Left: Ashikaga Takauji, originally sponsored by the Hojo, recruited a large samurai following and eventually placed the puppet ruler Go-Daigo on the throne.

sult of all the battles that the military class was now under no-one's control. Brigandage and piracy became more and more common, and was even used by the southern court in its later days when it carried out desultory operations against the northerners' maritime fortifications. Although by 1392 there was once again one emperor and one shogun, Japan was still at war with itself.

The Muromachi shogunate under the Ashikaga, successors to Takauji, was in some respects a return to the firm and efficient rule of the Kamakura shogunate under the Hojo regents. It would therefore seem like a contradiction in terms to describe this period as a time of unrest (*sengoku-jidai* as Japanese historians have it). But there were frequent disturbances and rebellions throughout the empire, despite the relative peace of the Kyoto region. The tact and skill with which the strife between the northern and southern courts had been brought to a close by the Ashikaga did create a feeling of security and reduce the marauding of mercenary bands around the capital, but in the provinces little had changed. Also, the meteoric rise of the Ashikaga had caused resentment among the other great provincial clans. Kyushu in particular was in turmoil of one kind or another for decades, and there were battles in the Kanto region between warring houses.

The palaces of Kyoto at this time are remembered for their magnificence above all. It was Ashikaga Yoshimitsu who had the Golden Pavilion (*Kinkakuji*) built in Kyoto, and many others were built, repaired or restored under his rule. Yoshimitsu, although a shogun, was not content with military power alone, as the Minamoto and many of the Hojo had been. He had himself invested with the highest court ranks, and relations between his household and that of the emperor were so close that it often seemed as though the two households were one and the same, all the more so as Yoshimitsu also held such ranks as gave him the power of overseeing many aspects of the imperial household. Yoshimitsu also took care to keep the goodwill of the monks; the Zen sect was now the most flourishing in Japan, and Yoshimitsu always had a Zen abbot as an adviser. Under Yoshimitsu foreign trade began to prosper, too. The influence of the Zen monks, who had usually studied in China, meant that this shogun was inclined to be favorably disposed toward China, and so trade increased and the *bakufu* also took steps to quell piracy, which was a great nuisance along the Chinese and Korean coasts.

It has been said that Kyushu in the south was generally in turmoil during the first half of the fifteenth century. The reasons for this are various, but mainly have to do with the large number of succession disputes

Below: A section of a map showing Edo (present-day Tokyo) and its surrounding provinces which provided a defensive ring around the capital.

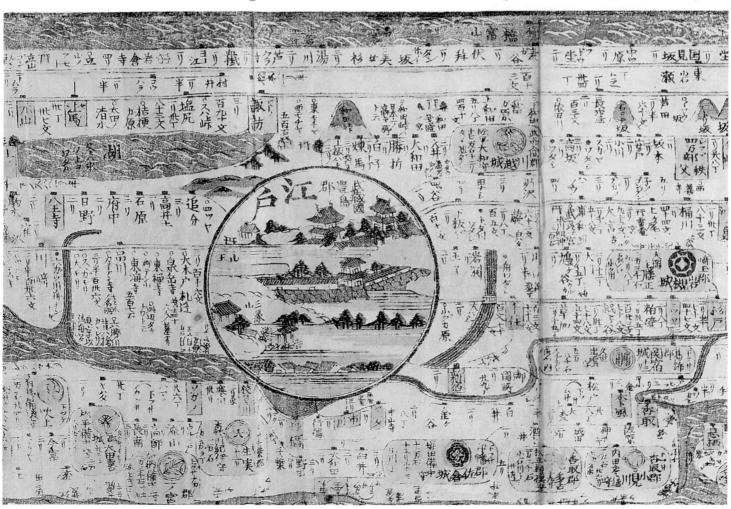

among the powerful clans in the region. At one time the chief shogunate official in northern Kyushu was actually compelled to flee his fortress and take refuge in Kyoto. As a result of this, many Kyushu samurai were reduced to beggary, and it was these who often took to piracy. Japanese chronicles of the time mention the reappearance of a Mongol fleet at Tsushima in 1420, and a Japanese victory there. But Japanese histories, then as now, are too often written without reference to Korean history, which is more closely bound with that of the Japanese archipelago than the scholars of the latter care to admit. Korean chronicles view the battle off Tsushima in 1420 as a punitive raid by Korean warships in reprisal for Japanese piracy.

Early in the Ashikaga rule there had been an Ashikaga lord in Kamakura as well as in Kyoto. Kamakura was much reduced from its former glory under the Minamoto and the Hojo, and was little better than a fishing village. But it was still the political center of the Kanto region, and as such it was important to the prestige of the Ashikaga to have a proxy shogun there. Kamakura became the scene of battle again early in the fifteenth century, when in about 1415, Uesugi Ujinori, being deprived of his deputy's rank at Kamakura, seized the town from Ashikaga Mochiuji. The Kyoto shogun, Ashikaga Yoshimochi, ordered the Uesugi to be crushed and his Ashikaga restored to his position. There was fighting in

Kamakura between branches of the Uesugi clan, and when Ujinori's branch was defeated, he and 40 or so of his followers committed *seppuku*. Ashikaga Yoshimochi in Kyoto found that his own brother Yoshitsugu was implicated in the affair, and had him put to death. Ashikaga Mochiuji, restored in Kamakura, plotted the overthrow of Yoshinori, now shogun in Kyoto. The Uesugi deputies in Kamakura supported the Kyoto shogun, however, and promptly betrayed the plot to Kyoto. An army was sent against Mochiuji, who committed *seppuku* in 1439. His eldest son and some other relatives committed suicide with him, but his three youngest sons escaped to the protection of the lord of Koga. The Uesugi attacked the Koga castle and killed everyone in it, only the youngest son of Mochiuji, a child of five, being allowed to escape. From this time on there were no Ashikaga lords in Kamakura and the highest office in that region was held unchallenged by Uesugi clan members.

Yoshinori's downfall came when he tried to break the power of the Akamatsu clan in the Bizen, Harima and Mimasaka regions. Yoshinori decided to attempt this not by military means but simply by partitioning the Akamatsu estates administratively to deny them resources. The Akamatsu clan chief made no protest at this, which alone should have made Yoshinori suspicious, but invited the shogun to a banquet at his Kyoto mansion in 1441. When all present

Above: A painted screen showing an attack on a fortified mansion. A horseman on the left wears a distinctive red *horo* (cape), which billows behind him.

were drinking and making merry, two Akamatsu retainers turned loose all the horses in the stables and drove them all at once into the yard of the mansion, where, panicked, they bit and kicked each other and created a terrific uproar. With this as a distraction, all the doors were shut and locked, and after a struggle the shogun was beheaded by two Akamatsu vassals. Akamatsu escaped with the head, but was soon attacked by other clans including the Yamana, and was forced to commit *seppuku* rather than acknowledge both defeat and treachery. Thus the power of the Akamatsu was broken, though at the cost of Yoshinori's life.

The next two shoguns, sons of Yoshinori, were children. This period, during the 1440s, was a particularly turbulent one. There were several clans which had failed to move against the Akamatsu when ordered to do so to avenge the murder of the shogun. The troops of the Ouchi clan were commissioned to punish them, and in this they were successful, but managed at the same time to enrich themselves and enhance their own reputations at the expense of that of the shogunate, whose centralized government was becoming weaker day by day. Fiscal administration malpractice had been partly responsible for the fall of the Hojo and now it seemed the Ashikaga were repeating their mistake. Taxes were punitive, and famines frequent and widespread. Fighting as such had comparatively little effect on the lives of the peasants, or at least they could recover quickly from it. If their houses were burnt down by soldiers, well then they were quick to rebuild, being constructed in a fairly flimsy manner because of the earthquakes and the summer heat.

It was taxes which could really impoverish a small farmer, and the tax burden was much greater under the Ashikaga than it had been under the Hojo, who had had Mongol invasions to contend with. When

famine struck, many of the poorest would go into Kyoto looking for food or work, and there are records of the disposal of whole families who could not be fed by their parents – the girls to the brothels and the boys to the monasteries, where they were often used as homosexual prostitutes by the monks. This practice, which begins to be generally reported around the time of the famines of the mid-fifteenth century, is recorded as having been widespread among the Zen priesthood much later, although perhaps the European missionaries who recorded it found it more noteworthy than would any Japanese of that time.

A major cause of disorder in the mid-century was rioting by the ordinary population. They too were suffering from the scourge of debt, and some clan chiefs began to take landless and indebted men into their service as warriors. The rest, however, were left with little recourse, and there were riots in Kyoto in 1447, 1451, 1457 and 1461, in which moneylenders' houses were burnt to the ground and the evidence of indebtedness thus destroyed. This was under the Shogun Ashikaga Yoshimasa, who was very much dominated by his counselors, and particularly by his consort Tomiko and other ladies. Taxes were raised at this time not only on land, as had always been done, but also in the form of extraordinary taxes, often raised on no pretext at all but simply to squeeze revenue from the population for the maintenance of the luxurious life of the *bakufu* and court.

The succession war known as the Great Onin War (1467-77) was just one of the bloody struggles which plunged the empire into disorder up to the end of the sixteenth century. It arose from a succession dispute in the Hatakeyama clan. Hatakeyama Mochikuni was deputy in Kamakura at this time and wished to make his son Yoshinari his successor. The shogun supported Mochikuni's wish, to the displeasure of other lords, especially the Yamana chief, Sozen, known as the Red Monk because of his priestly name and because of his highly-colored complexion. The shogun, Yoshimasa, was prevailed upon by Yamana pressure and show of strength to support their counter-claim for Mochikuni's nephew Masanaga. At this Yoshinari mustered troops to attack Masanaga, his uncle Mochikuni having since died, and the shogun once more patched up a peace between them, leaving the house of Hatakeyama divided.

Yoshimasa was of a changeable nature, however, and when some trees presented to him by Yoshinari all withered, he took this as a bad omen and caused him to restore Masanaga to high favor, much to Yoshinari's resentment. Meanwhile, Yamana Sozen, the Red Monk, had been gathering his own army to pursue his own aims, and threw in his lot not with Masanaga but with Yoshinari, having been impressed, it is said, by the latter's skill as a military commander. The Red Monk was remarkably successful in overawing the shogun's forces, so that he took over Harima province virtually unopposed. Yoshinari's troops fighting on his side gave him considerable advantages, and he was determined to supplant all other powerful chiefs and install himself in their place. The shogun had no son, but in 1465 his consort Tomiko gave birth to a boy. It was too late for the official succession; Yoshimasa had already prevailed upon his younger brother to leave the priesthood and undertake the succession, and Tomiko faced the prospect of her infant son being deprived of the office of shogun after so many years of intriguing to ensure herself a powerful position of influence in the *bakufu*. Tomiko therefore entered into secret negotiations with the Red Monk, who in his turn was quietly gathering troops and support to await the moment when it would be safe to defy the shogun. The forces opposed to the Red Monk were under the command of his father-in-law, a Hosokawa and chief minister. Neither at first dared to give battle, and their respective troops lay lined up opposite each other close to the *bakufu* buildings in Muromachi for some months.

The shogun had declared that the first to strike would be declared a rebel. But soon there began to be skirmishes between outlying parties of troops, and in 1467 Yamana advanced, quickly taking the imperial palace and temples in Kyoto. There were several more victories by the Red Monk's forces, but the Hosokawa forces, while defeated, managed to prevail upon the emperor to come under their protection, at quarters in the *bakufu* buildings. This made the Red Monk technically a rebel as he was now fighting against the emperor's forces. The Red Monk quickly began to lose the supporters he had spent so much time and trouble acquiring because of this simple but decisive move.

In 1471 the Red Monk resorted to the desperate measure of reviving the old southern imperial court. A pretender to the throne was brought into the Yamana camp, but little more is heard of him, and he may well have been executed as an embarrassment, as the two armies remained in stalemate around Kyoto, which was now virtually in ruins, for some time to come. The Hosokawa commander had failed to get any clear declarations of support from his supposed allies in the provinces, as all there feared the consequences to themselves of a victory by either side if they declared allegiances. The Akamatsu clan in particular, jealously guarding their fairly recently-acquired provinces, would have nothing to do with proposals of peace, nor would they lend military support to the Hosokawa side.

The Red Monk died in 1473 and Hosokawa only a month later, but the war dragged on until 1477, with the fighting becoming ever more factional and intermittent. The Yamana position became steadily less and less secure as the shogun stripped

Below: A Kunisada woodblock print of the warrior monk Yokogawa Kakuhan wearing Buddhist robes over his armor and carrying a metal pole. The techniques of whirling this long pole were much developed by warrior monks and greatly feared.

Far right: A reproduction of a Muromachi period suit of armor. It was made by Masuda Miochin Ki no Muneharu in 1860 and presented to Queen Victoria by the last Tokugawa shogun.

Below: Daimyo (large land-holders) and samurai aboard ship.

its leaders of all offices because of their rebel status, and had assigned their provinces to subordinates carefully chosen to be those most likely to undermine their influence in their home provinces. Eventually, in December 1477, the Yamana forces abandoned and set fire to their encampments around Kyoto. Thus there was technically a Hosokawa victory, but in fact the war had transferred itself to the provinces, over which the central government had by now very little control. In almost every province of Japan at the end of the fifteenth century there were wars, skirmishes and factional fighting between the clans.

Even before 1467 and the outbreak of the Great Onin War the central government's control over the provinces had become so loose as to be feeble. The long war destroyed that control altogether, and decrees from the shogun began to be ignored, so that it was soon realized that it was futile to issue them in the first place. Yoshimasa was a great patron of the arts, but he was inadequate as the leader of a military government. In this way the great military clans

had now become independent. They had stopped even pretending to pay taxes and dues to the *bakufu*, although peasants and traders of course still paid taxes to them. The only reason the military clan chiefs could not accurately be described as petty kings was that they minted no coins; but then, no coins had been minted in Japan for centuries, and such coinage as was in circulation had come from China. Japan was full of military rulers, owing not even nominal allegiance to anyone else, having absolute sway over those of other castes living in their domains, and having their own troops in their service. Both the emperor and the shogun had become more or less irrelevant under these circumstances, but it was their absence as a force in the land which allowed the country to slide into almost a century of civil strife.

Yoshimasa had nominally resigned in 1474 in favor of his son Yoshihisa, then nine years old. Yoshihisa showed promise as he grew up, but his mother Tomiko encouraged him in a predilection for drinking and women which characterized the Ashikaga men. Yoshihisa died, probably an alcoholic, at the early age of 25. Thereupon Yoshimasa adopted his nephew, Yoshitane, as his successor and made him shogun. He was no luckier, however, as the Hatakeyama family were then holding the post of chief minister and at the same time conducting a private war within their clan. Hatakeyama Masanaga prevailed upon the shogun in around 1492 to make his campaign against the rival Hatakeyama a national one and to march at the head of his troops on his rival in Kawachi. But the rival Hatakeyama had entered into alliances both with the military monks of the Kofukuji temple and with the powerful Hosokawa clan. As soon as the shogun reached Kawachi, Hosokawa Masamoto, who was in Kyoto, rose against him and seized the capital. Hatakeyama Masanaga committed *seppuku*, while the shogun fled to Etchu in the north. This left Hosokawa Masamoto in charge, and he set up a puppet shogun in the person of Yoshizumi, another nephew of Yoshimasa. Hosokawa Masamoto was chief minister (*kanryo*) from 1494 to 1507, during which time he placed his own adherents as officials in charge of the home provinces around Kyoto.

Masamoto was childless, as he was a believer in sexual abstinence as the path to spiritual fulfilment. He adopted two sons, whom he entrusted to the care of his two chief vassals respectively. These were deadly rivals but Masamoto hoped thus to guarantee his own succession by making it to the advantage of neither guardian to make away with his own or the other's charge. The plan failed, however, and Kosai Motochika, the guardian of Masamoto's adopted son Sumiyuki, fearing that the rival son, Sumimoto, was about to be declared heir, contrived to have Hosokawa Masamoto assassinated in 1507.

Above: The statue of Tokugawa Ieyasu at Okazaki shows him wearing the armor he is believed to have used at the Battle of Nagakute in 1584.

The former shogun, Yoshitane, had meanwhile gathered forces and marched again on Kyoto, first taking care to gain the support of the Hieizan (or Enryakuji) monks. Masamoto's forces had all the Hieizan priests' quarters burned down, but Yoshitane escaped, mustered a new army, and in 1508 marched on the capital again. The puppet shogun, Yoshizumi, had to flee and Yoshitane was restored to office in 1508. Hosokawa Masamoto had in fact adopted a third son, Hosokawa Takakuni; he had thrown in his lot with Yoshitane and the Ouchi clan. A few years later, however, in 1518, the Ouchi support was withdrawn as there was trouble in Ouchi's own provinces. In any case the Ouchi had been supporting the shogun financially to such an extent that the clan had become impoverished. Hosokawa Takakuni was now ruling Kyoto with a high hand, and the shogun began to feel his position was a ridiculous one. In 1520 Miyoshi Nagateru, guardian of

Hosokawa's adopted heir Sumimoto, reappeared in Kyoto with the avowed intention of driving Takakuni out. Yoshitane found it prudent to recognize Sumimoto as the head of the Hosokawa clan. But the offensive did not succeed. Miyoshi had insufficient forces to overcome those of Takakuni, and when his troops were surrounded he committed *seppuku*. Sumimoto the puppet died a few months later, leaving Takakuni in supreme control and Yoshitane's position untenable. Yoshitane fled in 1521, and Takakuni set up Yoshiharu, son of the former puppet Yoshizumi and then a boy of 11, as the new puppet shogun. Yoshiharu in his turn was driven into exile by another chief of the Miyoshi clan in 1539, when he became a fugitive. He resigned as shogun in 1545 but this did not help him and he was on the run until his death in 1550.

The Hosokawa fared little better. Takakuni was driven from Kyoto in 1527 by Miyoshi Nagamoto, and the Miyoshi were to be overthrown before long by Oda Nobunaga. These developments show how rapidly new feudal houses were displacing the great clans which had been so powerful for centuries. Most of the old clans retained precarious footholds, but in one or two provinces only. There were also hundreds of smaller clans existing and all were engaged in land-grabbing attacks on their neighbors. The position of these smaller clans was naturally even more precarious, as one of their land-rustling exercises might backfire on them at any time and cause them to be incorporated into one of the greater fiefdoms, or eliminated altogether in a battle with a neighbor. The smaller houses therefore had a tendency to commend themselves to the larger ones, and particularly to those which appeared to be prospering. This kind of feudal allegiance was not a strong bond, however, and was thrown off at the slightest prospect of greater advantage elsewhere. Within all the houses, of all sizes and status, there were continual succession disputes too tedious to chronicle. This is what is meant by 'a country at war'; there were constant small civil wars and internecine disputes, with no great purpose, but a similar effect to a unified war, thus having all the disadvantages to the general population of waging such a war without any general benefit to be gained from a victory.

The turmoil and political confusion of this age did have one redeeming feature: only the strong would survive when everyone's hand was set against his neighbor's and every house had to guard against attack, which might come at any time from erstwhile friends and allies. So all the clan chiefs, great and small, looked for warriors to serve them who had real ability; and in the absence of the strong social cohesion of previous centuries there was now no bar to employing those from obscure backgrounds. Also, every manor needed resources, and constant fighting tended to lay waste the rice-fields and encourage the tillers of those fields to flee across the border into an adjacent manor, where they would be welcomed and set to work to till the wastelands of that manor. So it became to the advantage of the military chiefs to stop treating the peasant farmers as slaves, from whom revenue must be squeezed without recompense. Also, in a time when soldiers were so much in demand, it became much more common for former peasant farmers to go into military service as *ashigaru*, lightly-armed soldiers of a lower rank than the heavily-armed samurai.

After the Onin War (1467-77) the samurai had abandoned the capital and gone back to the provinces, where, as we have seen, they engaged in their own wars. This left the capital virtually without warriors, and the imperial residence undefended. The building known as the Dairi, where the imperial family had their apartments, was surrounded by only a bamboo fence. The emperor himself had no income, and was reduced to selling samples of his calligraphy for a few coins. The irrelevance of the emperor can be seen in the fact that between 1465 and 1585 there were no abdications by emperors, and the succession passed in each case from father to son without dispute. There was no need for powerful leaders to set themselves up behind puppet emperors because the political and military happenings were elsewhere, in the provinces. When Emperor Tsuchimikado II died in 1500, it was 44 days before enough money could be collected to cover the funeral expenses. More than this, Emperor Nara II, Tsuchimikado's successor, had no coronation for 21 years because of lack of funds.

During all the provincial wars of this time, the feudal chiefs had the ambition to conquer all the lands which lay between their home province and Kyoto, and to give their wars of conquest legitimacy by gaining control of the shogun's person and then conducting those wars in his name. One of the most powerful of the chiefs who had this ambition was Imagawa of Totomi, who was in control of three provinces and who set out in 1560, having bled those provinces white to finance the expedition to Kyoto. But Imagawa did not get far. His army was defeated by the inferior force of a rather obscure chief called Oda Nobunaga. This Nobunaga had been so little respected in his younger days that he was called 'Lord Fool' (*Baka-dono*) by those around him. Nonetheless, by 1559 Nobunaga had increased, by conquest, his land holdings from a small part of Owari province to the whole of that region, and had beaten off land-grabbing attacks on it from the south too. Then in 1560 he created astonishment by defeating Imagawa's great army.

It is said that Nobunaga was able to devise the strategy which gave him his victory over Imagawa because he had, less than two

years before, taken into his service one Tokichiro, a small, almost dwarfish man of peasant stock, later known as Hideyoshi. In any case, Nobunaga's victory over Imagawa had great consequences for Japan's history. One of the feudal subordinates to Imagawa was Tokugawa Ieyasu, then 18 years old. The Imagawa clan chief died almost immediately after the battle in which the clan was defeated by Nobunaga's army. His son took charge, and straight away had a quarrel with Ieyasu. Just at this time the victorious Nobunaga was making overtures to all the small clans attached to Imagawa, so Ieyasu found this to be the right time to respond. The two made an alliance, the terms of which were that each was to make his own way toward Kyoto, making what conquests he could. The first to succeed in obtaining the shogun's commission would become the overlord and ally of the other. From this time on Nobunaga (ably assisted by Hideyoshi) and Ieyasu acted together.

In 1561 it was Nobunaga who arrived first in Kyoto, received the shogun's official sanction for the conquests he had made, continued to storm through the home provinces around Kyoto, and was ready to make an assault upon Ise. He seemed invincible, but still had the powerful cliques around the last of the Ashikaga shoguns to contend with. The fourteenth shogun, Yoshiteru, had been assassinated by two of his ministers in 1565. They set up a puppet shogun of their own, but Yoshiteru's younger brother, Yoshiaki, who had entered the priesthood, now re-emerged in search of allies to pursue what he saw as his rightful claim on power. He traveled around the provinces seeking support from the military lords there, all of whom tantalized him with promises of support which somehow were never forthcoming. At last Yoshiaki sent a messenger to Nobunaga to ask for support. Hideyoshi is said to have advised Nobunaga thus: 'Nobunaga can do

Above: In 1603 Ieyasu obtained the title of shogun, which continued in his family until 1868, at which time the shogunate was abolished. Ieyasu never put anyone to death from personal reasons, so consequently his friends and retainers had the greatest confidence in him. On the other hand, he never spared any of his own family or relations if their conduct endangered family solidarity and supremacy.

nothing without a name; if by espousing Yoshiaki's cause he could maintain that all his subsequent wars were waged in obedience to his command, he (Nobunaga) could conquer the whole empire.'

So Nobunaga lent his military support to the ousted would-be shogun, Yoshiaki, in exchange for the legitimacy that the shogun's authority still allowed. Nobunaga could thus continue his conquests. But there were two powerful lords standing in his way. One of these was Sasaki, and for the time being Nobunaga could see no way, save out-and-out military victory, of overcoming Sasaki, and he was not yet quite ready for this. The other was Asai, and here Nobunaga was on easier ground. He resorted to the time-honored ploy of using his female relatives to strike alliances: Nobunaga's sister was soon married to Asai, thus forming a political alliance between Asai and Nobunaga. Together they now had enough military resources to overcome Sasaki, and by the end of 1568 Sasaki's domains were no more, and Nobunaga and his allies had occupied Kyoto. Nobunaga himself was now vice-shogun, with the shogun himself as a puppet, and could resume his conquests in Ise province, which was soon overcome.

It has already been said that Japan was a battleground at this time with feudal lords fighting each other, and ready to make short-term alliances if it seemed to be in their interests to do so. Instead of being intimidated by this prospect of battle at every turn, as might have seemed appropriate for one whose rise had been so rapid and from such comparatively obscure origins, Nobunaga and his advisors simply used the mutual jealousy among the provincial chiefs to their own advantage. Nobunaga's alliance with Tokugawa Ieyasu was very useful here, in that Ieyasu was able to subdue the still-powerful Hojo family to the point where they could do no more harm. This left the two chieftains, Takeda of Kai

and Uesugi of Echigo, who were constantly warring with each other. They had mounted one expedition after another against each other since at least 1553. By 1560 they had come to stalemate, and were impoverishing themselves rapidly by long and expensive campaigns against each other. They therefore decided to settle the matter between them by single combat between their best warriors. This resulted in a victory for the Uesugi, leaving Takeda unable to pursue further campaigns against the Uesugi, and the latter pushing their conquest southward through Suruga. All this had the effect of protecting Nobunaga's rear and flank from either; the more so as, although Takeda had been left very much alone after his technical defeat by Uesugi and could in theory have either attacked Nobunaga or tried to interpose his armies in the way of Nobunaga's conquering progress, Ieyasu was still Nobunaga's ally, and had again made safe Nobunaga's rear by occupying the former Imagawa territories to the east.

Once Nobunaga was in possession of Kyoto and had set up the Shogun Yoshiaki, relations between them cooled. Nobunaga had great respect for the emperor, who had secretly encouraged him in his conquests, but little, it seems, for the office of shogun. Yoshiaki began to intrigue against Nobunaga soon after taking office, and Nobunaga had little compunction in deposing him in 1573. There were renewed military difficulties in his way. The warlords who had become his allies by virtue of conquest, notably Asai, who was married to Nobunaga's sister, now rose against him. Nobunaga's army, though made tough by experience, looked on the point of defeat when, as always, Ieyasu swung to his aid and turned the battle in his favor. But throughout the 1570s Nobunaga was engaged in almost constant battle against one or other of the provincial warlords, very often in the name of the deposed shogun,

Below: European settlers arrive on the mainland of Japan.

Yoshiaki. The consistent victories won by Nobunaga were at least partly due to the fact that Nobunaga and his trusted counselor Hideyoshi had been quick to recognize the superiority of firearms over swords, bows and arrows. Muskets had been introduced into Japan in the 1540s by the first European visitors, the Portuguese, part at least of whose mission was to introduce Christianity into the islands. The spread of Christianity was quite rapid at first – not least because it suited the purpose of leaders like Nobunaga to encourage anything which might lessen the power of the warlike Buddhist temples, some of which had been a continual thorn in his side.

It was not only the musket which gave Nobunaga his power. He seems to have been a man of great ruthlessness, even by the standards of the age, leaving no-one alive whenever he won a victory. He also appears to have been especially fond of penning defeated warriors into stockades and burning them to death, leaving their leaders scarcely enough time to commit *seppuku*. Nobunaga was not only ruthless but guileful. He made good use of espionage and counter-espionage. He was not the only warlord to do so by any means, but seems to have taken to subterfuge from an early age. There is a tale that in his teens, when he was newly married to Nohime, daughter of the Mino clan, and had just succeeded to the headship of his own family, Nohime noticed that he was absent from their bedroom for several hours each night. Whe she asked him where he went, he told her that he was plotting with two retainers of her father's household to kill her father and take over the domain, and had to be absent to watch for the arranged signal. He also warned Nohime that as his wife her loyalty should be to him and not to her father, and ordered her to say nothing to anyone. Nohime had in fact been ordered on her marriage to spy on her husband on her father's behalf, so she relayed this information to her father, who promptly had the two retainers put to death. In fact the story of the plot was a complete fabrication and Nobunaga had simply wanted the two powerful retainers out of the way so as to make the Mino domain more vulnerable to attack.

The Mino and other domains fell to Nobunaga one by one, and although there were many counter-plots by defeated lords who wanted to regain their territories, none of them was successful. In 1581 Nobunaga was left with only the Mori clan as a serious adversary. Mori Terumoto had conspired against Nobunaga with the former shogun, Yoshiaki, and Nobunaga was determined to exterminate his clan. Hideyoshi was, in 1581, engaged in a campaign against the Mori on Nobunaga's behalf.

Throughout Nobunaga's campaigns one of his most trusted lieutenants had been Akechi Mitsuhide. Akechi was a man of humble origin, who had nevertheless im-

pressed Nobunaga. However, it is said that Akechi never recovered from an insult by Nobunaga and sought revenge. During Hideyoshi's 1581 campaign against the Mori he had besieged their army at Takamatsu and sent to Nobunaga for reinforcements. Ieyasu had just returned from his campaign which finally eliminated the Takeda clan as a force in the land, and was resting, on Nobunaga's instructions, so Nobunaga decided to take charge of the reinforcement expedition to Takamatsu himself. Akechi Mitsuhide had gone on ahead of Nobunaga's troops, so that Nobunaga had only a small retinue when he lodged at the Honnoji temple in Kyoto on the way to join Hideyoshi's army. On 21 June 1581 the temple was surrounded by Akechi's army and Nobunaga was taken completely by surprise. With such a small retinue, and his

Above: A portrait of Toyotomi Hideyoshi. He rose from nothing, his father having been a peasant foot soldier to the *kampaku* (civil dictator). Despite his small stature – he was almost a dwarf – and his personal ugliness, described by one historian as 'a base-born, monkey-faced adventurer,' he could impress his rivals with his charm as well as his strength.

trusted men Hideyoshi and Ieyasu else-where, the situation was hopeless, and Nobunaga died in the blazing temple. He may have committed *seppuku*, but his body was never found.

The news of Nobunaga's death reached Hideyoshi the next day at Takamatsu. Hideyoshi prudently kept the news secret for the time being. Coming to terms with the Mori, he then took over Takamatsu castle, rode back to Yamazaki, southwest of the capital where Akechi was camped, and by the end of June had overcome Akechi's army and killed Akechi as he fled.

The succession to Nobunaga now had to be decided, although it was Hideyoshi who really had supreme power. Nobunaga had several sons, who were quarreling among themselves, so Hideyoshi, who was present at their quarrel, simply walked into the next room and came back with Nobunaga's in-fant grandson, Samboshi, in his arms and presented the child to them; they agreed to declare Samboshi heir to Nobunaga. Hideyoshi was now undisputed master of Japan. Only a year after Nobunaga's death he was in control of at least 30 provinces. In Kyushu and the Kanto region there were still military threats, but Hideyoshi man-aged to bring these regions too under his domination by 1590.

Ieyasu was not to be found in the months immediately after Nobunaga's death. He appears to have spent the time in the forti-fied town of Sakai enjoying the tea cere-mony and other civilized pursuits. He did speed to Hideyoshi's aid against Akechi, though, but arrived too late, and may have felt aggrieved against Hideyoshi for having stolen a march on him. At any event, in 1584 a breach appeared between Ieyasu and Hideyoshi. One of Nobunaga's sons, Nobu-katsu, had been intriguing against Hideyoshi, and Ieyasu, listening to him, went into battle against Hideyoshi twice in that year. Both battles were inconclusive but tending to give Ieyasu the advantage, but neither would withdraw, so the two armies faced each other in a stalemate for some time. Neither leader had his heart in another battle and it was Hideyoshi who offered terms. Ieyasu was at first too proud to respond, but by the beginning of 1585 the two armies no longer faced each other, but in the same direction, and Hideyoshi and Ieyasu were working together for the unification of the empire, as Hideyoshi put it. Their remaining task was to bring Kyushu and the Kanto region under their control, and this they did in a few short years with a number of well-fought cam-paigns. Thus, by 1590 they had a unified empire but nowhere to go. The warlords were under their command, but after so long a period of civil wars great and small they would remain under control only so long as they continued to be duly rewarded. But to do this Hideyoshi and Ieyasu needed spoils with which to provide them, and with the known empire already their domain

there was no scope for conquest.

Castle-building had been a preoccupa-tion of Hideyoshi's for some time; one of his successes had been the great fortifications at Osaka. But there was no internal threat worth the mention against which to fortify the empire; the answer for these proud and ambitious military leaders was a foreign war.

There is evidence that Hideyoshi had been planning an invasion of Japan's clos-est neighbor, Korea, as early as 1578, when he was not yet fully in control of his Japanese domains. He is believed to have said to Nobunaga around that date when starting his expedition against the Mori that he intended to take not only central Japan and then Kyushu, but to go on and invade Korea with warships, and from there, using Korean troops, to conquer China itself and make Japan, Korea and China one country. It is certainly true that in 1587 Hideyoshi sent a harshly worded message to Seoul to complain of the non-appearance of Korean ambassadors in Japan for some time past. The message was uncalled-for in that no protest had been made when the ambassadors first ceased to appear, and it would seem that Hideyoshi's reason for sending the message was simply to provoke the Koreans into some act of aggression to provide the pretext for an act of war.

At first the Korean king did not deign to reply but, in 1589, he agreed to send ambas-sadors on condition that some renegade Koreans, who had gone to Japan and from there had acted as mercenaries helping Japanese pirates raid along the Korean coast, be sent back to Korea to face their punishment. Hideyoshi was glad to comply, and the Koreans were duly sent back and beheaded. The Korean mission arrived in Japan in 1590 and apparently was treated in a gravely insulting fashion, with no cere-mony or proper entertainment being pro-vided for the Korean guests. This comes from Korean chronicles; Japanese histories are silent on the subject. Whatever the truth of the matter, the Korean envoys re-turned after a year's stay in Japan con-vinced that war was inevitable. The Korean king was offended by Hideyoshi's request that he join Japan in moving against China; Korea had been a domain of the Chinese emperor for too long to cope easily with the idea of a future outside Chinese domination.

Hideyoshi was serious in his plan, what-ever the Korean king may have thought, and set up a naval base at Nagoya, where he spent some time, giving out that he in-tended to command the war party himself. A naval expedition was rapidly equipped. The two chief divisional commanders were named Konishi and Kato, who between them commanded about 40,000 men in a total force of at least 200,000 troops. Kato and Konishi competed fiercely with each other as to who would be first on Korean soil, and in the event it was Konishi who reached Pusan first, on 24 May 1592. The day was misty, and it is said that the governor of Pusan was out hunting when the Japanese warships approached. He rushed back to prepare a defensive force, and only laughed at the Japanese peremptory request for surrender. The assault on Pusan by Konishi's troops was so savage that the city (then only a large fishing village) soon fell. The Japanese lost only 100 dead and 400 wounded, but the Koreans, who had put their best troops into the defense of Pusan, lost some thousands. From this point on there was such consternation throughout southern Korea at the Japanese approach that the five fortresses which lay between Pusan and Seoul simply opened their doors to the Japanese invaders. Konishi advanced northward by a westerly route, and Kato, who had landed at Pusan some days after Konishi, took the easterly route. They met at Mungyung on 5 June.

When the news of the fall of Pusan and the Japanese invasion reached Seoul, there was a frantic effort to raise the standing army. But this army really only existed on paper: those on its register were almost all unavailable for military service, having pressing commitments with their duties to their ancestors, their parents' funerals, and so on. Such Korean forces as there were, under General Yi Il, fled before the Japanese, and it was left to General Sil Yip, the vice-minister of war, to try to hold the Choryong Pass, without which Seoul could not be safe, against the Japanese. The Korean army was trapped at the pass and simply cut to pieces by the Japanese troops, no doubt overjoyed that they were dispatching the only army which lay between them and Seoul. An unseemly race then ensued between Kato and Konishi for the gates of Seoul — again Konishi was first. The Japanese occupied the city immediately, the royal family having fled north before them. Even as the king and his court were leaving the capital, flames were leaping into the sky behind them; these were fires set not by the invaders but by the city's inhabitants, who were losing no time in looting the granaries and the government houses where the deeds of slaves and bondsmen were kept.

The first reverse for the Japanese came just north of Seoul, in Kyonggi province. The Korean army had had time to gather some reinforcements from the north, and there was a fierce battle in which the Japanese were defeated. The Japanese were soon reinforced in their turn by the divisions of Konishi and Kato, though, and their next problem came with the crossing of the Imjin River. The Koreans, less seasoned fighters than the Japanese, were taken in when, after sitting for some time on the opposite bank, the Japanese set fire to their camp and retreated. The Koreans set off in hot pursuit, and the larger part of

their force was immediately cut down in an ambush. The Japanese did cross the Imjin, but were constantly harried, and the story goes that they were also impeded by quarrels between Konishi and Kato as to which road was the way to Peking. In mid-July Konishi arrived in Pyongyang, where the royal family had retreated, and there sent messages asking for safe conduct to Peking in exchange for no further molestation. The Koreans refused to parley while troops were on their soil. After desultory fighting, the Koreans fled Pyongyang, leaving their supplies behind, so that the Japanese could encamp there in comparative comfort.

Hideyoshi's plan had been that he would send reinforcements from Nagoya to join his troops at Pyongyang. Accordingly, more ships set off from Japan, and the Korean commander of Pusan harbor lost faith in his men's ability to defend the port. He sent urgently to the naval commander of Cholla province to the west, Admiral Yi Sun-shin, for aid. It was with this summons that the fortunes of the war changed. Yi Sun-shin arrived in force with his famous 'turtle ships' (*kobukson*), which the Japanese found invincible. They were ironclad warships, named for the shape of the hull, thought to resemble a tortoise shell. Their decks were convex and studded all over with iron spikes, making the ships impossible to

Below: Himeiji castle, known as the 'Heron castle' because of its white walls, was originally built by Akamatsu Sadanori in the fourteenth century.

Left: Toyotomi Hideyoshi, the great general who did more than any other to assure the unity of Japan under a military government. Hideyoshi was of peasant origin, and had a passionate and unpredictable temperament. Nevertheless, his political and military achievements remain unrivaled.

Right: A view of Osaka castle. After its capture in the great siege of 1615, it became a symbol of the power of the Tokugawa shogunate, which ruled Japan in strict isolation from the world for the next two centuries.

Far right: Tokugawa Ieyasu leads his troops at Sekigahara, the great battle in which Ieyasu's troops won a decisive victory against rival warlords in 1600. Ieyasu was a shrewd and cunning strategist, also known for his aphorisms. One of his famous lines is illustrated here: 'After victory tighten your helmet strings.'

board. The Japanese fleet was soon retreating in confusion, and at least one of its commanders committed *seppuku* in despair.

From this point on the invasion was doomed. The Japanese continued to fight on land, though defeated at sea. But the Koreans had recovered their morale; they made extensive use of sniper and ambush parties, and discouraged the Japanese whenever they camped for the night by surrounding the camp with small groups of men, each carrying a framework which supported five torches, so that their numbers appeared much greater than they really were. Japanese defeats in Cholla province caused them to lose ground which was never regained, particularly as Admiral Yi Sun-shin's fleet had made the arrival of further reinforcements from Japan largely impossible.

While the Japanese reinforcements were struggling to make their way northward, Konishi's division was still waiting in Pyongyang for the new divisions to arrive so that progress could be made toward Peking. Messengers were sent to Peking without reply; it was only when China heard that the king of Korea was about to take refuge on Chinese soil that the Japanese envoys were taken seriously. A Chinese force of about 5000 men marched on Pyongyang; but when they came to the city they found its gates open and no sign of life. It was of course an ambush, and over half the Chinese were killed in the first few minutes of fighting. But despite their victory at Pyongyang, the Japanese were cut off, and had come to realize it. They soon agreed to an armistice lasting 50 days.

In the dead of winter, late in January 1593, a massive Chinese counter-invasion force crossed the Yalu River into Korea, and after bitter hand-to-hand fighting the Japanese forces fled south. It was then, when the Japanese position was at its worst, that we hear of Commander Kobayakawa. He was an old man to be on active service, around 60 years old, but his command of strategy was such that he got the Japanese divisions comparatively safely back to Seoul, and then beat their pursuers just outside the capital, killing 10,000 Chinese in the mopping-up operation. But despite this, the Japanese position was now desperate. When peace terms were proposed by China in May 1593, the Japanese accepted immediately and ignominiously. The peace, however, was between Japan and China only, and Korea was not so happy to see the invaders go unpunished. It took a great many negotiations before terms could be found which were acceptable to the Koreans as well as to China and Japan. Eventually the Koreans achieved a form of words which stated that the Japanese were to leave Korea and never again to invade.

Meanwhile, Chinese envoys were in Japan for talks with Hideyoshi. These too ran into difficulties, partly because of a series of earthquakes which had left almost none of the magnificent buildings put up by Hideyoshi in a condition to receive foreign ambassadors. Even Osaka castle was partly destroyed. Another problem was that Hideyoshi steadfastly refused to meet any of the Koreans who had accompanied the Chinese envoys. In 1596 Hideyoshi was prevailed upon to accept their terms, which included a patent of investiture as king of Japan in Chinese terms. This meant receiving a crown and robe from China, together with a missive couched in not very respectful language which tacitly stated that Japan was now a vassal of China. The ambassadors returned to China with no reply from Hideyoshi. All they could do was report that he had accepted the crown and robe, though not before casting them on to the ground in disgust.

Hideyoshi was not one to be subdued by such a little thing as the defeat of his best troops in Japan's first foreign war, however. By March 1597 Japanese naval divisions were being armed for a new invasion of Korea — and this time they were better prepared. Also the Korean navy was no longer under the command of the great Admiral Yi Sun-shin of the turtle ships, who was old and in retirement. The Japanese won initial victories, although they were plagued by Chinese ships off southern Korea, and were able to set up fortified camps along the coast. But these were insufficiently supplied, and their garrisons began to suffer from famine. There are tales of Japanese soldiers stealing out from their camps at night to rifle the bags of dead Chinese soldiers in the hope of finding some uneaten rations.

In the spring of 1598 the Chinese received further reinforcements, and this prompted Konishi to advise evacuation of the Japanese camps and a retreat to Pusan. Admiral Yi Sun-shin had now been recalled from retirement to command the Korean navy, which was once more in fine fettle. Hideyoshi would not hear of a retreat, but ordered the Japanese to stay and fight. A great battle was fought at Sochon, where the Satsuma division commanded by Shimazu Yoshihiro slaughtered 40,000 men. Their ears were cut off, pickled in brine and sent back to Japan, where they were buried in a tumulus at Kyoto. The unexpected Japanese victory caused the Chinese to sue for peace, an overture which was most welcome to Konishi and the other commanders. Just at this time news arrived of the death of Hideyoshi. A general troop withdrawal was begun at once, but despite the conclusion of an armistice, there was another battle in which Korean and Chinese squadrons fell upon Konishi's and Shimazu's fleet. Korean accounts say the Japanese were forced to abandon several ships, but the Japanese say that they beat off the attack. Whatever the outcome, it was in this battle that Admiral Yi Sun-shin was killed by a stray bullet.

This was the inconclusive end of the Korean invasion which had lasted six years. Diplomatic relations between Korea and Japan were resumed by 1607 at the latest, although both nations bear the scars of the war to this day. At one time during the conflict there were 200,000 Japanese soldiers overseas, which was then the largest number of men ever sent abroad on a military mission by any nation. Hideyoshi's death lead to the usual struggle for power among sons, in-laws and their supporters, but Ieyasu was the strongest contender, and he was still a young man.

Hideyoshi had not been dead for long when the first rift appeared in the government of Japan. There was disagreement almost immediately on the best management of the withdrawal from Korea, but this was patched up in 1599. More important was the threat to Ieyasu's position, because this was bound up with the terms of Hideyoshi's will. Ieyasu had a sworn enemy in Ishida Mitsunari, who had been a favorite of Hideyoshi and was a master of intrigue. He was instrumental in having charges brought against Ieyasu for marrying off his children for political ends, a practice outlawed under Hideyoshi's will. Ieyasu had also aroused the suspicion, if not the enmity, of many others beside Ishida who professed to be faithful to Hideyoshi's memory. Ishida sought twice in 1599 to have Ieyasu assassinated, and, although the plots were discovered, Ieyasu saw fit to be lenient and have him imprisoned rather than executed. Ieyasu did take care, however, to pack the new Council of Regency with his own supporters, and was invested with the title of shogun in 1603.

The first true revolt against Ieyasu was planned by Uesugi Kagekatsu and Ishida Mitsunari. Uesugi Kagekatsu had been on the Council of Regency but had retired voluntarily to his estates, and was there biding his time. Ieyasu became aware that Uesugi was plotting against him and sent a message asking him to explain himself. When the reply was insolent, Ieyasu dispatched a 50,000-strong army with himself at its head against Uesugi. There is a poignant story that on his way from Osaka, Ieyasu stopped at Fushimi, where the warden of the castle, Torii Mototada, was an old friend. The two men spent the night in talk and reminiscence and parted at dawn, both knowing that Fushimi castle would soon be attacked and that Torii would die in its defense, but neither mentioning it to the other. Ieyasu made a slow and measured progress, having laid his plans beforehand, stopping for some time at Edo (now Tokyo), which he had made his base. In September 1600 he arrived at Oyama, where he received his first conclusive intelligence that Ishida Mitsunari was in full revolt against him. Earlier that month Mitsunari had in fact captured Fushimi castle after a siege and Torii Mototada had indeed been killed there. Mitsunari was representing his own

cause as that of Hideyori, Hideyoshi's son, and was marching from castle to castle mustering support. Not all the support he had counted on was forthcoming, however. It had become known that Ieyasu was well prepared for a battle, and not even those who counted themselves his enemies were sure they dared to face him. Among these latter was Mori Terumoto, who had charge of Hideyori and refused to move.

By mid-September Ieyasu was in his castle at Edo from where he launched a two-pronged attack, intending each wing to converge at Mino, where they would link up with his own army. This was in imitation of Nobunaga's strategy which had given him control of the home provinces around Kyoto. Ieyasu, having sent out his troops, did not commit his own forces until he had received enough intelligence to be certain of their loyalty and military competence. Ieyasu's army left for the front in early October, and camped on high ground at Akasaka on the 20th.

Mitsunari, meanwhile, had gathered as many allies as he could, and now had a force numerically superior to that of Ieyasu. They established themselves in positions which Ieyasu would have to take by frontal assault if he was to reach Osaka, but Mitsunari's lines looked impregnable. But, as Ieyasu knew, Mitsunari had traitors in his ranks. The battle began in fog and rain, so that it was difficult for either side to see its own men, let alone the enemy. After four hours of fighting, only about half of Mitsunari's troops had gone into action, while Ieyasu had engaged almost all his men, and the battle was turning against him. But Ieyasu was not perturbed. Kobayakawa, the veteran of the Korean invasion, who was ranged with Mitsunari's troops, was standing with several thousand men quietly on a nearby hill. Ieyasu had arranged with him beforehand that at a given signal he would change sides and join Ieyasu's troops in attacking the enemy from the rear. At first it seemed as though Kobayakawa would not respond to the signal, as he remained still while Ieyasu's men were pressed harder and harder. Ieyasu, furious, turned his guns on Kobayakawa's troops, and this spurred the latter into action.

Kobayakawa moved down the hill with 600 men, but Otani had already been suspicious of his good intentions and rounded on him straight away. Otani would have succeeded in preventing Kobayakawa's advance if the troops on his left flank had not then also changed sides and attacked his forces. Otani's division was routed, and seeing he had no chance, Otani committed *seppuku* on the spot. The change in the fortunes of battle caused Ishida Mitsunari's troops to be cut to pieces next. Only the Satsuma chief Shimazu, also a veteran of the Korean campaign, was left but his troops were utterly surrounded, and Shimazu himself turned and fled at the head of those of his men who were left. He escaped back to

Far left: The Battle of Sekigahara. After the death of Hideyoshi in 1598, the government of Japan was left to the Council of Five Elders (*Gotairo*) and the Five-Man Council of Commissioners (*Gobugyo*). The intrigue and rivalry between these two councils and their supporters threw up two rival leaders: Ishida Mitsunari (1560-1600), a favorite of Hideyoshi, and the senior warlord Tokugawa Ieyasu (1543-1616) who had at times been an ally of Hideyoshi. The struggle between the two factions led to the Battle of Sekigahara in which Ieyasu was victorious despite being outnumbered.

Above: Nagoya castle, with its massive fortified gatehouse, was built in 1610 by the first shogun, Ieyasu Tokugawa. Destroyed by fire during World War II, it was rebuilt in 1959 according to the original design.

Kagoshima by cutting his way through the enemy lines, galloping to Osaka and seizing the best ships in the harbor by force.

Ieyasu took a very considerable risk at the Battle of Sekigahara. It seems Kobayakawa was in two minds whether or not to keep his agreement to change sides. If he had not done so Ieyasu's forces would have been hard pressed and, what is more, there were at least 30,000 more enemy troops a few miles from Sekigahara. Not one of these men came forward, however, doubtless having decided to join Ieyasu before his march on Sekigahara began. Ieyasu at this stage of the battle was still waiting for his own reinforcements under Hidetada, Hideyori's father-in-law. But Hidetada was late in arriving, partly because he had been distracted by minor skirmishes for possession of small fortresses on the way, and partly because it seems he had received an invitation to join the Ishida side and it had taken him a little while to make up his mind. In any event, Ieyasu was so furious with Hidetada for his tardiness that he refused altogether to see him, although he was his own son. It was some days before

father and son finally met.

The victory at Sekigahara allowed Ieyasu to march on Osaka. He first instructed those who had come over to his side to finish off the Ishida camp, which they did, once again achieving their aim through treachery. The camp was defended by Ishida's brother, who being defeated killed Ishida's wife and children and then committed *seppuku* himself.

The inhabitants of Osaka were terror-struck when they heard the result of the battle at Sekigahara from the survivors who poured in through the gates of the city with the most horrific tales of disaster. But Ieyasu sent a message to Yodogimi, Hideyori's mother, to say that he was quite sure that neither she nor Hideyori had ever wished to be part of any conspiracy against him – news they welcomed with some relief. This left only Mori Terumoto of the chiefs opposing Ieyasu at Sekigahara and he, on receiving a message from Ieyasu which stated that if he now dropped any further campaigns against Ieyasu his domains would be left intact, retired to his private residence at Kizu. Three days later, on 1

November 1600, Ieyasu entered Osaka castle.

In 1605 Ieyasu, now growing old, resigned the office of shogun and obtained the appointment for Hidetada. Hideyori, son of Hideyoshi, was invited to the celebrations but refused to go on the instigation of his mother Yodogimi. Nonetheless, Yodogimi had to abase her pride as time went on. However much of a disgrace she may have felt it that her son and that of the great Hideyoshi had no preferment, it was the Tokugawa under Ieyasu who were rulers now. The contemporary histories say that Ieyasu longed to see Hideyori before he died, and finally did so in 1611, in what was to be the last meeting between them. Ieyasu is recorded as saying after their meeting that he had been impressed by Hideyori's intelligence. It would seem from this that Ieyasu had been consistently misinformed, to the effect that Hideyori was weak, effeminate and of no account. This reputation had been carefully fostered by Hideyori's

Above: The practice of sculpted portraiture which began during the Kamakura period continued in the following centuries. This sixteenth century portrait of a nobleman in lacquered wood has painted crystal eyes.

Left: Ieyasu's last resting place. Revered in his lifetime for his great victories, Ieyasu was idolized after his death. His remains are at the Tosho-gu shrine in Nikko, eastern Japan. The shrine is also home to a great library containing 7000 Buddhist sutras. Seen here are the stone lanterns which front the shrine's library.

Above: The figure of Tokugawa Ieyasu at the shrine built in his memory at Nikko. The unifying shogun of Japan is revered for his wisdom and nobility of character as much as for his military and political achievements.

during the Tokugawa period that the concept of absolute loyalty to a single lord came to be enshrined in this code, with the consequent emergence of heroic feats like those of the famous '47 *ronin*'. This concept of loyalty did not of course have to be tested in peacetime. It has already been seen how often allegiances were shifted in wartime, and Japan's wars were not quite over.

Hideyori was held in suspicion by Ieyasu and with some reason. By June 1614 Hideyori was ready to do battle against Ieyasu. He called to Osaka all the provincial lords who had suffered by the rearrangement of domains after the Battle of Sekigahara. There was quite a number of these petty lords, along with much larger numbers of samurai thrown out into the world as *ronin* (masterless samurai) as a result of the confiscations of 1600-02. The house of Toyotomi, to which Hideyori belonged, was closely linked by marriage to the Tokugawa, but this did not stop the Toyotomi from feeling the resentment which goes with lack of preferment. Among those lords of some consequence who shared this resentment, and therefore rushed to join Hideyori at Osaka, were Sanada Yukimura, Goto Mototsugu and Akashi Morishige. Sanada's family had been impoverished by the Battle of Sekigahara, and Sanada himself, having retired to a monastery, had great difficulty in escaping from there to join Hideyori. Goto and Akashi had connections with the Korean campaigns, but had failed to prosper.

Hideyori held a council of war, at which a defensive strategy was adopted which involved waiting for the enemy's attack on Osaka castle. This was opposed by Sanada and Goto, who wanted to advance on Kyoto and capture the emperor; in this way they could give their campaign legitimacy and brand the Tokugawa as rebels. But Hideyori was not sure enough of his support. Many of the provincial lords he had called upon had failed to respond, and some had sent his messages on to Ieyasu after killing the messengers. The main reason for this was that Ieyasu had been ahead of Hideyori. He had, well in advance, demanded and received written promises of loyalty from Shimazu, Hosokawa and 48 other lords in the western provinces, all of whom feared for the consequences if they were seen to be traitors. Also, by November 1614 Ieyasu was already mobilizing the Edo troops to march on and surround Osaka at some distance. The main Tokugawa force was under Hidetada's command, some 50,000 strong. Before it arrived in the Osaka area there had already been skirmishes between Tokugawa and the Osaka forces. By December 1614 the last of the outpost encampments around Osaka had been taken, and Hideyori's forces were forced back into the castle; however, this was not achieved without considerable loss and expense to the Tokugawa forces. Attempts to scale the castle walls were driven back by firearms, and the besieged made sorties out of the

guardian Katagiri, because it made Hideyori no threat to Ieyasu.

Between 1600 and 1615 Ieyasu consolidated his power over Japan. He was setting up a system, the Tokugawa shogunate, which was to last for more than two centuries and would preside over Japan's greatest period of isolation from the outside world as well as the development of a unique culture, one distinctly different from the Korean and Chinese which had given it birth. Ieyasu had his capital in Edo, present-day Tokyo. He maintained peace in the empire partly by the device of requiring the provincial lords to leave their families permanently there, and that they themselves should spend a substantial part of each year in the capital. This was intended to prevent the formation of hostile cliques in the provinces where they could not be monitored, and in this the policy was generally successful. The well-known policy of national isolation (*sakoku*) came a little later, toward the middle of the seventeenth century, and by then peace was well established. The absence of wars during the Tokugawa period meant that the samurai had the leisure, and the inclination, to formally set down the code of honor and conduct they had taken for granted before and which was known as Bushido. It was castle from time to time for a month or so, but soon determined to remain inside, where their position was impregnable.

Ieyasu soon realized that assaults on the castle would always be driven back, and he also knew that the garrison was well supplied. He therefore resorted to bribery, but when he offered Sanada the rich province of Shinano, he was harshly rebuffed and the incident was publicized in the castle. As well as bribery, Ieyasu used inducements. He continually sent messengers with offers of free pardon and restoration of property to any who would abandon the campaign. Hideyori even responded at one point, insisting on two provinces on Shikoku, an outrageous demand which brought the negotiations to an end. In January 1615 Ieyasu ordered the ladies' quarters in the castle, where Hideyori's mother Yodogimi lodged, to be fired upon. Two of her maid-servants were killed, and Yodogimi herself flew into such a panic that she begged Hideyori to make peace without delay.

Ieyasu's entreaties and importunings continued almost without cease. On 21 January 1615 Ieyasu succeeded, through treacherous intermediaries, in getting a solemn undertaking from Hideyori and Yodogimi to the effect that Hideyori would make no further rebellious moves against him, and that Hideyori should consult Ieyasu and no-one else. On the same evening it was proposed to make a sudden night attack out of the castle on the Tokugawa camp but this proposal was rejected after some discussion.

A few days later Ieyasu left for Kyoto, staying there only a week before setting out for eastern Japan. Hidetada remained at Osaka in command of the besieging forces and proceeded to fill in the castle moat and demolish its ramparts. There were immediate and strong protests from the Osaka camp that such acts were working against a successful conclusion to the peace negotiations. Some of the Tokugawa troops were sent home, and a peace of a kind was concluded; but Hidetada continued to besiege the castle. The whole procedure began to take on an air of farce, as those within the castle debated whether to begin digging up the moat again. By this time Ieyasu had at least one spy in the Toyotomi camp, and soon (May 1615) was able to gather evidence that Hideyori and Yodogimi were acting contrary to the spirit of the peace just concluded. Ieyasu had learned that Hideyori was once again calling on *ronin* to join him in Osaka. Ieyasu then asked Hideyori to withdraw to another place while the Tokugawa undertook to repair Osaka castle, whereupon Hideyori could reoccupy it, knowing full well that after the fiasco of the filling-in of the moat no-one in the Osaka camp would trust him for a moment.

Ronin were indeed flocking to Osaka once more to join Hideyori; accounts vary as to their number, but it seems to have been well over 100,000. But the castle's defenses, though partly re-erected, were flimsy compared with their previous condition, and morale inside was not good. There was some disunity and quarreling, and meanwhile Ieyasu was advancing on the castle with all the forces he could muster. By June there was hard fighting within ten miles of Osaka. Goto had sent out divisions to block the Tokugawa advance, but was routed, while Sanada failed to put a conclusive stop to the Tokugawa vanguard. The Osaka leaders were thus having no success in fighting in the open, but nonetheless, following another council of war, they decided to offer battle on the open ground to the south of the castle. It was arranged that Sanada and his fellow commanders should block the Tokugawa advance, while Akashi and his troops attacked from the rear. At the height of the battle Hideyori himself would emerge from the castle and put the Tokugawa to flight.

The Osaka plan failed, however. Akashi was stopped before he could reach the Tokugawa rear and the general battle was joined too soon – mainly because of the impetuous and semi-trained *ronin* who formed such a large part of the Osaka force. Only Sanada held firm and he, seeing that the strategy was failing, sent urgently for Hideyori to come out of the castle straight away. Sanada launched his troops upon the main Tokugawa body, and just as Ieyasu's forces were coming up to their rear to reinforce them, the Asano troops, on the Tokugawa side, swung round against them in what looked like treason. Panic began to ensue in the Tokugawa ranks, and it was only their weight of numbers which prevailed. The main Tokugawa body began to push forward again, and the Osaka troops were in retreat into the castle.

Although Hideyori had been summoned, he failed to appear and the Osaka troops began to buzz with rumors of treason inside the castle. Hideyori himself was affected and partly convinced by these rumors, and so hesitated – the Tokugawa masses then began to push the Osaka troops further back into the castle fortifications. Just at this moment, Hideyori's chief cook, it is said, turned traitor and set the kitchens on fire, causing even greater panic and allowing the Tokugawa troops inside the second ring of fortifications. Hideyori fled back inside to a storehouse comparative safe from the flames and sent out his wife to beg Ieyasu to spare her life and that of her mother-in-law Yodogimi (it will be remembered Ieyasu was Hideyori's wife's grandfather). On 4 June Hideyori, not receiving any reply from Ieyasu, committed *seppuku*, while Yodogimi was killed by one of his retainers. The 30 or so supporters who had gone with Hideyori into the storehouse also disemboweled themselves in the burning castle. The house of Toyotomi was destroyed and the Tokugawa shogunate assured in its mastery of Japan.

Overleaf: A rendition of Uesugi Kenshin, the warlord of Echigo. Uesugi is famous for his heroism in personal combat. Uesugi's arch-rival, Takeda Shingen of Kai, fought some well-documented battles with him at Kawanakajima in Shinano for possession of that region. It was Uesugi who formed the most serious threat to Oda Nobunaga during the latter's rise to power. For that reason Nobunaga formed an alliance with Uesugi's enemy Takeda Shingen. Nonetheless, when Uesugi died suddenly in 1577, Nobunaga is said to have exclaimed in relief: 'Now the whole country is on the way to peace!'

The Artistic Tradition

From early recorded times, there has been a strong tradition of poetical composition in Japan, particularly centered around the court. Indeed, it has been said that there has been no emperor or empress of Japan who has not been a poet; in 800, when Charlemagne could barely write his own name, the Japanese Emperor Saga was one of the greatest calligraphers of his age. The Japanese literary tradition is perhaps unique in the world for the very prominent part played by women geniuses. It has been speculated that, when the men were imitating Chinese composition — even to the extent of writing verses in praise of tea, which had not yet been imported into Japan and which they had never tasted — court ladies were writing brilliantly in the native Japanese language. It is thought that they may have saved it from being lost, at least as a vehicle for cultural expression.

When the warriors took over power from the court in the twelfth century, they still retained their awe of the cultural prestige of

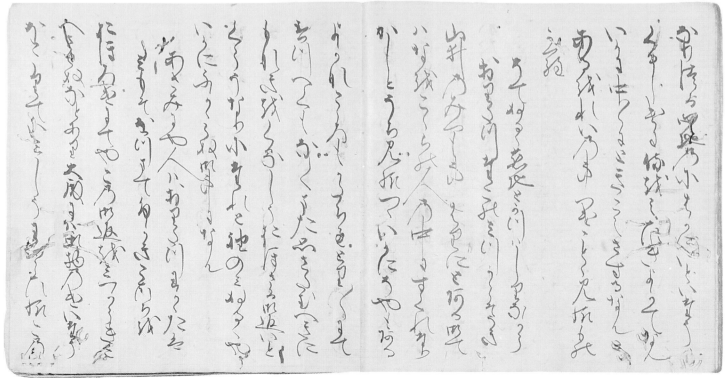

Previous page, below: A passage from the *Tale of Genji (Genji Monogatari)*, a very long novel of Heian court life written probably in the first quarter of the eleventh century.

Previous page, above: A kitchen in a samurai household. From a scroll illustrating the life of the samurai warrior.

Below: Ota Dokan shelters from the rain and a peasant girl offers him a flower in place of the straw raincoat he had requested. This famous story illustrates the poetic sensibility found even among supposedly illiterate peasants.

the nobles and the role of the emperor was maintained as a sort of figurehead. The warriors took part, with increasing success, in literary activities. One of the then important regular events in literature was the *uta-awase* (contest verses). These verses, called *uta*, were not spoken in Chinese, but in pure Japanese, though a few Chinese words were admissible. The presiding deity was the god of Sumiyoshi.

The *uta-awase* contests were often held after the end of one of the great Buddhist ceremonies; something of the solemnity of the occasion spilled over into the very strict formalities of the *uta-awase*. The competing poets and poetesses, all amateurs, were divided into teams, but there was no outright winning poem. The poets from the two teams were matched against each other individually, rather like a chess match today. The two poems to be judged were read out and, after consideration, a ruling was given: superior-inferior or, occasionally, a draw. The judge had to be a famous poet and he was supposed to be aided by a number of assistants, who were often partisans of one team or the other. The decision of the chief judge was expected to be in im-

pressively poetic form. For instance, one verdict was: 'The poem has put out leaves, but no flowers.'

One of the most famous poets, whose verses are in many anthologies, was renowned as a warrior, an expert in archery and a military strategist. This was Sato Norikiyo, born into a warrior family renowned for bravery in 1118. He was himself particularly notorious for his reckless courage. He became an officer in the bodyguard of the ex-Emperor Go-Toba, with whom he was a great favorite due to his gift for poetry. But Norikiyo did not care for honors or riches and was drawn toward a life of retirement from the world. The sudden death of a near relation and friend, a young man in apparent good health, impressed him profoundly with a sense of the transience of life. Although still in his twenties, he immediately resigned his post (in spite of his lord's strong protest) and became a priest with the Buddhist name Saigyo. His wife became a nun and led an ascetic life at the foot of Mount Koya, the seat of a great Buddhist monastery.

Saigyo spent the rest of his life almost entirely as a wandering priest. He traveled extensively, visiting Buddhist temples and composing verses wherever he went, becoming famous as a poet in his own lifetime. When he passed through Kamakura, he was pressed by the first shogun, Yoritomo, to lecture on poetry but declined to speak of poetry on the grounds that he was an amateur, and talked on archery and strategy with Yoritomo and others.

The following day, when he took leave of the shogun, the latter pressed on him a silver cat, as a token of his appreciation. Saigyo accepted it with some reluctance, and gave it to a little boy who was playing at the gate of the shogun's mansion.

Many of his poems concern the Buddhist sense of the 'passing of things,' but he had a very wide human feeling, and one of his masterpieces shows a woman's desperate attempts not to care:

Forsaken
Why should I feel bitter now he has turned
away?
There was a time when I did not know
him, or he me.

Another great Bushi poet of the same time was Minamoto Sanetomo, the second son of Yoritomo the shogun. To give some idea of Japanese verse and how it is appreciated, here is the original first:

Ame
Toki ni yori
Sugureba tami no
Hachi-Dai-Ryu-o
Ame tame yamae

Rain
The sudden flooding
Is making the people weep
O Eight Dragon Kings!
I beg you, stop the rain.

A Japanese critic says of this verse: 'It is both powerful and rhythmical, in that the fourth phrase consists of four sonorous Chinese words, and the last phrase is of three pure Japanese words, ending in the same vowel: *ame, tame, yamae.*'

From the early days, poetry developed in unique forms in Japan. For instance there was a form of competition in which the first line of a poem would be given, and then the participants were asked to complete it with a second line. One of the most famous 'completions' was to the first line: 'I want to kill him; I don't want to kill him.' The poet Issa supplied the second line: 'I caught the thief, and found – it was my own son.' To rank as good poetry, the completion had to be both unexpected and appealing. A charming example, from thirteenth century Kamakura, was to the first line: 'We have put a new roof on our house.' The second line which won the competition was: 'The swallows (who come to nest every year) seem a little bewildered.'

In the Japan of the thirteenth century, there are records of peasants who were able to compose short poems. When the monk Ryuson and a companion were traveling through the countryside, they entered a hamlet in Omi prefecture. Darkness fell and, as they could find no better lodging, they squeezed themselves into a hovel for the night. As they were leaving in the morning, their hosts offered them some coarse food, at the same time apologizing in verse, to which they suitably replied in verse. Another example was when Ryuson was traveling in the Musashino Plain. He became thirsty and asked at what appeared to be a shack for a bowl of water. From a window, a boy of 11 or 12 offered him some water in a bowl with a big chip out of it. Ryuson spontaneously composed a poem: 'As I hold it (the bowl) I had expected a full moon, but I got only a chipped moon.' The boy immediately capped the verse by replying: 'It is because the moon has not yet fully come out of the mountain ridge that it has a chip out of it.'

Even the peasants then, in certain places, were able to appreciate and to compose poems. There is a traditional incident concerning Ota Dokan, a famous warrior. Ota Dokan is one of the paragons of medieval Bushido and his life, possibly embroidered at a later date, illustrates some of the virtues and also, unwittingly, some of the defects of the medieval warrior's attitudes.

He was born in 1431 in the Kanto area, which was then ruled by the Hojo regents who strongly supported Zen. When he was young Ota Dokan had little knowledge of poetry, and was absorbed in mastering the military arts. There is an anecdote about his early years, concerning his humiliation by a peasant girl. It centers on a poem composed about 500 years previously by Prince Kane-akira. As the actual words are important, here is the Japanese in Roman characters. It will be seen that it is composed in

Above: A farmer wearing a straw coat (*mino*). This was the normal wear in rainy weather. Japan's lack of resources for cloth-making, made straw the ideal material for clothing.

one of the classical forms – five lines of 5, 7, 5, 7, 7 syllables respectively. A literal translation is given after each line, to illustrate the suggestive character of these verses:

Nana-e- ya-e (seven-fold eight-fold)
Hana wa sakedomo (though the flowers bloom)
Yamabuki no (of the *Yamabuki*)
Mi no hitotsu dani (even one fruit)
Naki zo kanashiki (there is not. Alas!)

There is a delicate play on words in this ancient poem. *Mi no hitotsu* means 'one fruit' (*mi*) but it could also mean 'one straw-coat' (*mino*). The straw-coat was the normal protection when it was raining. The verse has a second meaning that the poet had been caught in a shower and found himself surrounded by yamabuki flowers but, alas, not a straw-coat among them. The incident told of Ota Dokan occurred when he was out hunting with some retainers. They were unexpectedly overtaken by a heavy shower and he sent one of his men to a nearby peasant's hut to ask for the loan of a straw raincoat. To his amazement,

Right: A top-knotted warrior riding his horse is accosted by a lady, possibly a courtesan. Mount Fuji is visible in the background.

Below: A portrait of Minamoto no Kintada, a tenth century poet. The portrait is attributed to Fujiwara Nobuzune, of the Kamakura period and is therefore painted from the imagination. It is an example of 'likeness pictures' (nise-e) in which the artist strove to capture the essence of a personality with a few brushstrokes.

a young girl came out with a small tray and on it a beautiful branch of yamabuki flowers, which she humbly and silently offered him. Dokan shouted in annoyance, 'The girl's a fool — I don't want flowers!' and strode away to go back home in the rain.

Back in the castle, he was telling some of his other retainers what had happened and commenting on how half-witted some of the peasants were, when one of them, an old man, gently remarked that there might be something else. He then quoted to him in a low voice the poem of Prince Kane-akira and explained its double meaning. He further explained that the girl, not wanting to be so rude as to refuse his request directly, had tried to express delicately her regret that there was no straw-coat to offer him. Dokan was greatly ashamed at his ignorance, and began to study poetry. Afterward he became a prominent poet and left a number of well-known verses.

There are some extremely illuminating points in the above story. The first thing that may strike a Western reader is that a peasant girl, in no way distinguished and encountered by chance, knew by heart some of the poems of the *Go Shui Shu* anthology, and so well that she was able to find this appropriate one instantly. Then she had the creative poetry in herself to be able to use it to convey an unwelcome message in an indirect but beautiful manner. It may be that this particular story is apocry-

phal, but it has parallels in much of the literature of the time.

Ota Dokan was himself the author of some good verses; it is said that, at the moment of his death by an assassin's spear, he capped a mocking line of verse delivered by the assassin with another to the effect that he was unmoved even at the moment of death because he had practiced freedom from attachment to life throughout the living of it. This is echoed by the famous case of Nobunaga, trapped in Honnoji temple by a murderous rival, also a former ally. Nobunaga set the place on fire and then danced in the burning building until the flames consumed him. It is almost as if training in taking death not merely calmly

but also with apparent joy included an acceptance of the likelihood of the double cross by an ally, so frequent an event in Japanese military history.

It was expected that not only generals but also some of the lower-rank warriors should be able to reply in verse of their own composition. In fact, the Bushi were meant to be more than just warriors, they were also expected to have a knowledge of science and culture. This tradition of artistic creativity already existed in Japan but was particularly encouraged by Zen. This does not mean that all samurai subscribed to this ideal, but the key point is that they respected it and were slightly in awe of both learning and culture.

Below: A portrait of the warrior Tawara Toda Hidesato from the series *Twenty-Four Generals*. He is seen here with full weaponry, including one of the great *san-nin-bari* longbows. These were bows reputed to require the strength of three men to bend them.

Confucian Bushido

Historically, Bushido can be divided into three periods. First of all there was the 'Bushido of the Fighter,' which originated in the time of Yoritomo (1147-99), and it lasted until the end of Japan's civil wars (1600). This was followed by a re-shaped form of Bushido, an amalgamation of Confucianism and Zen, which appeared at the beginning of the Tokugawa era (1603). Finally, there was the legacy of Bushido, which coincided with the restoration of imperial rule at the beginning of the Meiji era (1868).

The 'Bushido of the Fighter' was prevalent in the era of Japan's civil wars, and focused on the standards of discipline required of a warrior. These can be summarized as:

To be brave in danger and ever faithful.
To be loyal toward his clan lord.
To content himself with a sober living.
To be just and have integrity.

Apart from this, the standards of Bushido were not expressly defined. It is only from other incidents that one understands Bushido. The book *Koyo Gun Kan*, written by Takasaka Danjo, a general under Takeda Shingen (1521-73) and a lord of the province of Koshu, is a typical work of this era.

However, when the shogunate of Tokugawa appeared (1603), it heralded a period of prolonged peace, and samurai were hard put to find a use for their swords. Many of them turned to agriculture; others became *ronin* (masterless – owing loyalty to no definite person); the majority at court became both soldiers and officials. As the old form of Bushido no longer matched the new spirit, Yamaga Soko (1622-85) and other Confucians sought to express what they considered to be the true nature of Bushido. The famous Zen priest Takuan (1573-1645) was also explaining Bushido from the point of view of Zen during this period. His concept is set out in a letter to Yagyu Tajima-no-Kami (1571-1646), a noble who was a famous master of swordsmanship. The letter is known as *Fudo Shin Myo-Roku*; (*The Secret Immovable Mind*); extracts from this are given later.

The *Budo Shoshin-shu (First Steps in Bushido)* of Daidoji Yuzan is supposed to have been written near the beginning of the eighteenth century. At first, this book had little success because it was thought to have been written in too popular a style, but this opinion soon changed and several provinces even adopted it as an official textbook. According to the account of an old man who had lived in the province of Matsushiro at the beginning of the Meiji era in the late nineteenth century, even the women there could recite the first chapter of the book by heart.

Here are some extracts from Daidoji Yuzan's famous work, *First Steps in Bushido*:

'The samurai must keep within himself, more than anything else, from the rice-cake ceremony on New Year's morning to the last moment of that year, all day and all night, the thought of death. It is only by never letting drop the thought of death from the forefront of consciousness that he can preserve in him the two fundamental virtues: loyalty to the lord, and honoring his parents. By this, he is at the same time free from vices, and also from accidents. He keeps a healthy body and can live a long, long time. The character becomes noble. Such are the advantages which the thought of death brings to us ... Let us explain further.

'The life of man is fleeting as the evening dew or the morning hoar frost. What can be more perilous than that of a samurai? Yet many there are who resolve to serve their lord and their parents, supposing that they themselves will live for a long time. In fact they neglect their duties while thinking this, both toward the lord and to the parents. When he realizes the contrary, that his life can end tomorrow, that the day he is living is perhaps the last time he will be able to receive orders from his lord, or see the faces of his parents, then he turns toward them with a heart full of sincere devotion. It is in this way that one can accomplish what is required for the loyalty toward lord and parents.

'But when one begins to forget the

Far left: The armor of the samurai warrior was designed as much to strike terror into the hearts of the enemy as to protect the warrior himself. He also devoted time before battle commenced to a recitation of his own prowess and that of his ancestors in order to encourage himself and demoralize his opponent. The fact that much of the fighting was hand-to-hand until the advent of the musket at the end of the sixteenth century meant that a samurai's 'face' or personal credibility counted for a great deal in battle.

Above: Samurai at table, from a scroll illustrating the life of the warrior. Modesty and good manners, without excessive attachment to the pleasures of the flesh, were highly prized. Below: The horse was a most valued possession of the samurai, as he was a mounted warrior *par excellence*. The six horses shown here are all well-groomed, and kept in comparatively luxurious quarters, though austerity was recommended for the living quarters of the warriors themselves.

thought of death, he becomes imprudent. He will lose the sense of modesty which is always necessary. He gets into quarrels over ideas which are not based on anything at all, and which are provocative. He argues back instead of letting other people speak. Then he will take to going freely to vulgar places of amusement, will consort with ne'er-do-wells, get into fights with them. Sometimes he even loses his own life. Thus he will taint the honor of his lord, and be creating worries for his parents. All these things are simply the result of this first failure, of having neglected to keep present in himself the thought of death. If one is always thinking about death, on the other hand, with a lively awareness of what the demands on a samurai are, then he will weigh his words before uttering them. He gives everything equal consideration, and he will be circumspect before speaking.

'If what he is going to say is true he will not get in meaningless quarrels; he will not go to bad places even though he may be invited there. He does not run the risk of unforeseen accidents and in this way he can keep himself from all evils and accidents.

'Right from the top classes of society down to the very lowest, it is by having forgotten the thought of death that they have delivered themselves to intemperance. They eat too much, they drink too much, they make love too much. In which case they get affected with illness and they die young, or at least if they are not completely extinguished, they remain with incurable illnesses which waste them away. A young man who is always thinking about death whilst he is still healthy and vigorous, takes care of himself, and will eat with moderation and avoid voluptuousness. He will be reflective and he will be modest. In that way he will keep himself full of vigor. In this way he will be able to live for as long as God may permit him. On the contrary if he is taken up with the idea of deliberately living for a very long time, then he will become the victim of all sorts of desires. He will get miserly, and want to get hold of other people's possessions, and he will not be willing to give to other people what belongs to them. His character will become like that of a do-nothing. But if one always holds the thought of death, miserliness disappears naturally, the vicious characteristics such as envy and avarice do not manifest themselves any more and the personality becomes noble.'

The 'Confucian' Bushido of the Tokugawa period was also discussed by Daidoji Yuzan. The military police of the Tokugawa, the new rulers of a unified Japan at the start of the sixteenth century, can be encapsulated by a humorous poem:

Boon-bu! boon-bu!
Even at night, the mosquitoes don't let you sleep.
(*Boon-bu* represented the sound of the

mosquitoes buzzing around the sleeper's ears and a play on the words *Bun-bu* which also gave some sleepless nights.)

This was a humorous poem about the policy of *Bun-bu* (literally, Learning-and-fighting-arts), which was strongly encouraged by the Tokugawa. The country was about to enter a long period of peace; there were to be no more wars. The samurai now had to develop a high degree of administrative skill in order to run the machinery of government. In fact, they showed themselves sufficiently flexible to do this — the *Bun* (learning) gradually tamed the *Bu* (fighting) tendency.

The process took place over many years — in fact, it was never total, because the warrior was not encouraged to forget his martial skills. They were strictly controlled, but they were still polished to a high degree of efficiency if needed. The samurai always retained the deference of the commoner classes, though some of the merchants might be far more wealthy than the samurai, who had only their official salaries. The samurai, constituting about 10 percent of the population, were quick to punish (sometimes with the spilling of blood) any sign of insolence from their inferiors. And threats were occasionally used to improve the work efficiency of those inferiors. For instance, a doctor might be told that if he failed to cure some eminent personage, his own life might be forfeit. The *Bu* was always there, symbolized by the two swords which the samurai carried. But the fact that there was only one major rebellion in the 250-odd years of Tokugawa rule shows that the *Bun* did in fact exercise restraint. The local lords (*daimyo*), though

Below: An example of Japanese calligraphy. The thickness of the stroke is said to reveal the character of the artist; the density of the ink indicates the depth of emotion.

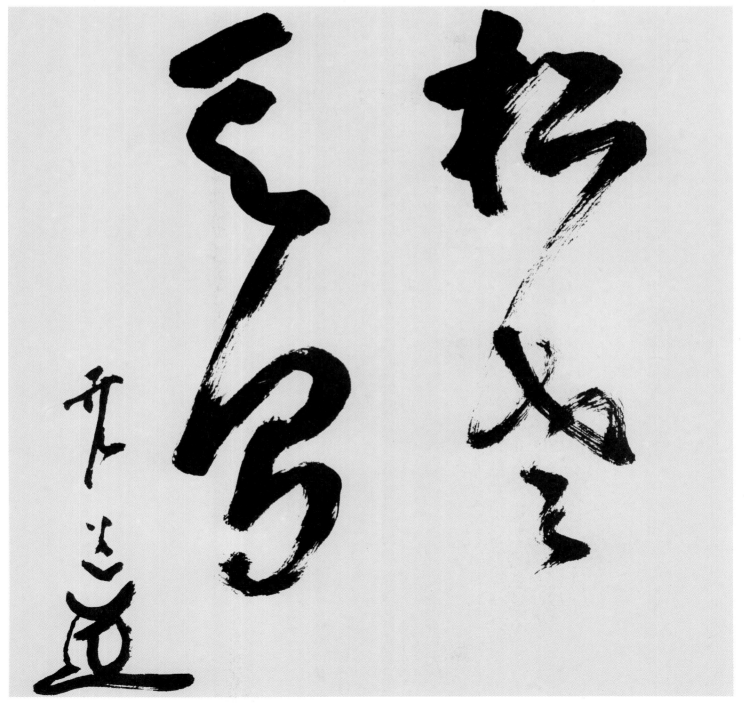

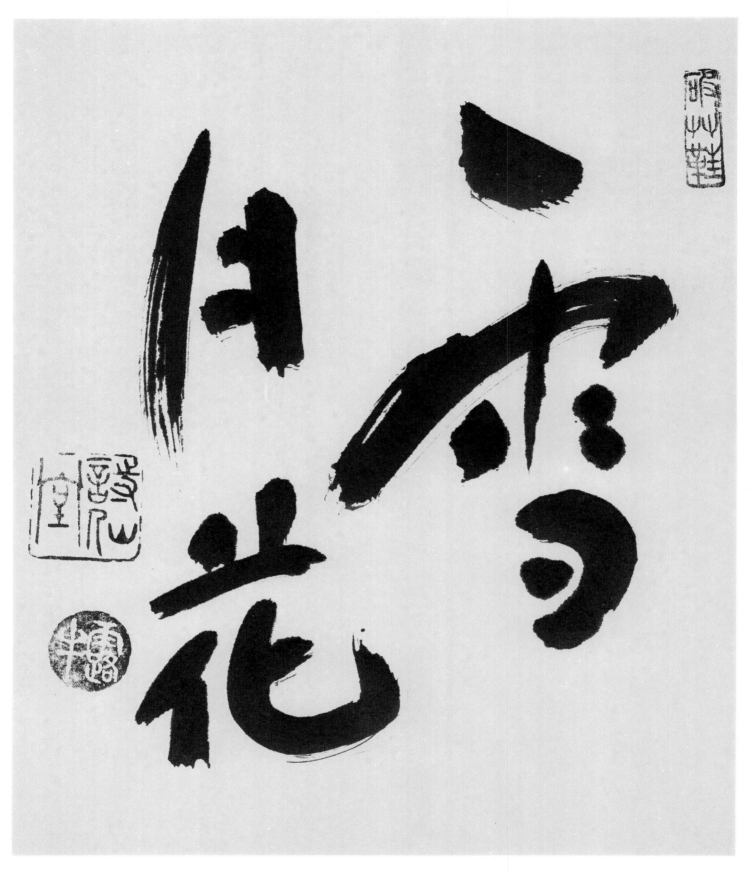

Above: The art of calligraphy is still practised in Japan. More than 1000 artists take part in the New Year exhibition in Tokyo.

Right: An illustration by an unknown sixteenth century artist of the *Tales of Ise*. Like the *Tale of Genji*, it is a romantic story of ancient court life in Heian Japan.

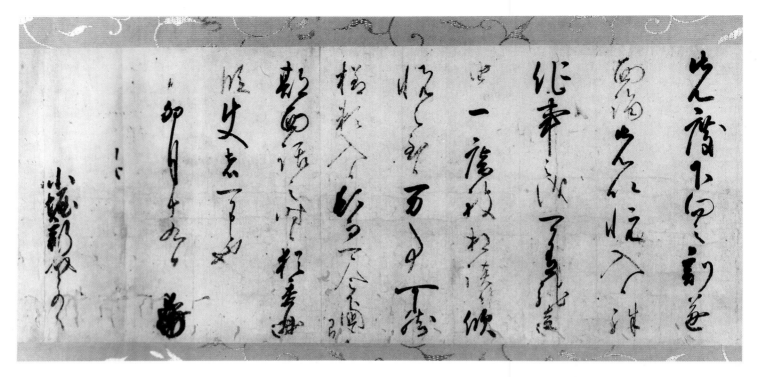

Above: With the tea ceremony, calligraphy was one of the most highly prized arts of sixteenth century Japan. It was at this time that the great schools of calligraphy began to emerge, some of which still dominate the art in Japan today. The sample illustrated is by Shoren-In Sancho (1552-97), abbot of Tendai.

Right: This sample of writing is by Honami Kosetsu (1558-1637) and dates from the early seventeenth century. Honami was one of the greatest calligraphers of his time. The illustration is from a poem on the subject of cherry blossom.

retaining a good deal of autonomy, were forced to leave some of their family in the capital under the eye of the shogun's government – in a way they were hostages for the *daimyo's* good behavior.

Samurai who left (or were dismissed from) the service of their local lord could take to trade and other occupations. In one sense, they were not a part of the Bushido ethic which laid great stress on loyalty to a lord. Some of them, of course, did find employment in the service of another lord, or were taken back by their own former master after a period of 'exile.' The successful transformation from mainly *Bu* to *Bun-bu* is a good example of the flexibility and adaptability of the samurai class, and in the following extracts from Daidoji Yuzan's influential manual of Bushido for young samurai, it can be seen how the *Bun* element is stressed, though never at the expense of the *Bu*. For instance, although poetry was so much extolled, there are warnings against losing martial vigor by plunging headlong into poetry alone:

'There is a saying – a bit light and vulgar but I approve the spirit of it – which runs:

The undercoat, and the official, are white when they are new.

'Let us explain a little further. The undercoat when it is new is a very smart formal garment, but when you have used it a long time, the collar and the sleeves begin to become soiled. Their color turns grey, and so it becomes unpleasant and unattractive. It is the same with the official. At the beginning his attitude is straightforward and naive. He will faithfully follow the orders of his lord, taking care over the smallest things, and keeping above everything the spirit of the oath which he has sworn on taking up the post. He keeps the rules of the position. He will carry out his task with respect and reserve; he is careful to keep all the rules so that nothing can be said about him in reproach. He does get frequently praised by one and all as a good officer, fair to all and a man of integrity.

'But when he has been a good time in the same position and gets to know all the ropes, he becomes clever at maintaining a good appearance while beginning to commit injustices which he would never have done before. Whereas at the beginning he was esteemed for his excellent manners and his way of accounting carefully for presents received, and keeping his oath; now on occasion, he feels that he cannot refuse to accept a present on the spot, and he takes it intending to return it perhaps at some other place and time.

'So it is that there comes about a change, without anyone being able to say just when it is, that he is taken by a desire to make a fortune by profiting from his position. He still refuses presents, with a manner and words showing that he cannot ever be easily tempted with presents, but the knowing ones guess his inner thought, and affecting to know nothing about it at all, they make their presents in various indirect ways. These he accepts with a show of reluctance, and begins to favor one side and so deceive his lord.

'By this sort of conduct he becomes like a dirty sleeve. And whereas in the case of the sleeve it is only dirt and dust, and a good cleanser will make it white again, the heart of man is often so polluted and soiled by the infiltration of thousands of taints, that no cleanser can restore its whiteness, so strong are they. A sleeve is washed once or twice a year. The heart of man should be examined morning and evening about all incidents, without negligence. In spite of all one's vigilance it can easily become dirty and very quickly spoilt.

'And there is a choice among cleansers for

the white undercoat and sleeve, there is also a choice of cleansers for the heart. The cleansers in this case are: loyalty, virtue, and courage. Among defilements, there are those which are to be washed off by loyalty, and others by virtue. Defilements which are the most tenacious, and which can resist loyalty have to be forcibly and cleanly removed by courage, by valiance. These are the secrets of the washing of the heart of the samurai. I have written all this so that the young samurai should know what should be their character.

'Although Bushido involves first of all training in use of force and in courage, the samurai must not confine himself to becoming strong like a farmer. Apart from the necessity of studying the various branches of knowledge, he must use at least some of his leisure time to practice the art of poetry, and to get to know the tea ceremony. If he does not make himself well-informed, he will not know either the reasons why the things of old were as they were, or why things are as they are today.

'Without knowledge, however clever and experienced he may be, he will be at a loss when difficulties arise. If he knows at least the essentials of sciences like medicine, and something about foreign countries and also his own country, and if he leads his own life with full respect for the three elements of time, place and rank, he will almost never go badly wrong. And this is why I speak first about the necessity of studying the branches of knowledge.

'Now a few words about poetry. To compose poems is a custom of our country. Among the celebrated generals of the past and present, there have been, and still are, many skilled in poetry. Even a samurai of low rank should be knowledgeable about the art of poetry, and able to compose a verse himself, even though it may well be undistinguished. However, if a samurai gives up everything else to plunge into poetry, his heart and even his expression become weak; without realizing it, he gets like one of those courtier samurai, that is to say a samurai of the (effete) nobility, and thus he loses his proper warrior's dignity.

'Then again among those who are clever at composing the *haiku* poems, there are a number who like to make comic verses, or play with the verse forms. They themselves think they are producing masterpieces, and they do this even on formal occasions when proper ceremony ought to have been observed. These verses, though they may amuse their audience for a moment, are indiscretions that a samurai should avoid.

'Now as to the tea ceremony. It has always been the great pleasure of the samurai. It already existed in the period when the shoguns lived at Kyoto (1392-1573). It may not be necessary to practice it in one's own home, but at least one has to be able to take part in it without embarrassment, when invited for tea at the home of an acquaintance, or when one is on a visit as one of the

retinue of a great noble. There are many aspects of the tea ceremony: how to enter the small tea-house itself, how to look at pictures and ornaments displayed, how to accept the food itself, and how to drink the

Above: Tea bowls of Raku, Karatsu and Bizen ware.

Right: Tea drinking was originally associated with Zen and the monastic life. But it was gradually adopted by the warrior class.

Above right: A tea party at night. Moonlight through a *shoji* (paper screen) was thought to lend a special quality to the experience of drinking tea.

tea. A samurai needs to have had lessons from a master of the tea, so that he knows at least how to make the proper movements without drawing attention to himself. The tea-house should be a place to enjoy peace and silence, away from luxuries or ostentation, although in fact they are also to be found in the homes of rich men and nobles. The tea-house should be surrounded by a garden which gives the impression of mountains and hills. It will have its pillars of wood with the bark still on and a roof of thatch, windows of crossed bamboos and a door made with interlaced branches, so that in every detail it is simple and subdued. Then the utensils used are also to be of an elegant simplicity, equally removed from ostentation and mere crude banality.

'The tea ceremony, which aims at sober feeling, is very useful in the cultivation of the Bushido spirit, and a samurai can have made a tea-room of his own, very plain in construction, and furnished with new hanging scrolls and new tea cups and an unglazed teapot. However, studied simplicity can often lead to expensive tastes. When he sees in other places, some of the famous Ashiya glaze for example, he may become dissatisfied with his own unglazed teapot. He may come to feel that he would like better things himself, and begin to look out where he can pick them up cheaply. He begins to notice the utensils in his friends' houses, and soon he is asking to make an exchange for one or two of his own – taking care to do well out of the bar-

Above: The Momokawa tea-house at Edo. Tea-house was often a euphemism for brothel, and so-called 'tea-house girls' were really prostitutes, though often of a high-class kind.

gain. In the end he begins to look like a courtier, though his soul is becoming that of a plebeian; he loses the fundamental spirit of Bushido, and is untrustworthy. So it would be better in that case that he remained a samurai not too well up in the tea ceremony than to become a tea fancier like that. Even if a samurai should happen to become a bit embarrassed about how to behave when he has to serve a cup of tea at a ceremony, still that will not taint his Bushido at all. I have written this so that the young samurai should know what their character should be.'

Although the Tokugawa government made Confucianism the official state doctrine, the influence of Zen on the samurai class was preserved to some extent by priests like Takuan (1573-1645) who accepted Confucian ideals willingly in his presentations of Zen. This was again in the Japanese tradition of eclecticism. One of Takuan's pupils was the famous Yagyu-Tajima-no-Kami, teacher of swordsmanship to the shogun himself. There is a famous letter written by Takuan to Tajima-no-Kami. Here is an extract from the letter, which is in fact a short treatise:

'Merely to have Zen realization is not enough unless we make it practically effective in life. Merely talking about water will not satisfy our thirst, nor will talking about fire make us warm. Both Buddhism and Confucianism explain what the mind is, but unless it is made to shine in our daily life, we cannot be said to have a realization of its truth. The main thing is to meditate on it all the time, trying to realize it in yourself.

'Where should the mind be placed in a duel with swords? If it is set on the opponent's movements, it stops there; if it is set on his sword, it stops there; if on the thought of killing him, it stops with that thought; if on one's own sword, it stops there. If set on the thought of not being killed by him, it stops with that thought. Where should it be set if one wants it to function, freely without check?

'Some people say, then isn't it better to keep the mind on the *Tanden* just below the navel point? This is indeed good, but it is not the highest attainment. The mind is still restricted by that very thought of the *Tanden*. In fact if it is set anywhere, you will be restricted. The answer is, to have no idea at all about setting the mind. If you can avoid setting it in any particular place, it will pervade the whole body, down to the tips of the fingers and toes. If hands are to move, they obey the mind at once; if the eyes are to look about, they instantly follow the order of the mind. Therefore the mind is not to be focused on any part of the body.

'It is the same with an art like dancing. You just take up the fan and move the feet naturally; but if you begin to think how to move your limbs best to create an effect, your mind begins to stick, and your dance is spoiled. Perfect freedom means perfect forgetting of your personality and all that relates to personality.'

Much of Takuan's thought appears also in *Heihokadensho*, written by his pupil, the sword-master Yagyu Tajima-no-Kami. We may note the spirituality and humility of this master warrior, as shown in the first sentences which indicate that weapons are unblessed instruments. The priest Hakuin (1685-1768) also had a profound influence on Zen and helped in its revival in Japan. After undergoing a mystical experience in 1708, he joined the Rinzai sect and unlike many of the other supercilious priests who served the shogunate, he lived in great poverty among his followers. His fervent belief, goodness, modesty and contentment attracted a large following in Japan which became the core of a new Zen movement. Hakuin was also a famous Zen artist and calligrapher. In Zen painting the important thing is not what is actually represented on the paper but the picture that is conjured up in the viewer's mind. With a minimum of brush strokes the Zen artist hopes to produce a spark that will give an insight into another world.

Hakuin believed that it was possible for anyone, high or low, to obtain 'knowledge of the truth,' and taught that a moral way of life must be part of religious practice. The following extracts are from a letter he wrote to Lord Nabeshima in 1748 outlining his principles on the practice of Zen:

'The essential thing is this: whether you are reading certain parts of the sacred teachings, or pondering the principles of the holy doctrine, or sitting for long periods in meditation without lying down, or walking throughout the day, your vital breath, *Ki*, should always be concentrated to fill the sea-of-energy (*Kikai*) just below the navel. Even if you are hemmed in by worldly cares or tied down by guests who have to have a lot of attention, the source of strength, the sea-of-energy, just below the navel, must be habitually concentrated and filled with vital energy. The attention must not be allowed to wander from there. There will be a swelling in the abdomen which is like a new football that has never been kicked before.

'If someone can acquire this kind of concentration of the energy, then he can sit in meditation all day long without ever getting tired. He can intone the sutras from morning to night without being fatigued, and write all day long without any trouble, and talk all day without tiring. Even if he is taken up with good works day after day, he will not have any feeling of getting weary. In fact, his mental capacities will increase and his vitality will always be strong. In the hottest day of summer he will not sweat or have to use a fan. On the coldest night of deepest winter he does not have to wear socks or warm himself. If he lives to be 100 years old he will keep his teeth. And provided that he does not relax his practice of this inner concentration below the navel, he will live for a long time. If man masters this method, then what can he not do? What can't he keep to? What meditation can't he practice? What virtue can't he fulfil?

'When I was young I was practicing the *Koan* meditation, but I used to think the source of thought had to be made absolutely tranquil and that that was the Buddha way. So, I despised being active and always used to seek for a quiet place, some dark and gloomy refuge, and there I would sit silently. But all sorts of trivial things would press on me and I found my heart was getting agitated and I could not enter properly into the active practice of Zen. I got irritable and sometimes fearful. My mind and body were always weak and there was sweat pouring from me; my eyes used to fill with tears; I was depressed and did not make any advance at all in the practice. But, later on I was fortunate in getting the instruction of a good teacher. He showed me the secret of turning the attention within (*naikan*) and for three years I devoted myself to meditation practice on these lines. The serious disease from which I suffered, and which up to then I had found so difficult to cure, gradually cleared up, like frost and snow melting in the rays of the morning sun.

'The problems with those terrible *Koan* riddles, [is that they are] so difficult to accept and so difficult to penetrate, so difficult to understand, so difficult to enter! Up to then it had been impossible to get any hold on it at all. But now all that has passed away, like casting off an illness. Even though I am past 70 now, my vitality is 10 times what it was when I was 30 or 40. My mind and body are strong and I never have the feeling that I must lie down to rest.

Below: A screen of the Muromachi period (1472-1525). The painting is attributed to Soami (d.1525) and is one of a pair entitled 'Landscape of the Four Seasons: Spring and Summer.' Soami is known to have followed Chinese masters and was a critic as well as a painter. He was also associated with Zen, the tea ceremony and the arts related to incense, as well as with flower arrangement (*ikebana*) and gardening.

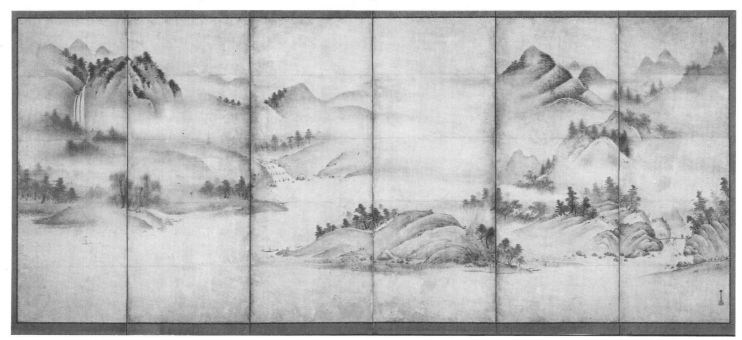

Should I want, I find no difficulty from keeping from sleep for three to seven days without suffering any decline in my mental powers.

'I have over 300 Zen students who require my supervision and instruction; sometimes I lecture on scriptures and the sayings of the masters for 30 to 50 days in a row, but it does not exhaust me. I am quite convinced this is all due to the power gained from practicing the method of turning the attention within.

'Sometimes you may feel you are getting nowhere with your practice of meditation in the rush of life, whereas when you sit quietly, you get some results. But, be sure that those who sit quietly can never hope to enter into meditation in activity. Meditation in the midst of activity is immeasurably superior to simply sitting quietly. If you do not become able to meditate even within your worldly duties your progress is almost impossible. I am not trying to tell you to give up sitting quiet completely and to look specially for active situations to practice your meditation. The important thing is, just to meditate and try to solve your *Koan* riddle without caring or being aware of whether you are in a quiet situation or interacting with other people. So it has been said, the monk who really practices, does not know that he is walking when he is walking or sitting when he is sitting.

'A lotus that is grown in water may bloom, but if it comes near fire it shrivels up, because fire is its deadly enemy. But a lotus that has been grown in the midst of flames simply becomes all the more beautiful and fragrant as it comes close to fire. The man who carries on his practice from the very beginning, keeping away from all outside things, may get insight into the way, but he is like the lotus that has been grown in the water. If he comes out from his solitude into the middle of activity he is lost, and most of his vitality disappears. He is like the lotus that withers when faced with fire. But if you bravely keep trying to meditate on the *Koan* riddle in the midst of ordinary things, if you devote yourself to meditation and persevere, you will be like the lotus that has been grown in fire, and in confronting any difficulty, you will blossom all the more.

'I cannot emphasize enough that the true practice of turning the attention within is absolutely essential and must never be given up. The practice means meditation on the *Kikai-Tanden*, the field of the elixir (*Tanden*) in the energy-sea (*Kikai*).

'What is this true meditation? It is to make everything — coughing, swallowing, waving your arms, moving, keeping still, talking, acting, the evil and the good, prosperity and shame, gain and loss, right and wrong — into one single *Koan*. Make the space below the navel, the *Tanden*, as though a lump of iron was settled there. Take the shogun as the main object of worship, the various ministers and high offi-cials as the many *Bodhisattvas* that appear in the world, engaged in the same work as you. Consider the various *daimyos*, the lords, great and small, attending on the lord or living at a distance, the great disciples of the Buddha like Shariputra. Consider the multitude of the common people as sentient beings eligible for salvation, who are to us as children and for whom particular benevolence must be felt. Think of your robes as a monk's robes; think of your two swords as if they were a table for studying the scriptures. Make your saddle your meditation cushion. Take the mountains and rivers and earth as your place on which you sit for meditation. Make the whole universe your personal meditation cave. Think of the workings of Yin and Yang as the two meals of gruel which we have in the monastery every day. Heaven, Hell, pure lands and the impure world, take as if they were your stomach and intestines and your gall bladder. Think of the 300 pieces of your music on formal occasions as the sutra reading and recitation morning and night. Think of the countless million Himalayas fused into your single backbone; all the court ceremonies and studies of the knightly arts as the mysterious operations of countless good deeds of the *Bodhisattva*. Affirming — brave mind derived from faith, combine it with the true practice of focusing the attention within. Then rising or keeping still, moving or not moving, at all times keep alert that you do not lose the true meditation. This is the real practice of the sages of the past and of today.

'You must be prepared to undergo great austerities in your practice. The famous monk Daien went to pay a call on Zen master Yozan to talk about his understanding of Zen. But Yozan reviled him, hit him and drove him away. Furious, Daien went on that very day to a bamboo grove and sat in meditation absolutely naked. At night swarms of mosquitoes surrounded him and covered his skin with bites. Striving against the terrible itching, he gritted his teeth, clenched his fists and simply sat. Several times he almost lost consciousness, but then, unexpectedly, he suddenly experienced a great enlightenment.

'The Buddha himself underwent painful austerities in the Himalayas for six years, until he was only skin and bones. A disciple of Bodhidharma cut off his arm at the elbow, and only then penetrated into the depth of his true nature. At no time has there ever been a Buddha, a patriarch or a great sage, who has not had to struggle to see into his own nature.

'But it seems to be the custom nowadays to depend on just your ordinary understanding, things foolishly thought up by your own mind. Yet they think they have arrived at some sort of realization. But, they will never be able to break the evil net of delusion. A little knowledge is a hindrance to enlightenment and this is what these people possess.

'In the Middle Ages, when Zen flourished, the samurai and the high officials whose minds were dedicated to true meditation, would, when they had a day off from their official duties, mount their horses and, accompanied by seven or eight soldiers, gallop about places crowded with people. Their purpose was to test the quality and validity of their meditation in the midst of disturbance.

'In the past Ninagawa attained a great awakening while involved in a fight. Ota Dokan composed poems when pinned down by an enemy on the battlefield. My own teacher Shoju, at a time when his village was beset by a pack of wolves, sat for seven nights in the graveyards. He did this while the wolves were sniffing at his neck and ears, in order to test the validity of true meditation, continuous and without interruption. What good can possibly come from piling up wealth and then more wealth, not realizing when you have enough?

'Or seeking fame and then more fame without ever being satisfied? Only you, my lord, see that wealth is like imaginary flowers in the sky; that fame is nothing but an illusion. You have always wisely devoted your thoughts to the unsurpassed great way. You have already called on my simple hut three times.

'The essence of our teaching cannot of course be given in words. But, if you keep up steadily the core of your Zen practice then you will spontaneously awaken to it. When you have leisure, call a few of your faithful retainers and some perhaps of the older ministers together, and have read to them what I have written here. And you yourself, seated on your cushion, will help to heighten the feeling for the true way. If you pass calmly half a day in this way, you will be appreciative of the Buddhas teaching and you will all come find joy in meditation.

'How much better to spend the time in that way than on the vulgar and luxurious parties, and the trivial and extravagant dissipations, and monstrous and vicious illusory sports of the world, where the ears are captivated by music and the eyes blinded by the many dances. What use indeed even to consider such things. Please give careful consideration to what I have said.

'They say that when their general is strong, the soldiers are not weak. When the benevolence of the lord and the benevolence of the Buddhist teaching are handed down together, your samurai are well cared for. Who of them would begrudge giving his life to such a lord if the fear of birth and death is no longer present? What need is there to seek for Nirvana? All the directions of the compass dissolve before the eyes. Your one thought pierces, past, present and future, and this is from the power of true meditation.

'At such a time the warriors are filled with respect, the commoners feel close, the prince acts with kindness, the ministers are motivated by truth. The farmers have sufficient harvests, the women have enough cloth. All, high and low, feel love for the Buddha way. The country is at peace and will continue vigorous for 10,000 generations. This is the highest achievement of man and heaven.'

It was in the Confucian period of peace throughout much of mainland Japan that the various practitioners of the multitude of Zen 'ways' could develop their artistic and military techniques.

Below: Between 1615 and the end of the nineteenth century Japan was at peace almost continuously. Battle paintings were still popular, however, though more and more stylized due to the absence of real contemporary battles on which to base them.

The Ways

The use of the word 'way' means it is regarded as a means to train and move toward something else — an ideal. The word Way, (*Do*) is the same as the word generally spelled *Tao* or *Dao* in Chinese meaning, 'the Way of the whole Universe.'

To understand Bushido it would help if we compared it with the ideal of sportsmanship. Sportsmanship is practiced in games of various kinds, for instance tennis. Here the purpose is not to become skillful at tennis, although players try very hard and keen ones practice the different shots. The ultimate purpose of sportsmanship in tennis is to be a good winner or a good loser. In other words, to be able to retain a calm enjoyment irrespective of the result, though one has tried to win — this is sportsmanship. This is not easy to understand. Many people play games in order to win. They are furious if they lose and they are exultant when they win. So we can see that sport has an ideal which periodically lapses into the practice of the thing. In the same way Bushido is meant to be a 'Way of the Warrior' and it is meant, through the profession of being a warrior, to lead to a calm, benevolent and wise spirit, aloof from winning or losing. This was meant to be Bushido. Periodically it lapsed and the warrior lost the way and simply became a warrior. He simply wanted to win, however ruthlessly, and gratify his lust for power and possessions, and sometimes reputation. The conclusion is, just as you can be a very good tennis player but a rotten sportsman, so he could be a very successful and ruthless Bushi warrior. As an example we can look at the story of the 47 *ronin* (47 masterless samurai), a story that is one of the most famous in Bushido.

In 1701, Lord Asano was the *daimyo* of the western domain of Ako. During the course of a visit to Edo (Tokyo) to study the intricacies of protocol, he felt for some reason insulted by his tutor Kira and drew his sword, cutting him on the shoulder and forehead. Asano had committed the unpardonable crime of assaulting a high *bakufu* official within the precincts of Yedo castle and for this he was ordered to commit *sep-puku*. When news of his death was received in Ako, his retainers considered mass suicide and even an attack on Kira's home, but they decided first to await the shogunate's decision as to whether the Ako domain would be confiscated or pass to Asano's younger brother. After a year it was decided that the domain should be forfeited, which automatically reduced all of the Asano retainers to the status of *ronin*.

On hearing the news, 47 of the 100 Asano *ronin* determined to revenge their lord by assassinating Kira. The story is told that they went to great lengths to make it appear that they were not concerned about what had happened and only wanted to live their lives as peaceably and happily as possible, but secretly they were plotting their revenge. They separated and disguised themselves, some becoming carpenters, others merchants; and their chief, Oishi Kuranosuke, who left his wife and children, is said to have taken to frequenting brothels and wine houses, determined to thoroughly delude the enemy. On one drunken spree he fell down asleep in the street and was seen by a man from Satsuma who accused him of not having the courage to avenge his lord and thereby being unworthy of the name of samurai, and he trod on Kuranosuke's face and spat at him. When Kira's spies reported this back to him, he was relieved and felt secure from danger.

Left: Woman practicing kendo (the Way of the Sword).

Below: A scene from the story of the 47 *ronin* (masterless samurai) which has become a model tale of samurai loyalty as the 47 avenged an insult to their lord. The tale is famous in Japan to this day.

Above: The 47 *ronin* take their revenge by killing Lord Kira. They cut off his head with the same dagger with which their own lord, Asano, had been forced to commit *seppuku*.

Right: A hanging scroll by Kenzan Ogata (1663-1743), 'The Fourth Month' from his series 'Flowers and Birds for the Twelve Months.' The painting is in an unromantic, restrained style. Kenzan was a Zen follower and also painted in a manner which found favor with the masters who sought scrolls of the correctly austere manner.

The attack on Kira finally took place on 14 December — the same day of the month that Lord Asano had died. The *ronin* found Kira hiding in a small charcoal hut in a courtyard. They treated him with great courtesy and invited him to commit *seppuku* but when he refused Kuranosuke forced him to the ground and cut off his head with the same short sword with which his Lord Asano had killed himself. Later that night they took his head to Sengakuji temple, placed it on Asano's grave and then surrendered themselves to the authorities.

Although they gained public sympathy the supreme court decision was that they were to disembowel themselves. After this was done their bodies were carried to Sengakuji temple and buried in front of the tomb of their master. Many people came to pay respect to their graves, including the Satsuma man who had trodden and spat on Kuranosuke. In atonement he killed himself and the chief priest of the temple taking pity on him, buried him beside the *ronin*, making 48 graves in all.

If we look at this incident from three standpoints of Bushido — Zen Bushido, Confucian Bushido and Fanatical Bushido — we find that all three of them disapprove of this story.

Zen Bushido would disapprove because as the poem has it: 'Though hated, do not return hate. For hating and hating again there will be no end.' So the Zen influence would have disapproved of the revenge motive of the 47 *ronin* and indeed of Japanese warrior life as a whole. Confucian Bushido would argue against them when the shogun had to decide what to do with them; they had carried out their revenge in loyalty to their master. The great Confucian Ogyu Sorai, who was himself one of the upholders of Bushido and used to undergo austerities in order to train himself in the warrior spirit, nevertheless insisted that they should be executed for having broken the law, whatever the motives. Lastly, and perhaps surprisingly, Fanatical Bushido also condemns them because of their cunning and waiting. Practitioners would say

they should simply have thrown themselves into an attack on Lord Kira, and whether they were cut down or cut him down, would not matter.

There were Confucian works on Bushido which, though heavily influenced by Zen, still sought to distinguish Bushido from Zen by emphasizing the importance of technique. One of the best of such works was *Tengugeijutsuron* (1730) and here is a crucial section of that book taken from *Zen and the Ways* by Trevor Leggett:

'Question: What of the stories of fencers of old who met a Zen priest and came to realize the ultimate of fencing?

Answer: A Zen priest teaches not the ultimate principle of fencing but that when the heart is right it adapts to things, whereas hanging on to life only makes life a suffering. And he shows how the heart may be deluded about life, as if the three worlds were a dark cave.

When one has devoted himself many years to fencing, not really resting even in sleep or sitting, when he has been training his *ki* and mastering all the techniques, and yet he is still without inspiration in actual contest — months and years of frustration — now if he meets a Zen priest and from him grasps the principle (*ri*) of life and death, and realizes how the 10,000 things are only transformations of the heart alone, suddenly his heart is illumined and his spirit composed, so that he abandons all his hankerings and makes himself free. It is one who has for many years trained his *ki* and studied all the techniques who makes a warrior of this kind, and it is not to be attained in a moment. His long training in fencing corresponds to the training of a Zen pupil under the stick of the Zen master, and realization is not to be had while one is still busy learning the techniques. One whose art is still immature will never get enlightenment from the wisdom of even the greatest priest.'

The word '*do*', the last syllable of Bushido, means literally 'way.' In Japan, as in China, this word has many meanings, but when it is the final syllable of a word like Bushido, it has a specially important association with what might be called inner training.

It is useful to look at the uses of '*do*' at the end of a word. It contrasts with '*jutsu*,' which means an art of technique. There are several well-known 'ways': Judo is the way of softness or pliability (*ju*); Ken-do is the way of the sword (*ken*); Kyu-do is the way of archery (*kyu*); Sho-do is the way of calligraphy; and Sa-do is the way of the tea ceremony (*sa*). In many cases, these 'ways' are contrasted with the corresponding '*jutsu*' or technique. There is ju-jutsu and ken-jutsu, and for instance so-jutsu or techniques of using the spear which is contrasted with so-do, the way of the spear. What then is the difference between learning and perhaps finally mastering one of these techniques and practising the way?

The practices and the ideas behind them

have not been systematically developed in the West, and sometimes attempts to explain them in terms translated from the Eastern languages end up in vagueness and confusion. It is useful to consider a somewhat parallel case: the contrast between sport and exercise. Some people take up a sport, especially when young, in order to excel at it. They do not necessarily have great ambitions, but like small children, they want to beat their friends. To do this, they need to learn some skill and have a certain will to win. There are others, who play the game as a means of getting exercise for themselves in an interesting way. They do not much care whether they win or lose, and once they can perform reasonably, they have no particular interest in improving their skill. They just want to be good enough not to be a nuisance when playing with their friends, but they do not keenly want to beat them. Still, they have to have a certain amount of will to win, otherwise the game itself becomes boring. These two classes one can call the competitor and the hobbyist. We may note that the hobbyist is not really devoted to getting fit, which few games can bring about on their own.

Above the categories of competitor and hobbyist is the true sportsman. He takes the game intensely seriously and tries hard. But whatever the result, he has enjoyed the contest. And he can even congratulate his opponent on a good win. This concept of

sport is extremely difficult for children to understand, but many of them come to respect it, even though they may not be able to practice it. The difficulty that many have found in understanding the idea of sport can be compared to the difficulty of comprehending the meaning of the word 'do,' to someone from outside Japanese culture. There are many examples of this confusion.

In 1912, Edward Lasker, a young German chess master, paid a visit to London, and was introduced by a German friend to the

Above: Two samurai practice kendo with wooden swords (*bokuto*).

City of London Chess Club. Lasker spoke no English, but his friend found him an opponent. Lasker won this game by a series of brilliant moves and later wrote about it in his memoirs:

'I am sure none of the onlookers realized what a deep impression my opponent made on me when, on being checkmated, he smiled and shook hands with me. He said: "This was very nice." Only after my friend had translated these words to me, and had slowly repeated my adversary's name, did I realize that I had been playing the champion of London, Sir George Thomas. For him to take this defeat so graciously was a fine example of British sportsmanship. It was an attitude which I had hardly ever experienced during the years I had lived in Berlin. Had I won this game against one of the leading amateurs there, probably his only comment would have been "You are just lucky! Had I captured with my knight on move 18, you would have lost." '

In a sense, a good sportsman is able to rise above circumstances, and laugh even when his own self-esteem or gain are affected. Some Zen teachers in Japan highly esteem the spirit of sport, when they understand what it is, but the concept and practice of 'do' goes far beyond this. Something becomes a 'do' when it is consciously used as a training ground for calm concentration, inspirational action, creativity, and finally illumination and freedom from fear, including the fear of death.

To paint pictures, to create beauty, to express inner conflicts, or make money, is not a 'do.' However, to paint pictures so that when the brush moves, the painter feels that his whole life is staked on it, consigned to the inspiration of its movement, is a 'do.' Similarly, the delicate and precise movements of the tea ceremony may be mastered for their own sake and that is an art; but if the practitioners whole life is serenely concentrated on the act, then it becomes a 'do.' Warriors in the early Kamakura period used to perform the tea ceremony just before a battle and occasionally even during a lull in the fighting. The movements cannot be executed with precision if there is the slightest tremor in the hand or body. In this way samurai practiced the tea ceremony as an aid to making themselves tranquil at a time of crisis. To the trained eye, the movements which flow from this spiritual freedom convey a special meaning. There is an early record from the Zen temple of Enkakuji in Kamakura which at the end poses the question of the meaning of the cup of tea.

In the spring of the first year of Ryakuo (1338), the imperial tutor Lord Tadanori traveled to Kamakura from Kyoto to teach the Confucian doctrines to the warriors of the government there. By the Jowa era (1345) there were over 360 pupils studying under him, among them the Jomyoji temple librarian Tachibana, who showed great talent for study. However, Zen master Tentaku, the forty-first master at Enkakuji,

admonished him saying: 'You have talent for scholarship but no bent for Zen. Perhaps you will not be able to pursue the Holy Path. The Confucian scholars say that the way has its basis in heaven, but cannot speak of the way before heaven and earth were separated out. If you want to know the true source of the way, you must sit in meditation on the mat in the meditation hall till the perspiration runs from your whole body.'

The librarian reported this to Lord Tadanori, who was angry and went to Enkakuji to see the teacher. He asked him about the way, to which the master replied: 'Confucius says that if one hears the way in the morning, one can die in the evening content. This is the way which is the basis of the whole universe. How does your honor explain it?' The nobleman opened his mouth to speak but the teacher waved his hand and said: 'The source of the way is before the three powers (heaven, earth and man) exist; how can your honor explain it by mouth and tongue?' The imperial tutor retorted: 'Then how would a priest point out the way?' The master at once put a cup of fresh tea before him and said: 'Do you understand?' The nobleman was at a loss, and the teacher said: 'My Lord, you have not yet the talent for knowing the way.'

There are examples in Chinese and Indian classics which depict freedom of inspiration in everyday actions, but there is an important difference here from the ways developed mainly in Japan. Take this famous example of the cook from the early Chinese Taoist classic *Chuang-tze*. His cook was cutting up an ox for the ruler Wanhui. Whenever he applied his hand, he leaned forward with his shoulder, planted his foot, employed the pressure of his knee, and in the audible ripping off of the skin and slicing operation of the knife, the sounds were all in regular cadence. Movements and sounds proceeded as in the dance of the 'Mulberry Forest' and the notes of Ching Shau. The ruler said, 'Ah, admirable! That your art should have become so perfect!' The cook laid down his knife and replied, 'What your servant loves is the method of the way, something in advance of any art. When I first began to cut up an ox, I saw nothing but the [entire] carcass. After three years I ceased to see it as a whole. Now I deal with it in a spirit-like manner, and do not look at it with my eyes. The use of my senses is discarded, and my spirit acts as it wills. Observe the natural lines (my knife) slip through the great crevices and slides through the great cavities, taking advantage of the facilities thus presented. My art avoids the membraneous ligatures, and much more the great bones.

'A good cook changes his knife every year — (it gets blunt) from the cutting; an ordinary cook changes his every month — it gets broken. Now my knife has been in use for 19 years; it has cut up several thousand oxen, and yet its edge is as sharp as if it had newly come from the whetstone. There are the interstices of the joints, and the edge of the knife has no thickness; when that which is so thin enters where the gap is, how easily it moves along! The blade has more than room enough. Still, whenever I come to a complicated joint, and see that there will be some difficulty, I proceed cautiously and carefully, not allowing my eyes to wander from the place, and moving my hand slowly. Then by a very slight movement of the knife, the part is quickly separated and drops like a clod of earth to the ground. Then standing up with the knife in my hand I look round, and in a leisurely manner and serenely I wipe it clean and put it in its sheath.' The ruler Wanhui said, 'Excellent! I have heard the words of my cook, and learned from them how to cultivate inner vitality.'

This passage shows important elements of the ways, but their application to the ordinary affairs of daily life was not systematically cultivated in the Chinese traditions. There are more of these stories in Taoist classics, but they are only fragmentary hints. The operations of the cook are beautifully described – 'like a dance, movements and sounds in rhythm,' showing that the whole body took part as a unity. As a rule in such operations the lower part of the body remains fixed, with the arms and shoulders alone active. To overcome this great defect is essential in cultivation of the ways.

We may also notice that though the cook says, 'I do not look at it with my eyes,' he later remarks that when there is a difficult place, he does not allow his eyes to wander away. And though he says 'my spirit acts as it wills,' he also says that in those difficult places he proceeds cautiously. The inspiration is not like automatic writing, or a sneeze, where something happens that does not involve the whole of the man. The point is that the Chinese ruler appreciated the actions of his inspired cook, but he did not himself practice cookery as a method of training for himself. So cooking was not, for him, a way. For the cook, on the other hand, it had been. He had not merely skill in cutting, but created beauty and harmony all around him even in what many would think of as a brutal occupation. However, the text does not give much in the way of hints as to what his training had been.

All ways have techniques, sometimes, as in Judo, they are very elaborate and potentially almost infinite, and sometimes, as with the spear, extremely simple. In a sense, the inner side of the way appears more clearly in the case of a simple technique. The respective techniques have to be

Below: Some of the 47 *ronin*. This representation of some members of the loyal band shows that the 47 are seen as having individual and widely differing characters, as well as being a collective and symbolic entity.

learned from a teacher. To master them is to be a technical expert, as one might become a master-surgeon or master-carpenter, but if the teaching leads to awareness of a way, then the training will give courage and inspiration in the matters of daily life altogether outside the particular art. Instruction in the ways is partly concerned with the isolation, harmonizing and training of what is called *ki*, (vital energy) and partly to do with what can be translated as 'spirit.' We can take a brief look at vital energy, though it is mainly concerned with the practice of the individual arts.

Rather than using abstractions, look at an account of a crucial long putt in a golf championship, given by a well-known player. He said to the reporter: 'It is something that doesn't happen often, but it happened then. I get into a sort of cocoon of concentration; nothing else exists except the club, the ball, the line to the hole, and the hole. Perhaps this next bit sounds incredible, but as I am there, bent over the putter and before the club moves, I can sort of feel the ball going along the line into the hole. It's not that I judge it will, or hope it will or expect it will. I know it will. I actually feel it, before the putter moves. In a way the whole scene is part of me. There's not a separate me making the putt.'

Compare this experience with the extract from a Kendo classic text of 1811 which explains what winning by the *Seigan* (a posture with the point of the blade between the eyes) sword means. 'You must feel your *ki*-

Above: The samurai tradition lives on in the ritual and practice associated with judo, now an Olympic event.

Right: A stylized form of fencing unique to Japan, kendo (the Way of the Sword) nevertheless uses real (not bamboo) swords which are unguarded.

Above right: A kendo practitioner in full armor.

Far right: The practice of kendo: the combatants engage each other in a bout at the end of which neither will be dead but one will be the victor.

energy pervading the sword from the grip down through the blade up to the point, and you feel it leap from the *ki*-energy and strike the enemy. He who thinks the sword is a sword and that there is a will to win separate from the sword can do little.'

The difference between these examples is that in the golfer's case this happens only by chance: he does not know what it is, nor where it comes from, nor how to bring it out from where it comes from. In the way, there is a method of training and some rough indication about what is happening. The traditions of the ways, however, stress that it is not easy, and that not many students achieve it. The training of *ki*-energy is not part of Bushido as such, but to give some idea of its importance here are two exercises which are given in many of the ways and which are not related to their individual techniques:

1. 'Sit on the ground on a folded blanket, upright, with the chin a bit pulled in. Bunch the fingers of the right hand, and apply them to the abdomen about an inch below the navel. This area is called the *tanden* (elixir-field). Press in slightly so that you can feel it. Breathe in slowly and fully, and feel a current moving down with the in-breath, filling the abdomen. It is easiest at the beginning to feel that it is the breath itself that does this. As the abdomen swells, feel it pressing against the bunched fingers, which do not give way. When the in-breath is complete, hold it a second or two, and push the fingers in, tensing the muscles of

the abdomen to meet them. This gives quite a vivid sensation. Relax the pressure with the out-breath, but keep a residual tension in the abdominal muscles, to hold something of the after-sensation. Relax the muscles, and begin a new in-breath.'

If this practice is successfully pursued for a long time, there will be a permanent center of attention just below the navel. When aware of this center, the body moves from it, and is used as a unity. This last element is rather difficult for an ordinary person to attain. Physiologically, the center of the body is poorly represented in an average brain, both for incoming and outgoing; some Japanese researchers have speculated that attention on the *tanden* may help to rectify this. It may also produce a calming effect by activating the sympathetic system. However, these are speculations.

In the traditions of the ways, this practice will not be fruitful in invigorating and harmonizing the body-senses unless there is a background of calm self-control. This means, in fact, austerity. Some teachers insist on early morning practice, every day, without heating in the winter. Some used to insist on occasional practice kneeling on a bed of pebbles, alongside the teacher. He was unaffected by the pain, but many new applicants would leave, according to the old accounts. On which the teacher would say: 'That has got rid of them.' There are concealed references to the practice in the symbolic representations of the divinities related to the warriors.

2. 'Sit on the ground upright as before, and stretch the arms out sideways toward the walls. As you breathe in, feel the current going down the arms to the fingertips. Feel that the fingertips themselves are going through the walls. When this becomes vivid the movements of the upper body become invigorated and precise.'

Here again, the test is the actual result, one which does not come about in an agitated person or a lethargic one. Anyone can feel a tingling or other unusual sensation, but unless the effect comes such things are meaningless.

In the ways much importance is also placed on posture. In feudal days in Japan the samurai made sure that they maintained an upright posture and good balance, which left them free and unrestrained, not only when practicing with their weapons but also when sitting in their room or at a table.

The posture in all the arts, even playing the shakuhachi flute or the Koto, the tea ceremony or dancing with a fan, is of extreme importance. It is supposed to be such that if he were suddenly attacked, the performer would be in a position to meet that attack. Compare a picture of somebody playing the shakuhachi flute with that of say a violinist in an orchestra, who has his legs pushed forward in front of him and is often leaning against the back of the chair. The shakuhachi flute player could spring forward or to the side, and even use his flute as a weapon; the same applies to a calligrapher. There are reports of a famous calligrapher who, when writing, was attacked by a man with a sword. He flicked his brush so that the ink went into the attacker's eyes and escaped.

The great tea master Rikyu was not a samurai, but one of the chief retainers, Kato, was very jealous of him and there are a number of stories of how the retainer wanted to kill him. On one occasion he came alone to the tea-house where Rikyu was preparing for a tea ceremony, and asked for a cup of tea. Rikyu realized that the man intended to kill him but he nevertheless invited him in. Then, Rikyu upset the tea on to the hot charcoal which created a thick smoke. His would-be assassin was taken aback and Rikyu escaped.

During these years of danger for Rikyu, Hideyoshi, the military lord who was the master of both Rikyu and the retainer, called his followers' attention to the posture of Rikyu. He said, 'You see, there is no possibility for attack. Although Rikyu himself is not a swordsman, if you look at him from the point of view of a swordsman, you will see that there is no opening.' However, on one occasion, the jealous Kato thought that he saw an opportunity and planned to stab Rikyu with his fan. But Rikyu sensed something, spun round and confronted Kato. He gave him a piercing look and said, 'Kato is an excellent retainer.' Kato found himself deprived of breath and unable to make the thrust.

Another account tells of a famous swordsman who went to see a performance of a great dancer with the intention, as a swordsman, of seeing if he could find an opening to attack. Sitting in the audience to watch the performance, for a long time the swordsman could see no opening until suddenly the dancer faltered, whereupon the swordsman shouted, 'Got him!' Afterward he confronted the dancer, who said that he had been disconcerted because he had been moving on to a part of the stage where he had not been before and saw that it was dirty. Then, the account says, he offered to commit *seppuku* because of his lapse during the performance but the penalty was not insisted upon.

There is no question that such stories were widely believed. Not only villagers, but also professional fighting men and sophisticated scholars and officials credited those who meditated and practiced the Zen austerities and disciplines for a long time with unusual powers. It may be argued that such things were effective because they were believed. But they were widely believed, it may be argued, because at some time they must have been effective. Many of the stories concern professional fighters who would not have been easily overawed by impressive posing. After all they did a lot of it themselves.

The importance of posture, balance and

general behavior in oneself, as well as that of an opponent, is discussed in many of the texts on the ways. This is an extract on swordsmanship from the Jojo (Ever Pure) school; the date is 1811:

'You can judge a man's skill with the sword from his general movement. One who always is hitting things with his head or knocking against things as he turns round, or who touches a screen as he gets up or kicks against tables, or slips on a patch of mud, is one who will be muddled in technique. So in the sword art, one should always observe a man's movement, and rate him accordingly. A man who is set on moving very quickly, since he is relying on himself, is in fact slow; the one who invariably acts in reliance on the way, though his technical movement may not be quick, is in the end the fast one.

'When you stand in *Jodan* [sword raised above the head with no defense – relying on getting in first] you should not be observing your opponent's sword, but be in a state of *Mu-shin* [poised awareness]. But when you strike his sword it should be like a gun going off when the light is put to the powder, without any thoughts at all. Like Marishi, the war god, or some other god, you should strike as with the divine power of Gods and Buddhas. It is not right to feel

that you strike by your own power. This must be thought over.

'People think they can win in swordsmanship by surprising others with some unexpected trick. This is something that clouds inspiration. Therefore the movements in training are mostly standardized and there is nothing extraordinary about them; it is the two swords, one against the other, with nothing unusual.

'If you train in the standard movements, and go right through them with an understanding of the principle (*ri*), you will come to understand in yourself not only the standard lines but all the "secret traditions" as well. Hearing this now you may not have faith in it but when you have practiced and made it your own, you will come to believe these words. Therefore even at the beginning you should, by concentration, penetrate right through to *ri*. When you have done that, you will always be able to confirm it in your actual contest. Even an expert fencer, if he explains things which he cannot perform, or if he can perform things which he cannot explain, has not yet obtained the way. There is no hidden trick in the art of the sword.

'People suppose that if a man has had his mastery attested by an *inka* [diploma awarded for mastery given by the teacher]

Left: Family armor of the Date clan (sixteenth century). The body was constructed largely of wicker, and the whole was intended to look as fearsome as possible; the samurai warrior was well aware of the psychological advantage a terrifying appearance would give him before combat was ever joined.

Below: A battle fan used by Mori Motonari (sixteenth century). The fan shows the sun emblem (*hi-no-maru*) now of course the symbol of Japan itself.

then even if he were drunk he would never lose a fight. I will say something of my own knowledge. While my experience was yet shallow and my technique clumsy, I received the *inka* from my teacher Jokeishi. I thought I must not behave like a vulgar man; even if the people do not know it, I shall know it in my heart. If one sinks into drunkenness, the hands and feet lose their speed, and then the stupor becomes so great one could not even make out an enemy if he appeared. In such circumstances, how could there be any trick of winning? In this scroll of the secret tradition of the Shinkageryu which Jokeishi has granted me it says that it is to be given to one who follows tradition, who is skilled in both technique and in the *ri*, and who needs no urging to train. Unless, quite apart from his training and experience, he is one to whom it would be proper to give such a scroll, it is not to be given. However skillful a man may be, if his behavior is not correct, if his heart and will are not straightforward, it should not be given.

'As to the point about not being defeated even when drunk, there is this story. A samurai named Ishikawa Idafu was a master-swordsman. Once after he had been invited to go drinking and was on the way home he splashed through the puddles and went from side to side along the road. The servant walking behind him thought: "The master is always talking about swordsmanship, but if an enemy came now, what could he do? But perhaps there is some trick which one could not even guess at...." The doubt did not clear up. When the master got home he turned round and said to the servant: "You have been behind me looking at how I am today and wondering whether there would be some secret by which I would win at such a time. But all this, is simply that I relax for the sake of ignorant people."

'There are many schools of swordsmanship now which have arisen from the special development of some technique by their respective founders. But if you penetrate to the *ri* in them all, all the schools are the same. This you can know by long practice. Each of the styles has its strong and its weak points which the pupils argue over, but they do not know the truth. Whatever the school, when the time comes the more skillful wins, but above this is fate, which is above all. Understand that one who is without sin or disloyalty, if he fights through the way, will have victory granted to him by heaven.

'A man must be able to see all that is within visible range. If he is in a drunken stupor, his mind will not be able to know what is going on round him. It is only to a man always of good character, who is aware of what is around him, that an *inka* should be given, and not to others. I once heard it said, "You can tell the emptiness or completeness of a man by the way he opens and shuts the door. One who does it with a bang is empty within; but he who, however quickly he wants to go out or come in, still opens or shuts it with care, is called a man of completeness." I have considered this over a long time and now with the experience of a long life I can say I approve it. By this one thing, one can know a man's quality. Swordsmanship is an unruffled heart, but it is rare to find one who knows that.'

Archery is one of the most ancient and traditional of the military arts, one practiced not merely for fighting efficiency but also as a means of inner development. First of all, it is associated with horseback riding in one of the earliest phrases for Bushido *Kyu-ba no Michi*, which means literally, 'The Way of Bow and Horse.' So the earliest traditions of the Japanese knight were associated with being mounted and with skill in archery. Archery is a good example of the Japanese concept of inner training from a worldly activity. In archery a great problem occurs the instant when the arrow is released: aim has been carefully taken, and the body is quite still, but the decision to release the arrow nearly always means a willed movement which disturbs the aim. The decision is connected with the inner state; if that is disturbed, the release itself is disturbed.

These pages: The techniques of swordsmanship in action.

Of course archers all over the world have been aware of this situation. Robin Hood is credited with saying that he doubted whether any arrow had ever been perfectly released. He knew the problem, but no solution is recorded. Similarly a Chinese classic says: 'When they shoot for a clay prize, they shoot well. When the prize is silver, they shoot badly. But if it should be gold, they shoot as if blind.' From early times Japanese archers sought to discover how the arrow could be released without a conscious 'effort,' and to relax the hand holding a fully stretched bow-string. Here is a summary of the instruction in one of the 'secret scrolls.' It is difficult to fix a date but it might be as early as the fourteenth century, and it embodied material worked out well before that.

In archery the question of breath arises in a single form because the archer can take his time. Breathing in is represented by the sound 'um.' The student is made to listen to the sound of the in-breath, and to verbalize and prolong the out-breath: 'u-m-m-m-m.' At the same time his attention is held on the *tanden*. The mind is steadiest when the body is full of breath and by meditation on the *tanden* the mind can be kept steady all the time. In Japanese fencing and allied arts, the ideal is to attack, when full of breath, an opponent who has just finished breathing out.

Archery practiced only on the range is liable to become, in the language of the ways, 'dead.' Archery classics tell the student to imagine that the target is alive, that his own bow protects his body, and that his arrow is capable of splitting mighty rocks. This is an important part of the training. One of the teaching stories is that a warrior was riding through a forest when he suddenly saw a panther crouching on a rock. He quickly grasped his bow, took aim and shot. When he went toward the rock, he saw that what he had 'shot' was not a panther

Below: Kyudo (the Way of the Bow) is practiced in Japan today as a physical and mental discipline, as well as a sport.

but only the outline of a panther in the form of the rock. To the samurai's surprise he noticed that his arrow had gone through where the panther's heart would have been. Amazed that his arrow should have penetrated the rock cleanly, he thought he would try to do it again and rode back to where he had first seen the 'panther,' put another arrow in the bow and loosed it. But it only bounced off the rock. He tried two or three more times with the same result. This is meant to illustrate that complete conviction and wholeheartedness and determination in what one is doing will produce miraculous results. But the next time he had doubt, because he knew that it could not happen, and so his arrow was only an ordinary arrow.

Japanese archers draw to the shoulder. It is a more powerful but less accurate technique than the Western method of drawing to the cheek or ear. A Western archer in the 1930s demonstrated this fact to some Japanese master-archers, but they remained unimpressed. When he commented on their conservatism, one of them explained that the mental training was the main thing, and suggested a duel. They would stand at opposite ends of the range, and shoot at each other. 'If you are the better archer you will win.' The challenge was declined. This last story gives a hint as to traditional Japanese thinking, which indeed has relevance today. The challenge to a duel does not actually meet the point, which is the abstract question of which method of drawing the bow is the most accurate. It has nothing to do with courage or recklessness (depending on how it is viewed) of archers. But the old Japanese archer's thinking rejected abstraction: to him the technique, and the one who was to apply it, could not be separated. In fact the inner state of the archer was the most important thing. Without inner firmness, technique would simply crumble away.

Below: Young archers drawing the bow. For success, the archer must learn that the technique and the practitioner are one.

Fanatical Bushido

What may be called Fanatical Bushido is typified by a book of maxims and anecdotes, produced in the eighteenth century by a retired samurai scholar in a clan fief in Kyushu, the western island of Japan. By this time the land had been largely at peace for a century, and the clan lords were looking for highly educated, rather than militarily competent, samurai to help in administrative work. The book was called *Hagakure*, which can mean Leaf-hidden, but could also mean hidden under the leaves, implying modesty, and even someone who hides under the leaves.

The Nabeshima clan to which the author belonged, and whose clan lord, Nabeshima Mitsushige, he served for a long time, was not in favor with the hereditary Tokugawa government, which had been set up 100 years before. This was because Nabeshima Naoshige, in one of those sudden changes of side so frequent in Japanese history, had been with the losers in the decisive Battle of Sekigahara in 1600. He had had to submit to Tokugawa Ieyasu, and the displeasure of the Tokugawa regime lay heavily on the Nabeshima in succeeding centuries. However, at the time of *Hagakure*, the clan was not economically distressed, Mitsushige having proved a capable administrator during his 40 years of headship.

The author of *Hagakure*, Yamamoto Tsunetomo, had a great devotion to Mitsushige, and when the latter passed away in 1700, Yamamoto shaved his head and went into a semi-Buddhist retirement. During this period he dictated the material which later became assembled into the 11 books of *Hagakure*. It cannot be held against the author that though he spoke so often of death in service of the clan lord, he himself never took part in a battle: there were few samurai of the time who had done so. Under the Tokugawas, except for one rebellion the land was at peace for some 250 years.

Hagakure consists of some 1300 mostly short sections, some of them of only a few words. They are not systematically arranged, though there are some vague groupings into subjects. The main message of the book can be summed up in its famous opening two paragraphs:

'Bushido, or setting the mind in the Way of the Warrior, is nothing strange, yet these days people do not seem to be much concerned with it. In fact, if you ask what they think is the great purpose of Bushido, there are few who can give an answer right away. This is because they usually do not think about it. Because they do not realize that they are thus neglecting the Way of the Warrior, all the time they get negligent with everything else.

'What is called Bushido is simply choosing death. In general, it means that when the moment of decision comes, you simply act so as to die quickly. There are no complications about it. Set yourself firmly, and dash forward. They say that just to die without having achieved some purpose is a meaningless death, like that of a dog, but this is the Bushido of the city people. After all, usually one cannot know, at the time of the decision, whether the purpose will be achieved.'

We can see in this brief passage the great difference of this Fanatical Bushido from the inspirational Zen Bushido of the fourteenth century and the factional Confucian Bushido dominant under the Tokugawa. They have in common the absolute necessity of freedom from the fear of death. But in the Zen Bushido there was to be an experience of passing through death while in this very life, giving the inspiration to live life fully as there was no shrinking from death. In the Confucian doctrine, vivid awareness of possible imminent death in execution of duty was held to give freedom from many vices: selfishness would become tenuous, and in the ordinary way a samurai free from fear of death would be vigorous and live long. The historical records do in fact show that many of the leading figures in all three forms of Bushido did live to an advanced age, often into their eighties, which was then a real achievement.

The spirit of the *Hagakure* piece is a sort of hunger for death in service of the clan lord. In a way it is a kind of local religion with a martyr spirit. In fact, the desire to

find some great ideal or figure, and sacrifice one's life for it, has always been a strong element in Japanese character. It was only in Japan that the Jesuit and other missionaries, during the period of persecution which proscribed Christianity and tortured those who persisted in the faith, had to urge their converts not to proclaim themselves openly. The proscription in Japan was due to political fears: the Japanese government learnt that in the Philippines, conversions had led to conquest by the Spaniards. The fears were not altogether unfounded. The one great rebellion under the Tokugawa rule, which lasted over two centuries, was the 1636 Shimabara Rebellion, an uprising of Christians.

The Christian martyrs, however, held the conviction of a glorious reward in heaven. In *Hagakure* there is not such definite promise. The background is Buddhist, and there are many references to the Buddhist ideas that this world is a sort of illusion, comparable to a puppet performance. The conclusion is drawn that samurai should play out their part with nobility, and not set their hearts on anything worldly, but make an exit with panache. In a sense, the *Hagakure* ideal is to be a sort of rocket, one launched either by the clan lord or even self-launched to destroy any obstruction to the lord's policies. The rocket fulfills itself in destroying itself. Even if it misses, it has still carried out its mission, and the existence of such rockets will strike terror into potential adversaries. Among the translators of selections from *Hagakure* into English was Yukio Mishima. Here is a selection of some of the more important comments in the book:

GENERAL: 'It is said that a warrior will be of no use at all if he considers the matter of life or death. If he can free himself from the thought of either of these he can accomplish any feat. In this manner the martial arts can lead to the way.

'There was in China once a man who loved pictures of dragons; even his clothes and furniture were decorated with them. The Dragon God heard of this and one day a dragon appeared at the old man's window. The old man died of fright. Probably he was a man who spoke big words but when he had to face up to the real thing acted differently.

'One should pay attention and avoid saying anything that might upset others. You will make enemies by saying some unnecessary thing and create ill-will. At such a time it is better to stay at home and compose poetry.'

BUSHIDO: 'At the end of each meeting of the group under Oki Hyobu he would say, "Young samurai need to vigorously discipline themselves in purposefulness and courage. They can only do this if their hearts are set. If their sword is broken, they should fight with their hands. If their hands are cut off they should pin the enemy down with their shoulders. Should their shoulders be cut away, they should bite through the enemy's neck with their teeth. Such is courage!"

'A general told his soldiers, "When you must test your armor, you should only test the front. Also, whilst decoration on the armor is unnecessary you should take care about the appearance of your helmet. It is that which goes with the severed head to the enemy's camp."

'A samurai should avoid too much sake, egotism and luxury. In times of unhappiness they will not bother you. But if you become elated these three things become dangerous. It is unseemly to be proud and extravagant when things are going well. Therefore it is better to have some unhappiness whilst one is still young. If you never experience bitterness you will not be able to settle down. A man who becomes depressed when he is unhappy is of no use.'

LOYALTY: 'Among General Takeda Shingen's men were many of unflinching courage, but when Katsuyori fell at the Battle of Tenmokuzan, all but one fled. Tsuchiya Sozo, a warrior who had been in disfavor for many years came out alone. He remarked, "I wonder where the men are who daily speak of bravery? I shall repay my master's kindness to me." Alone, he fell fighting.

'The first thing a warrior should do each morning is to pay reverence to lord and parents and then to the patron gods and Buddhas. In revering his lord first, he will please his parents and receive the approval of the gods and Buddhas. For a warrior there is nothing else to think of other than his lord. If he is resolved in this, he will always be mindful of his master's welfare and not be separated from him even for a second. What is more, a wife should put her husband first, just as he does his lord.'

COMPASSION: 'To look on all with an equal eye and feeling, in that they are of service to the lord, is great compassion. Great spirit is great compassion. Compassion is the basis of both wisdom and courage. There is no one who has not got some virtue, who is not good for something. To see that and bring it out in service to the lord, is great compassion. Lord Naoshige, when he sat in judgment, sought to avoid giving the sentence of death. When in consultation with his senior counselors on points of judgment, he used to say that they should avoid the sentence of death.'

VENERATION FOR IMPERIAL HOUSE: 'The original account should be read of how, when Emperor Godaigo gave a rescript expressing his wishes to both Akamatsu and Masashige, Akamatsu prostrated himself and retired straightaway, but Masashige asked for more detail as to the imperial wishes, thereby showing his loyalty.'

Left: A medieval samurai holds the head of his decapitated enemy between his teeth.

WORSHIP OF GODS AND ANCESTORS: 'You should ensure that you have not been negligent in your daily prayers. Impurity is hated by the gods. If you only pray for good fortune when you are desperate and covered with blood your prayers will not be answered. You must also pray when not in need.'

STRAIGHTFORWARDNESS: 'There are times when a person gets carried away and talks without thinking. When he is being frivolous and not telling the truth, others will notice it. It is better at such times to express one's true feelings, to say what is in one's heart. One should consider carefully, even when just making a greeting so as not to cause injury to a person's feelings. What is more, should someone be critical of the way of the samurai or one's own country you should not stand on ceremony but speak to him severely.'

SELF-CONTROLLED ENDURANCE: 'Training never comes to an end. From yesterday there is today, then everyday, until the end of one's life, to improve. A very experienced swordsman said this: "During one's whole life the training goes forward by degrees. The unskilled lower grade practices but he does not actually grasp what he is taught. He thinks he is unskilled and that others are unskilled as well. At this level his fencing is quite unreliable. When he reaches middle grade, he still can not be relied on but he comes to see some of his own defects and those of others. When he gets to a high rank and begins to achieve success he enjoys being praised and feels sorrow when others fail. At this level his fencing is certainly reliable. He can see the skill in himself and others — most fencers reach this stage. But he can go one more stage, to the way. If he can delve deeply into this he will find that the way has no ending. He will discover where he himself is lacking. After a lifetime of training he will not have thoughts of pride or humility. All these things will have disappeared and he will have found the way." Today I should become better than yesterday and so day by day make progress. In this way training has no end.'

TEMPERING THE WILL: 'Winning is defeating one's enemies. Defeating one's allies is to defeat oneself. Defeating oneself is to overcome one's own mind. It is as if a man were surrounded by 10,000 allies but not one was following him. Only if he has previously mastered his mind and body can he overcome the enemy. There is nothing that man cannot achieve. If he is determined he can move heaven and earth. But he fails because he lacks resolution, he cannot set his mind to it. But if he makes the effort and concentrates it can be achieved.

'What one dreams can become reality. If

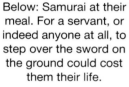

Below: Samurai at their meal. For a servant, or indeed anyone at all, to step over the sword on the ground could cost them their life.

Left: A girl of the Genroku period (early eighteenth century). The first half of the eighteenth century is known as the Genroku period, and is the time associated in the Japanese mind with the 'floating world' of the pleasure quarters, immortalized both in literature and painting. The values of the time, as embodied in those works, were worldly, cynical and humorous. Nothing was sacred but pleasure.

in a dream one is dying in battle or committing *seppuku*, by courage one can alter the dream.'

INCOMPETENCE: 'There is a saying that a great man is a late developer, and shows himself in the end of life. Someone who, when he is 20 or 30, is doing things superficially, will never have great achievements later on. It is the same with services of the lord. If people are hasty and become attracted to something outside their own particular duties, they get talked about as a bright young fellow. They begin to get excited and want to appear skillful in everything. Then their minds are distracted, they become frivolous, and in the end they are despised by others. They have to learn to "break their bones" in training and not be surpassed by others in their duty, otherwise they will not be good for anything.'

HOSPITALITY: 'Before calling on someone it is best to give advance warning. To pay a sudden visit not knowing whether the person is busy or has some urgent business is inconsiderate. Nothing is worse than to go somewhere when you have not been invited. However, you should not be brusque toward a person who has come to visit, even if you are busy.'

BRINGING UP CHILDREN: 'How to bring up the child of a samurai. From the time they are small one should encourage bravery and avoid lighthearted teasing or frightening. If as a child he is affected by cowardice, it remains with him for life. Parents should not make their children fear lightning or prevent them going into dark places, or tell

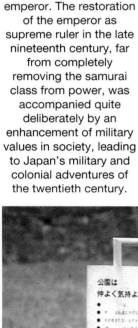

Below: An early-morning jogger pauses outside the Imperial Palace to pray for the health of the emperor. The restoration of the emperor as supreme ruler in the late nineteenth century, far from completely removing the samurai class from power, was accompanied quite deliberately by an enhancement of military values in society, leading to Japan's military and colonial adventures of the twentieth century.

them frightening things in order to stop them crying. Severe scolding will make them timid.

'Never allow them to form bad habits. If you do, then no amount of admonishment will correct it. Gradually teach him correct speech and good manners. Teach him not to be greedy. If you do this, and he is a normal child, he should develop along the lines you have taught him.

'Where there is a bad relationship between parents, the child will be unfilial, which is natural. Even birds and animals are conditioned by what they are used to seeing and hearing from the time they are born. The father-to-child relationship could deteriorate if a mother is foolish. A mother loves her child above all else and will side with him when he is scolded by the father. By becoming the child's ally she will create discord between him and the father. Because of the shallowness of her mind, a woman sees the child as her support in old age.

'In bringing up a boy you should first encourage a sense of bravery. From an early age he should liken his parents to the master, and learn everyday politeness and etiquette, how to serve others, correct speech, patience and even the correct way to walk down a street. His elders would have been taught in the same fashion. If he does not put an effort into things, he should be scolded and given nothing to eat for a whole day. One would also discipline a retainer in this way.

'The most important thing for a girl is to teach her chastity. She should never be less than six feet distant from a man, should never meet his eyes or receive anything

directly from his hands. She should not go sightseeing or take trips to temples. A woman who has been brought up strictly and experienced suffering at her own home will not suffer from boredom even after she is married.'

FAMILY VIRTUE: 'You should use rewards and punishments when handling younger children. If you fail to ensure that they do as they are told they will grow up thinking only of themselves which will later lead to their being involved in wrongdoing. Parents need to be extremely careful about this.'

MISCELLANEA: 'When Bokuden and a number of passengers were crossing Lake Biwa in a rowing boat, among them was a rough-looking arrogant samurai. He was boasting that he was the best swordsman in the land and everyone was eagerly listening to him. Everyone except Bokuden, who dozed as if nothing was going on. This annoyed the samurai so much that he approached Bokuden and shook him saying, "You have two swords, don't you have something to say?" In a low voice Bokuden answered, "My art is different to yours; it consists not in defeating others, but in not being defeated." This infuriated the samurai, who asked "What is your school then?"

"The school of Mutekatsu" [defeating the enemy without using one's hands, ie, without using a sword].

"But you carry a sword?"

"This is to do away with selfish motives not to kill others."

His anger mounting the samurai exclaimed, "And you really mean to fight me with no swords?"

"Why not?" said Bokuden.

'The samurai told the boatman to row to the nearest landing point, but Bokuden suggested an island farther off that was virtually uninhabited and therefore unlikely to attract other people who might get hurt. The samurai agreed and the boatman headed toward the island. As soon as the boat reached the shallows the samurai jumped off, drew his sword and prepared for a fight. Calmly, Bokuden withdrew his swords from his *obi* and handed them to the boatman and gave the impression he was about to follow the samurai. But, suddenly, he snatched the oar from the boatman and in seconds had pushed the boat out into deep water safely away from the samurai. "This," said Bokuden, "is my no-sword school."

'Bokuden had three sons who were all trained swordsmen. One day he decided to find out what they had learned through their training. He put a little pillow above the curtain at the entrance to his room, and arranged it so that anyone touching the curtain even slightly would have the pillow fall on their head. Bokuden's eldest son was the first to be called. As he neared his father's room he noticed the pillow on the curtain, took it down and after entering the room replaced it above the curtain. The second son was called and as he touched the curtain to enter his father's room he saw the pillow coming down and caught it in his hands. He too then carefully replaced it in the original position. The swaggering third son came in, touched the curtain and the pillow hit him squarely on the back of the neck. He cut it in half with his sword even before it had touched the floor. Bokuden gave his judgment. To the eldest son he gave a sword and said that he was well qualified for swordsmanship. His advice to the second son was to train even harder. But the youngest son was severely reprimanded and pronounced a disgrace to the family.'

The idea of *Hagakure* although unknown in Western history, can be illustrated by the case of the Norman court poet Taillefer who came with William of Normandy's invading army to England in 1066. He petitioned for permission to strike the first blow at the assembled Saxon army, and on receiving permission, rode out far ahead of the other horsemen. He was singing traditional songs of chivalry about Charlemagne and Roland and, while he sang, was throwing his sword into the air and catching it in juggling whirls. He dispatched a Saxon knight who came out, and then another. Finally he charged into the midst of the Saxon host, where he was cut to pieces.

The author of *Hagakure* would have understood Taillefer perfectly. The punctilio of asking for permission to be the first to strike at the enemy would be attractive to him, and the singing of traditional songs of chivalry of heroes of the past would not only establish him as a warrior of dignity and culture, but demonstrate that his voice was unaffected by any nervous tremor or tightening. This was reinforced by the juggling with the sword, recalling how the samurai, from the Kamakura times onward, used to perform the tea ceremony before a battle, the movements had to be made with perfect precision and any nervousness at once made itself apparent. Taillefer's determination to die would seem to be a useless loss of a brave man, but it demonstrated that among the Normans there were those absolutely undeterred by death, and indeed resolved to die in the coming battle. But Taillefer would have been relegated to an inferior status, as he was not serving the Lords of Nabeshima.

This last point may seem absurd, but in fact *Hagakure* was intended to be a local cult. For a long time, the book was not widely known in Japan. Marquis Okuma, one of the great statesmen who brought about the Meiji Restoration in 1868 and founded the famous Waseda University, remarked drily of it: 'It says that sages like Confucius, and our great heroes of history like Takeda Shingen, were only of the second rank, since they did not serve the Lords of Nabeshima. From this, one can judge the quality of the whole book.'

Anti-Bushido

The Meiji Restoration of 1868 might be thought to have initiated an anti-warrior movement, in that it put a final end to government by the military – or so it was believed at the time. The emperor was restored to his place as the true sovereign of the nation, as he had been in ancient times in Kyoto, but the restoration was carried out by the warrior class itself, or at least one sector of it. Also the presence of the emperor in the consciousness of the people did not prevent the rise of military rule in Japan in the twentieth century. The Showa era, under the long reign of the emperor better known in the West as Hirohito, was the first in which the Japanese ruler was a world figure; he was able to become such a figure because of the effects of the restoration of his grandfather Meiji.

Around the beginning of the present century there were three unrelated events which coincided to help establish the widespread view of a Bushido spirit of nobility and faithfulness even to death. One was Nitobe's book *Bushido: the Spirit of Japan* published in the United States in English (1899); the second was the first performance of Puccini's opera 'Madam Butterfly' (1905); the third was H G Wells, who that year brought out his story *Modern Utopia*. In this he has a short chapter concerned with the Plato-like 'guardians' of the 'Modern Utopia,' who are strong and noble; Wells calls them 'the samurai.' He later confessed that he was then under the spell of what he had read of the ideals and practice of the 'ancient swordsmen of Japan,' the high point of self-sacrificing loyalty to the community state. Some parts of his description of the training and austerities of his samurai read very like passages in Nukariya Kaiten's book *Religion of the Samurai*. This was also published in English; Nukariya was a famous historian of Zen and himself a most influential Buddhist priest. His book, first published in London, attracted considerable attention: it was the Zen of the Soto school, and though a few *koans* were mentioned, it did not have the overwhelming impact of Dr T Suzuki's much later presentation of Rinzai Zen.

The historian Yagiri Tomeo makes much of the fact that Nitobe's book was first published in English, and had an immediate success, quickly running to several editions. It was then translated into Japanese. Yagiri believes that Nitobe almost created the legend of the noble samurai, and especially the myth of *seppuku* as a voluntary gesture instead of a fictional dressing-up of what was in fact an execution.

In his highly skeptical and critical book, *The Aesthetic of Hara-Kiri (Seppuku no Bigaku)*, Yagiri Tomeo (1971) remarks that *Hagakure* used to mean a man who at the time of battle hid himself under the leaves, and Yagiri thinks the title of the book shows that it was in fact written to persuade perhaps rather reluctant samurai not to try to become chief retainers and finally seniors in the service of their lord but to die like madmen in battle, or in any other way that seems to be connected with the service of the lord.

In another section he says that he traveled to Canada and looked at the original manuscript of Nitobe's *Bushido: the Spirit of Japan*, and discovered that it was written in English and that it contained a good many alterations. After looking at the nature of the alterations and the corrections he says that it seems very likely that the book was written by a Canadian woman based on the accounts given her by Dr Nitobe. Yagiri believed it very likely that this manuscript was the original text of the book and was later translated and became famous in Japan because of the interest shown in it by foreigners.

In another section, Yagiri says that *Hagakure* was written in fact by a very ambitious man, who from childhood had the wish to become a high retainer of the feudal lord. He was a scholar and he became a librarian, and Yagiri says he was a poetry consultant who failed in his chief ambition. Yagiri postulates that after his retirement, when he was perhaps completely disillusioned with life and wanted to die, he decided to dedicate his book to people who wanted to achieve a form of fame from death.

Left: 'The Restoration of the Imperial Rule' by Murata Tanryo. The restoration of the Emperor Meiji in 1868 was a paradoxical political move. It was led by disaffected samurai. But they did not see their action as in any way treacherous to their social grouping; on the contrary, they sought to restore Japan's prestige by reinstating the emperor to what they saw as his rightful place as the head of the nation, instead of merely a cultural figurehead as had been the case for centuries.

Above: Emperor Meiji with his wife, daughter and his eccentric son and successor after his restoration in 1868.

Right: Ehon Taiko-ki shows a samurai applying a jujutsu armlock to a victim.

Far right: Emperor Showa, known in the West during his lifetime by his personal name Hirohito, at his enthronement in 1925.

Yagiri makes a good deal of the remark in Nitobe's preface thanking Anna Hartsthorne – 'my friend' – for 'suggestions.' He says that his impression from examination of the original manuscript is that it is to a considerable extent the work of a Western writer, probably Nitobe's future wife, made up from what he had told her from answers to questions. Yagiri points out that the writer had a very detailed knowledge of Western literature, as shown by the very many quotations and Western historical references. However, this might be met by pointing out that Nitobe was a considerable scholar of both English and German, and had lived many years abroad. It was then the fashion to reinforce a thesis with many quotations.

Yagiri also points to a certain vagueness that he discerns occasionally in connection with the descriptions of Japanese things, which contrasts with the exactitude of the knowledge displayed of Western things. He does not give examples, but he may have a point. For instance, take his description of *jujutsu*, specifically selected by him as one of the elements of samurai training. At this time the first demonstrators of *jujutsu* in the West, among them Yukio Tani and Taro

Right: A samurai prepares to commit *seppuku*. The samurai is shown with no second to decapitate him, either for reasons of artistic composition or to emphasize the ancient virtues.

Miyake, were performing what seemed miraculous feats against wrestlers and boxers. The naive audiences assumed that a small man like Tani could defeat his relatively huge opponents only by in some way paralyzing them; the principles of balance and technique were poorly understood as applied to antagonists. In fact there are methods of striking at what are called *kyusho* (vital points), but they are not easy to apply, and are not the central part of *jujutsu*. But here is Nitobe's description:

'Jujutsu may be briefly defined as an application of anatomical knowledge to the purpose of offense or defense. It differs from wrestling, in that it does not depend upon muscular strength. It differs from other forms of attack in that it uses no weapon. Its feat consists in clutching or striking such a part of the enemy's body as will make him numb and incapable of resistance. Its object is not to kill, but to incapacitate one for action for the time being.'

Certainly this description would seem to come from someone who had never seen *jujutsu*. It is much closer to what the West then conceived as a subtle Japanese art of combat, by which the weak could mysteriously defeat the strong. Nitobe's description shows ignorance of a fundamental principle of *jujutsu* – namely to turn an opponent's uncontrolled force against himself.

It can be shown, however that such beliefs were part of a general international view of Japan. This is reflected even in humorous literature. If we take a skit from as far back as the *Hood's Annual* of 1882, we find that most of the elements of the so-called myth must have been familiar to the general public. The scene is set in the mansion of a Japanese samurai, Ti Trai (Tea Tray). The story is illustrated with line drawings in a 'Japanese' manner, and Ti Trai is shown with his two swords. In his household are his wife, Satsu Mama (Satsuma), and an aunt, No Kanni (whose picture lives up to her name). Their daughter, Yama, is loved by a young samurai named Fuji. The parents like Fuji, but are enchanted by the Western glamour of Ay Kad (A Cad), who alone of all the characters wears Western clothes. His collars are described as 'throttling him impressively.' In this the writer shows himself well-informed – *hai-kara* (high collar) was then, and still is, a Japanese import meaning sophisticated elegance.

Outclassed, Fuji sits down to sharpen his sword for the 'Happy Dispatch,' watched by Ay Kad from behind a bush. Fuji endlessly tests the blade, always finding that it is not yet sharp enough. Auntie No Kanni steals up and, with a negligible glance at the fretting Ay Kad, whispers to Fuji, who goes off with her. No Kanni later tells Ay Kad that Fuji and Yama have planned a secret marriage that night; Fuji will come silently at midnight in a rickshaw, and Yama will steal out from a side door, in a dark veil. The priest in the temple on the hill has agreed to marry them. Auntie No Kanni tells Ay Kad that she will make arrangements to delay Fuji, so that Ay Kad can come at midnight instead. She warns him to keep silent and show no light, in case Yama sees his foreign clothes. The priest has agreed to marry them in semi-darkness.

Ay Kad duly comes, takes the little hand to help Yama into the rickshaw, but does not speak. They are married, and the priest unexpectedly says, 'Well, that's the second pair done.' Ay Kad's new bride slips off her veil, and he finds he has married Auntie No Kanni. Fuji and Yama were married an hour before. 'A dead sell,' mutters Ay Kad in English. When the parents find out, Ti Trai draws both his swords, but it is only to cut the wedding cake. This comical little tale, in a not particularly intellectual volume of 1882, shows that British readers were acquainted with some features of the Japanese scene, including *seppuku*.

And so we come full circle; well into modern times Japanese sages discuss the

Below: Samurai in full armor on the coast of Japan.

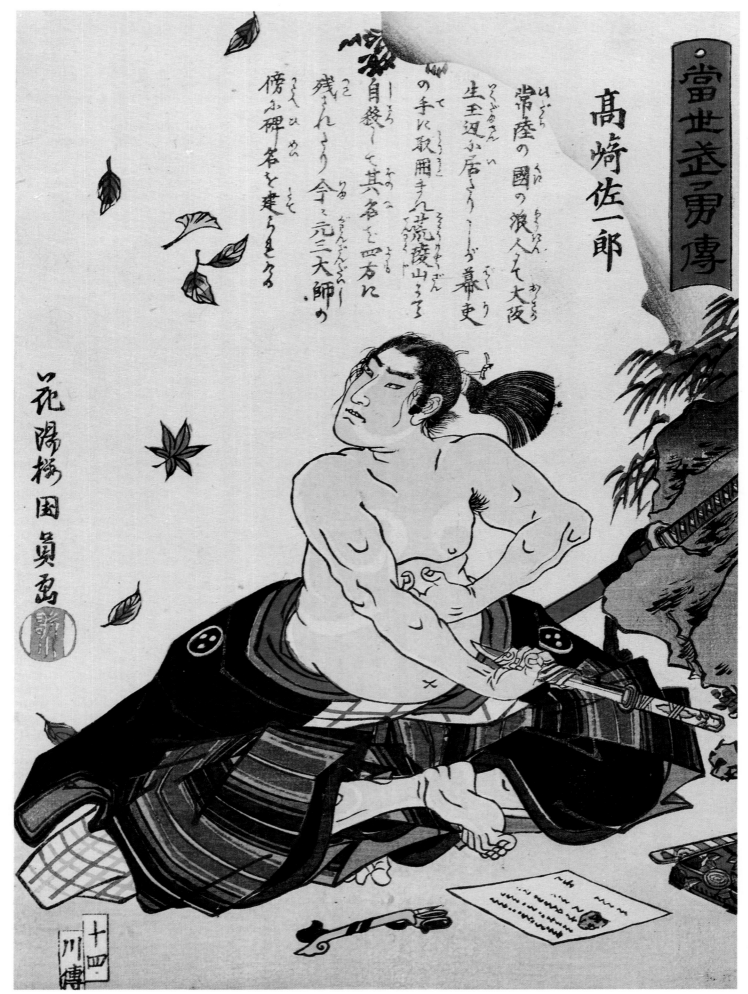

aesthetics of Bushido, the spiritual foundations of military tradition, and so on, as they had done in the eighth century. The practice of *seppuku* is a case in point. In his book, Yagiri Tomeo maintained that the idea of *seppuku* as a traditional Japanese method of 'happy dispatch' as it was called in the West by those gulled by an illusion, was a fiction. The cut was never in fact made, but the *kaishaku* or executioner took off the head of the condemned man when he stretched out his hand to the dagger. The idea of an actual cutting, said Yagiri, was built up by the Tokugawa propaganda machine as a terrifying threat, even to the extent of inventing accounts that it had actually happened. He points out that most of the cult was based on oral tradition, and was popularized by the dramatic performances of *kabuki*, popular novels and so on. He dismissed reports in *Hagakure* again as simply oral tradition.

There was a certain amount of speculation about the name Yagiri Tomeo, which read quickly in a certain way could mean 'Stop the Killing', but the book had considerable vogue as it discussed the ritual suicide of the Japanese author Yukio Mishima in 1970. Yagiri said that Mishima was a victim of illusion too. In fact, he said, *hara-kiri* was a form of execution, one which allowed the fiction that a samurai was not executed, but voluntarily killed himself as an act of repentance. The *kaishaku* simply 'helped' by cutting short the lingering death which would result from cutting open the belly. He points out that there are no large arteries in the abdomen and a cut would have to be very deep indeed (he gives the centimeters) to bring about a quick death. There was the possibility of cutting the throat as a conclusion.

One great obstacle to Yagiri's theory is the account by Mitford in *Tales of Old Japan*, published in 1871. Mitford attended the *seppuku* of Taki Zenzaburo as an official witness for the British Government, along with his fellow diplomatic representatives. Here are two extracts from Mitford's account of what he witnessed:

'. . . drawing near to the foreigners they saluted us in the same way, perhaps even with more deference; in each case the salutation was ceremoniously returned. Slowly, and with great dignity, the condemned man mounted on to the raised floor, prostrated himself before the high altar twice, and seated himself on the felt carpet with his back to the high altar, the *kaishaku* crouching on his left hand side. One of the three attendant officers then came forward, bearing a stand of the kind used in temples for offerings, on which, wrapped in paper, lay the *wakizashi*, the short sword or dirk of the Japanese, nine inches and a half in length, with a point and an edge as sharp as a razor's. This he handed, prostrating himself, to the condemned man, who received it reverently, raising it to his head with both hands, and

placed it in front of himself . . .

'. . . bowing once more, the speaker (Zenzaburo) allowed his upper garments to slip down to his girdle, and remained naked to the waist. Carefully, according to custom, he tucked his sleeves under his knees to prevent himself from falling backwards — for a noble Japanese gentleman should die falling forward. Deliberately, with a steady hand, he took the dirk that lay before him; he looked at it wistfully, almost affectionately. For a moment he seemed to collect his thoughts for the last time, and then stabbing himself deeply below the waist on the left-hand side, and, turning it in the wound, gave a slight cut upward.'

Yagiri points out that the phrase like 'bowing twice to the Buddha (high altar)' and 'then seating himself with his back to the Buddha (high altar),' are more appropriate (as he says sarcastically) to a description of the rituals at the beginning of a Thai boxing match. Then he seizes on the phrases 'looked wistfully, almost affectionately,' and adds: 'This is not a description of something he saw. He was told about the affair by someone else, or supplemented it from some Kabuki performance he had seen.'

But Mitford made a formal report to the Foreign Office, and the words of the report are almost exactly those of the account in *Tales of Old Japan*, except that the words 'wistfully, almost affectionately' do not appear in the handwritten report, and the account in the book has obviously been written to make it slightly more colorful and descriptive for Western readers. Here are two reports of what actually occurred as reported to the British Foreign Office by Sir Harry Parkes, the then British ambassador to Japan, and the formal witnessing of the event by Mitford:

Letter from Ambassador Parkes to Lord Stanley, 11 March 1868, Hiogo.

MY LORD,

In continuation of my despatch No 42 of the 25th ultimo, relative to the proceedings then pending in the matter of the Bizen outrage, I have the honor to report that Date Iyo no Kami the ex-prince of Uwajima, who is one of the leading ministers for foreign affairs in the Mikado's government, arrived at Hiogo on the 29th ultimo charged to offer to the foreign representatives the apology of the Mikado's government and to inform them that the execution of the principal offender would be immediately carried out at Hiogo.

On the 1st instant, Date Iyo no Kami met all the foreign representatives. He stated to us that the Mikado felt deeply pained that such a wicked outrage as he termed it, should have been committed upon foreigners just at the time that new relations with them were being initiated, and reforms being introduced into the administration of the country. The offense was calculated to bring discredit upon the Mikado's

WHY COUNT NOGI DIED: THE SOUL OF A SAMURAI

Is it a piece of Buddhistic pessimism when I say that life itself is a tragedy from which only death is deliverance, and that therefore death is not life's end, but the hope and beginning? It is, verily, often proved here that death is not a cowardice or act of negation; even as an apology it has the highest possible dignity. Certainly there are various degrees of intensity in feeling life's tragedy, according to personal temperament and circumstances, or to the nature of the age and race with which a man happens to bind himself. There are some who, appearing outwardly most rugged and insusceptible, are in their heart of hearts most tender and compassionate, and such an one was General Nogi, the famous Japanese soldier, known in the West as "the hero of Port Arthur," who committed suicide, or *junshi*—to use a Japanese word meaning a royal death, in following his master (the late Mikado) to the other world—on the very same evening when the Imperial hearse left the Palace.

Although it seems he already keenly realised the tragic side of life in his young day, and that, as he wrote in his will, he wished to find the opportunity of death ever since he committed a disgraceful act in allowing the colours of his regiment to be seized by the Satsuma rebels in 1877, I think that his great decision—I mean, his thought of suicide—was firmly formed during the late Russia-Japan War, or soon after that war. As the whole world knows well, he fought the hardest battle at Port Arthur, with many succeeding sad failures, and as a natural result lost many thousand brave young soldiers. He was criticised, even bitterly, by many in the Western Press: while he would not have feared the foreign criticism, how, he thought, could he see and face the fathers and mothers of those dead soldiers? In fact, he wrote the following lines when he returned from the field—making the so-called "Triumph" return:—

Hazu ware nanno kawo ka rofu wo min,
Seisen konnichi ikunin ka kayeru.

(What shame! Oh, what face have I to see their old fathers! 'Tis a "triumph" return; but to-day how many return?)

That was this brave soldier's saddest cry of heart. I can understand well why he placed his two sons—Lieutenants Katsusuke and Yasusuke Nogi—in the hardest, most exposed situation at Port Arthur; and, as he wished, they died the bravest tragic death. He could not have stood, above all things, against the criticism—if there was to be criticism—that his father's selfish love covered his sons from danger and death: it is said that he only smiled—not shedding even one tear (he acted differently in other cases)—when his last son's death was reported, and even forbade that his body should be put in a beer-barrel or orange-box, but commanded that it should be left on the field, to become a

prey of birds. It was in those days that the following popular song was sung in the streets:—

You cannot cry, saying that he was your only son;
Here is even one who lost both his sons.

That one who lost his two sons was, of course, General Nogi.

When he returned from the field, it was said he often confessed to his friends that he felt as if his heart's shoulders were lightened by the death of his sons, as he thought it was a punishment for his lack of tactics or wisdom in losing so many soldiers and making their mothers cry. "That was the little apology I could offer," he used to say. While the other generals seemed to be proud of their own war fame, and went round amid the banqueting and wine-drinking after peace had been regained, it was only General Nogi

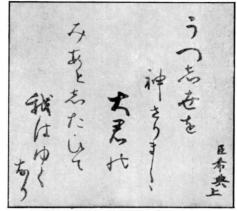

GENERAL NOGI'S FAREWELL "UTA" POEM
The verse, which is in the General's own handwriting, runs thus: "Utsushi yo wo, Kansari maseshi Okimino, Miato shitaite, Ware wa yuku nari." (After the great Lord who has passed from the floating world, I would go following his holy shadow.)

who shut his gate tightly against visitors, and hated and most bitterly objected to listen to and accept the words of praise. "*Sumanu*" was his usual word whenever the war talk, particularly on Port Arthur, happened to come up; that "I regret" was short, but by that one Japanese word General Nogi wished to express all things and everything of his true heart. When he told his family not to make the formal funeral service for his lost two sons, he thought that

the service would not be complete without the third coffin—that was himself; but to-day even the fourth one—that of Countess Nogi (what a great Japanese woman that was!)—has been added to the funeral of the Nogi family.

Why did not General Nogi die, if he had already decided to die, at the end of the war? That was because he was afraid it might be said that he had gone mad from the loss of his sons, and followed after them, and because, above all, there was the Mikado, who fully trusted in him, and to whose service his whole life was offered. Although he wished to die, to make the apology for once and all—I mean, to the fathers and mothers of the lost soldiers—he was so situated that he could not so easily die; and he was patiently waiting for the fit opportunity to make his life's final exit. I have some reason to imagine that he grew doubtful and suspicious of the true meaning of Humanity when his fighter's fame became greater and ever greater in the West; I believe he often asked himself why he was entitled to such a distinguished fame while he acted nothing but a series of brutalities at Port Arthur, although it was not from his own free will. This feeling—I mean, the distrust in general humanity—was intensified, I dare say, when he appeared in Europe in company with Admiral Togo a year or two ago, and was received with the greatest honour as the nation's hero; he became a thorough pessimist, and his pessimism was deepened when his beloved Mikado passed away. The only reason why he prolonged his life lay in the fact that the Mikado was living; he thought it proper and right to die with him.

If General Nogi's life-tragedy and his human side were clearly and intelligently told, I think that he would be more prized as a humanity-loving soul than as a "war-god." When we call him a true Samurai, it was because of his true love of peace: only the man with the real love of humanity can become the true fighter on the battlefield. General Nogi died as a protest against the modern tendency of imbecility and effeminacy, and as the encourager of the old Bushido precepts. He was right when his old Samurai heart grew restless and wounded from seeing the real fact that, not to China this time, but to Western nations, we were making kowtows and indiscriminately importing their literature and philosophy, even the dangerous individualism which would upset the Empire's spiritual foundation; and he saw enough, I fancy, to know that even the soldier class, who have promised life's whole devotion to the Mikado and his country, were growing to be lovers of money and Western luxuries, and I believe that he wished to warn us of the danger, and to point out to us, before it was too late, the true, only road we should follow, as Japanese. And for making that warning, he took the most terrible way in *junshi*, when our mourning hearts were gathered round the royal family.   YONE NOGUCHI.

---

government and could only be properly expiated by the signal punishment of the offenders. In accordance therefore with the laws of Japan, Taki Zenzaburo, the officer who ordered his soldiers to fire upon the foreigners, was sentenced to cut himself open and Hiki Tatewaki, the *karo* or minister of the prince of Bitzen, who was with the train at the time the attack was made, was condemned to a term of confinement for not having at once disavowed the violence of his men and endeavored to restrain them. These sentences, of which Date Iyo no Kami produced copies, had been made publicly known at Kioto, and he was now prepared to direct the execution of Taki Zenzaburo as soon as the details of the time and place of punishment could be arranged with the foreign representatives.

The latter expressed themselves gratified at the regard for justice which had characterized the action of the Mikado's government in this affair, they deeply regretted that it had devolved on them to demand that this severe example should be made, but were satisfied that in the end it would prove to be both a wise and humane measure. They left it to Iyo no Kami to name the time and place of execution, but requested that confiscation of the property of the condemned which sometimes attaches to such sentences might not in this instance be imposed. Iyo no Kami thanked

the representatives for their consideration and stated that their request should be complied with. It was eventually arranged that the execution should take place on the evening of the 2nd instant at the Temple of Seifukuji.

Execution by Harakiri or disemboweling is a privileged form of punishment which, as is well known, is common to the samurai of Japan. I enclose a valuable note on this subject which has been prepared by Mr Mitford, and which clearly establishes the judicial character of the process.

The sentence was carried out, in the manner arranged, in the presence of officers from each of the Delegations. Mr Mitford and Mr Satow attended on my part, and a full and forcible report supplied to me by the former, of which I enclose a copy, furnishes a complete description of this deeply interesting event. While drawing your lordship's attention to the remarkable fortitude with which the condemned man met his fate, and his public acknowledgement of the justice of his punishment, I should not omit to mention, as equally worthy of admiration, that on taking leave of the men of his clan immediately before the execution, he urged them to be warned by his example, and not to harbor any resentment against foreigners because he had suffered for attacking them.

In conclusion, I have to place before your

Above: The death by *seppuku* of General Nogi, the hero of the Russo-Japanese War, was an act of loyalty on the death of the Emperor Meiji, and was seen at the time, and can still be seen, as a samurai's death *par excellence*. The general chose not to die at the end of the war, in which both his sons were killed, but on the death of the emperor, his true lord and master.

Left: Samurai figures from the life of Miyamoto Musashi, a famous duellist who killed 53 people.

lordship translation of the letter of apology from the Mikado's government, which was accepted by the representatives as satisfactory, and a copy of the sentences which it encloses. Had it not been for the tragic event which has since occurred, and which I am reporting in another dispatch of this date, I should have been disposed to have anticipated from this proof of power on the part of the Mikado's government, and of their desire to cultivate cordial relations with foreigners, better prospects of security to the latter and of immunity from outrage by the two sworded class that have hitherto existed in this country. The catastrophe referred to however proves only too plainly that even this signal and recent example of punishment is not sufficient to deter that unruly and ferocious class from indulging in those feelings of savage animosity toward foreigners by which they have so long been actuated.

I have the honor to be, with the highest respect,

My Lord,
Your Lordship's most obedient
Humble Servant.

At the end of his report the ambassador included some notes on the various forms of *hara-kiri* (translated by Mitford) which were as follows:

1. Ceremony observed in the case of a Hatamono being compelled to perform Hara-kiri incursion:

Six mats are spread in an extensive yard in the prison, in front of the mats sits an *ometsuke* who fills the office of *kenshi* (sheriff), and with him are a *kashimotsuki* and a *kobimetsuke* (2d and 3d class *ometsukes*). The person who is to undergo *hara-kiri*, dressed in his clothes of ceremony is made to squat in the center of the mats. At each of the four corners of the mats is an official of the prison. Two officers of the governor of the city who act as *kaishakus* (executioners or rather seconds) take their place on the right of the condemned person. The *kaishaku* who stands on the left addresses the condemned person and, telling him his name and surname, offers to carry out his last wishes. The offer is accepted or not as the case may be. Then the condemned person bows to the sheriff, and a wooden dirk nine inches and a half long wrapped in paper and lying on a wooden stand of the sort used for offerings in temples is placed at a distance of three feet from the victim; as he stretches out his head leaning forward to take the dirk the *kaishaku* on his left hand draws his sword and cuts off his head. The *kaishaku* on the right takes up the head and shews it to the sheriff, and the body is given to the relations for burial. The property of the deceased is confiscated.

2. Hara-kiri as performed by a *Daimio*'s retainers:

Four mats are placed in the yard of the *yashiki* where the ceremony is to take place. The condemned person in his dress of ceremony is placed in the center of the mats, in front of which are a sheriff and his assistant. Two *kaishaku* stand one on the right and the other on the left, and four officials at the corner of the mats. The last will of the condemned is taken by the *kaishaku* on the left hand, and a dirk nine inches and a half long is placed wrapped up in paper before him. In this case the dirk is a real dirk, and the condemned person, stabbing himself on the left side of the belly below the navel, draws it across to the right side. When he bows his head in pain the *kaishaku* on the left-hand side cuts his head off, and the *kaishaku* on the right shews it to the sheriff. The body is given to the relatives to bury. In most cases the property is confiscated.

3. Self-immolation of a *Daimio* on account of disgrace:

When a *Daimio* has been guilty of a breach of etiquette or treason against the shogun, the whole family is disgraced, and it is not a matter in which an apology can be accepted. Accordingly the prince performs *hara-kiri*. When the time arrives he sends for his *karo* and delivers to them his last will and testament for transmission to the shogun. Then putting on his court dress, he first disembowels himself and then cuts his own throat. His retainers then report the matter to the government and a coroner is sent to investigate the affair. The retainers hand to the coroner the testament of their lord, and the coroner sends it in to the *Gorojiu*, who after consultation shew it to the shogun. If the prince's crime has been very heinous such as to merit the ruin of his family, by the clemency of the shogun half the property may be confiscated and the other half is left to the son of the deceased. In cases where the offense has been trivial, the family do not suffer.

In all cases where a guilty person of whatever rank performs *hara-kiri* before an investigation has been held and uncondemned, inasmuch as the crime can no longer be brought home to him, it is considered as not proven and his property is not confiscated.

Translated (**signed**) A B MITFORD.

Mitford's report on witnessing execution of Taki Zenzaburo.
Hiogo, 3 March 1868

SIR,

I have the honor to report that, in compliance with your instructions, Mr Satow and myself witnessed last night the hara-kiri or execution by disemboweling of Taki Zenzaburo, a retainer of the prince of Bizen, who gave the order to fire on the foreign settlement at this place on the 4th ultimo. A witness attended on behalf of

Left: Samurai with longbow and swords pose for a photograph taken in the 1870s. These men's sons might have seen Japan's defeat in World War II and heard the emperor's voice on the radio exhorting the people of Japan to 'bear the unbearable.'

each of the foreign representatives – seven foreigners in all.

The ceremony took place at 10.30 at night in the Temple of Seifukuji, the headquarters of the Satsuma troops. A crowd which lined the approach to the temple showed that the execution although conducted in private was a matter of public notoriety. The courtyard was filled with infantry and lighted by large fires and lanterns. We were conducted to a room in the temple where after some delay Ito Shunske, the provisional governor of Hiogo, came to us and took down our names, and told us that himself and another officer on the part of the Mikado, two officers of Satsuma, two of Choshiu and a representative of the prince of Bizen would act as *kenshi* – sheriffs or witnesses. Seven were appointed probably that their numbers might tally with those of the foreigners present. Ito Shunske further asked whether we had any questions to put to the condemned. We replied in the negative.

Below: The great warrior Takeda Shingen in belligerent stance. Takeda Shingen is remembered not only for his military victories but also as a wise lord of his domain in the province of Kai. As recently as the turn of the present century old people in the region would refer to him with affectionate respect as *'Shingen-Ko'* (Prince Shingen).

A further delay then ensued after which we were invited to follow the Japanese witnesses into the principal hall of the temple. On the raised floor, immediately in front of the high altar was placed a rug of red felt. The temple was dimly lighted with tall candles. The Japanese witnesses took their places on the left and the foreigners on the right of the raised floor. No other persons were present in the hall.

After an interval of a few minutes Taki Zenzaburo, a stalwart, noble-looking man, walked into the hall attired in his dress of ceremony and accompanied by his *kaishaku* and three attendant officers dressed in the *jimbaori* or war surcoat. The term *kaishaku*, I should observe, is one to which our word executioner is no equivalent: the office is that of a gentleman, usually filled by a friend or kinsman of the condemned, the relation between them somewhat resembling that of principal and second. In this instance the *kaishaku* was a pupil of Taki Zenzaburo chosen by the friends of the latter for his skill in swordsmanship. Taki Zenzaburo advanced slowly with the *kaishaku* on his left hand toward the Japanese witnesses and bowed before them, then drawing near to foreigners he saluted us in the same manner, perhaps even with rather more show of respect; in each case the salutation was ceremoniously returned. Slowly and with great dignity he mounted on the raised floor, prostrated himself twice before the high altar, and seated himself on the felt carpet with his back to the altar, the *kaishaku* crouching on his left-hand side. One of the three attendant officers then came forward bearing a tray on which wrapped in paper lay a dirk; this he handed with a bow to the condemned man, who received it reverently raising it to his head, and placed it in front of himself.

After another profound obeisance the condemned man in a voice of some emotion and with just so much hesitation as would be natural in a man about to make a disagreeable confession, but with no sign of fear either in his face or manner, spoke as follows – 'I and I alone unwarrantably gave the order to fire on the foreigners at Kobe as they tried to escape. For this crime I disembowel myself and I beg you who are present to do me the honor of witnessing the act.'

After delivering this speech, he allowed his upper garments to slip down to his girdle, carefully tucking his sleeves under his knees that he might die as a samurai should, falling forward: he remained naked to the girdle. Deliberately, with a steady hand, he took the dirk that lay before him. For a few seconds he seemed to collect his thoughts and them stabbing himself deeply below the waist on the left hand side he drew the dirk slowly across to the right. As the dirk reached the right side he gave a slight cut upward and then leant forward stretching out his head. An expression of pain for the first time crossed his face, and

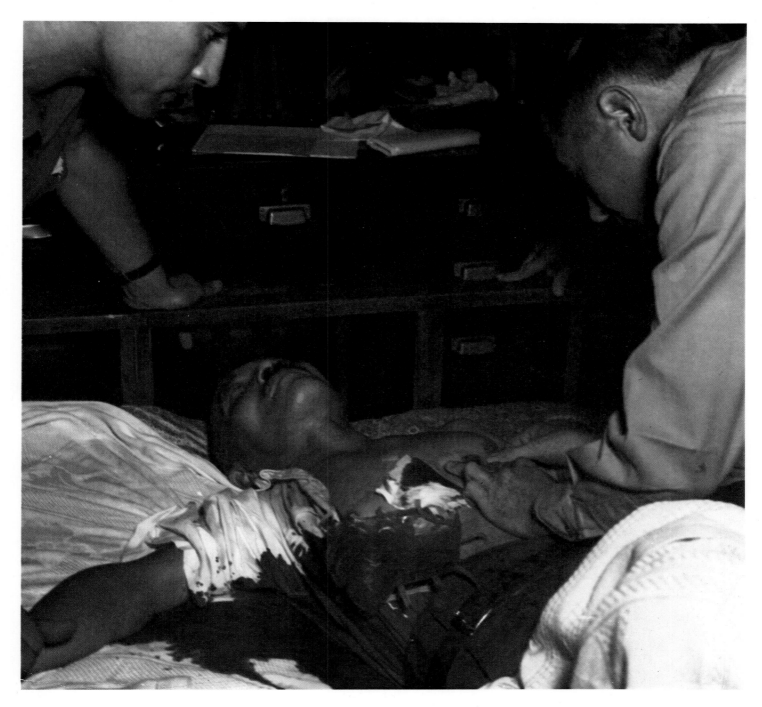

the *kaishaku*, who had been keenly watching every motion, sprang to his legs, and poising his sword in the air for a second, with one blow severed the head from the body. During a dead silence the *kaishaku*, having wiped his sword, bowed solemnly to the witnesses, and the dirk was removed as a proof of the death of Taki Zenzaburo.

Ito Shunske and the other representatives of the Mikado left their places and advancing to where we sat called us to witness that the execution had been faithfully performed. We then left the temple.

The ceremony, to which the place and the hour gave a most solemn effect, was characterized by that extreme dignity and punctiliousness which are the distinctive marks of a Japanese gentleman of rank, and it is not unimportant to note this fact, because it carries with it the conviction that the dead man was indeed the officer who com-

mitted the crime and not a substitute.
I have . . .

(*Signed*) A Mitford.
The above is a faithful description of the execution of Taki Zenzaburo.
(*Signed*) Ernest Satow.

Yagiri quotes sarcastically some of the minute regulations laid down for the *kaishaku*: that in a particular action of wiping the sword, the cloth must be taken away from the body, and not toward it. He says: 'One wonders why it had to be in that particular direction.' But this attention to ceremonial detail is not confined to *seppuku*, it is a general characteristic of other Japanese formal occasions. In fact the minute directions always given are supposed by some Japanese commentators to be an example of a strong feminine element in Japanese thinking.

Above: Tojo, Japan's ex-premier and a convicted World War II criminal, attempted suicide at his country estate near Tokyo. He is seen here being examined by Captain James Johnson, a US surgeon who was the first to reach him after the attempt.

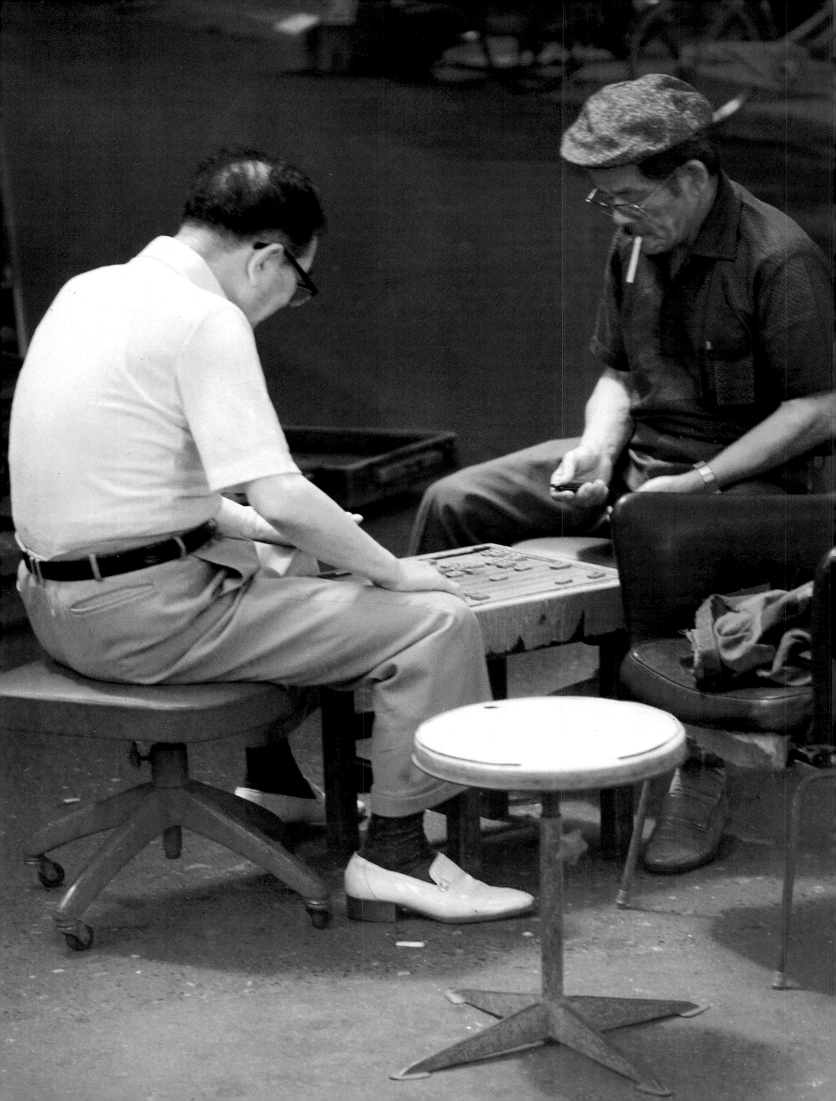

The Legacy of Bushido

Certain aspects of Bushido, surprising to foreigners, show themselves clearly in many of Japan's traditional arts and games. For instance the game of *shogi* (Japanese chess), has certain unique characteristics which appear in no other form of the game. Chess spread from India, to the West through Persia and the Arabs, and to the East through China and Korea to Japan. The game is recognizably the same, though the Chinese form has a river (which the elephant pieces cannot cross), cannon (which must fire over another piece), and an enclosure which the king-general cannot leave. In all the variations, except the final form in Japan, the pieces are gradually killed off until the king is checkmated (from the Persian *Shah Mat*, the King is Dead).

In the Japanese form, a piece which is taken is not dead. Instead, it becomes a soldier fighting for the side which has captured it. The pieces are not distinguished by color, but only by the way they face. When side A captures a side B piece, say a knight, that knight is put on a stand beside the board. At any time, in lieu of a move on the board, side A can drop that knight on a vacant square on the board, and it now points toward the enemy and functions as a side A piece.

Another manifestation of this fundamental, widespread willingness to 'sacrifice' oneself for a cause was seen a few minutes after noon on 25 November 1970, when the 45-year-old Japanese author Yukio Mishima committed *seppuku*. It took place in the office of the commander in chief of the National Defense Force Eastern Corps in Tokyo. The aim of Mishima and the four comrades from his private army called *Tate No Kai*, the Shield Society, was to arouse the members of the National Defense Force into action in order to effect a revision of the provisions of the constitution which had been 'degrading' them, and also so that they might be restored to the position of 'glorious duty' to defend the fatherland as the army of the emperor. Mishima planned this action as a samurai, and put it into practice with the determination to administer justice upon himself as a samurai when his mission was completed.

Mishima's death is understood to have observed the ancient formalities of Bushido prescribed for *seppuku*, but actually it was made complete when Masakatsu Morita, 25, a member of the Shield Society, assisted by ritually beheading him. Morita himself then performed *seppuku* and died when another member beheaded him.

Here are extracts from Mishima's appeal to the Defense Forces:

'We [Shield Society] dreamed of the true Japan, which no longer exists here outside Self Defense Force (SDF) compounds. Here we know the tears of true men, which we had not known since the end of the war. The SDF were the fatherland for us. It was the only place where we could breathe an air of intensity in the lukewarm Japan of today. The affection shown toward us [the Shield Society trained with the SDF] by the instructors is immeasurable. . . .

'We have seen Japan become intoxicated with economic prosperity, forget the fundamental principles of the nation, lose the national spirit. . . .

'We dreamed that today, the spirit of the true Japan, the true Japanese and the true samurai remains only in the SDF. . . .

'The first principle of the establishment of the Japanese army lies solely in the 'defense of Japan's history, tradition and culture, centering on the emperor.'

'Let us return Japan to its true form, and let us die for this. Will you only value life and let the spirit die? We will show you the existence of a value which is greater than respect for life. That is not liberty, and that is not democracy, it is Japan. . . .

'Is there no one who will fling himself at the constitution which has emasculated Japan and die for this end? If there is such a person, let him stand together with us, and let us die together. We are taking this action out of our great desire that you, who have the purest spirit, will be reborn as a man and a true samurai. . . .

'We will wait for another 30 minutes. Let us rise together for justice, and let us die together. Let us return Japan to its true form, and let us die for this. . . .'

Left: *Shogi* (Japanese chess) has many similarities to the Western game, both having originated in India. Each player has 20 pieces, distinguished by the ideographs drawn on them, and tries to checkmate his opponent's king; but in the Japanese game a piece which is taken becomes one of the opponent's pieces and fights against its former master.

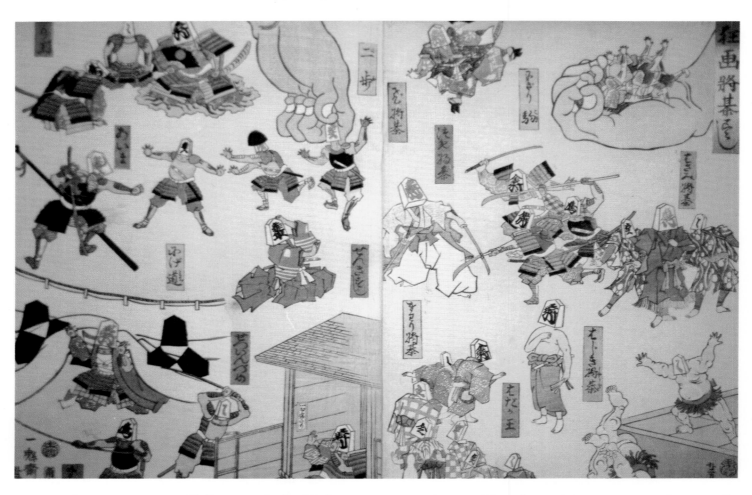

Above: *Shogi* pieces placed on human forms to illustrate their playing power.

Unfortunately for Mishima not a single member of the SDF agreed with him and after waiting 30 minutes he and his comrades committed *seppuku*.

Two other examples of 'sacrifice' involved Japanese soldiers: one was Sergeant Shoichi Yokoi who until 1972 had remained hidden for 28 years in the jungle on the Pacific island of Guam, unaware of Japan's surrender, and the other was Lieutenant Onoda, who spent 16 years in the Philippines until his surrender in 1960. Both men were praised for having shown the true 'Japanese spirit.'

The phrase 'Japanese spirit' originally meant a mysticism attached to the land, the imperial house and the people, combined with an aesthetic sensibility. The concept became Bushido, understood as the samurai's joy in dying in service of the feudal lord; this was later extended to service of the country as a whole, and finally extended to include Japanese of all classes, and not just the samurai who were less than 10 percent of the population. The suicide pilots who blew themselves up with their targets were showing this spirit. It was then called *Gyoku-sai* (literally, jewel

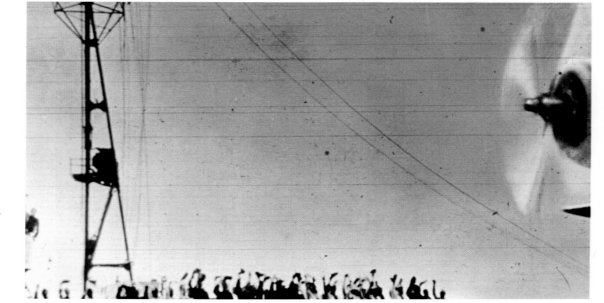

Right: A suicide plane takes off from a Japanese aircraft carrier in World War II.

Far right: Man playing *shogi* on the 81-square board *Nagoya*.

Above: A suicide plane hits its target.

crushed), deriving from an old Chinese phrase, 'Better a jewel crushed than a tile intact' – that is, better to die as a hero than live as a nonentity. The instructions to the Japanese armed forces in World War II made no provision for surrender. The view was, that if a soldier is permitted to surrender, he will not fight so hard as a man who knows that he cannot do so. Both Onoda and Yokoi probably made a picture in their minds of their superior officer – representing the emperor – giving them orders. They must have made up their minds never to question them; they had to be prepared to sacrifice themselves.

This willingness to sacrifice one's life for a belief, a cause, has always been part of Japanese tradition and deserves some further explanation. In the 1960s a number of books appeared with titles like *Medicine & Zen* and *Psychology & Zen*. The Zen posture is used by some Japanese doctors; for instance at a well-known hospital in Tokyo, which specializes in treating those who are overconscientious and neurotic. This is quite a common ailment in Japan, where people suffer from obsessive conscientiousness attitudes which are often felt to be imposed by society. One of the methods of treatment is to teach the patients how to sit in the Zen posture, in which the patient sits on the ground on a cushion with his legs crossed and one foot up on the opposite thigh. It can take loosening-up practice to achieve it, but when attained it is a stable position which the Zen practicants use as the standard meditation position.

The hospital doctors say they have found there is something about the posture which produces calmness. Dr Tomonari Suzuki has found that neurotics who have no interest whatever in Zen nevertheless find that this posture relieves their anxieties, so they master it. Dr Suzuki has remarked that some of his patients take to sitting like this for two or three hours a day. He also added that it is a great bonus for the nursing staff: they know where the patients are and patients do not need attention whilst they are sitting in Zen posture. Of course this it only one element in the treatment.

In the books on medical Zen, the Zen practice of meditating, especially directing the attention to the *tanden* 'Field of Elixir' just below the navel point, has been analyzed by some doctors, and noted by psychologists like Dr Sato Koji. One supposition for its success is that it may bring into

Left: A Japanese suicide pilot maneuvers his plane onto a vessel of the US fleet to cause maximum damage.

Right: Films depicting the valiant samurai of old are still highly popular in Japan.

Below: Sanjushi shrine was erected to commemorate the soldiers of the Russo-Japanese War, who destroyed the Russian fortifications at Port Arthur by carrying land torpedoes up to the walls and destroying themselves along with the fortifications.

tion for its success is that it may bring into play the para-sympathetic system, which has a calming effect on body mechanisms, such as blood pressure and muscle function. Some very elaborate and carefully controlled studies have been done on Zen monks in meditation and the electro-encephalograph, that is, the so-called 'brain waves,' do show a marked calming, but also interestingly also show a lack of habituation. The control subjects, who are mostly students, sit with their eyes closed, or half closed, and then a click is given and this produces a considerable upset in the 'brain waves' which lasts for several seconds. Then, at an interval when the next click is given, there is again an upset. But at the eighth or ninth regular click the upset is becoming small, and finally when the click is given it hardly disturbs at all. With the trained Zen subjects, the first click is noticed and there is a slight reaction, dying away very quickly. The same thing happens each time there is a click – there is slight reaction to the stimulus, no more but no less.

In one of the books on medical Zen, the author, a doctor, reported an experience.

The president of a very big Japanese company used to attend the medical examination of new entrants. At one point the candidates had to strip naked. The president would quietly come in and when the doctors had finished but before the entrants had dressed, he would say, 'Just a moment. Will you close your eyes and stand absolutely still. Right, you understand?' 'Yes, I understand.' Then the president would suddenly grab the entrant's testicles. If the man cried out or made a convulsive movement of defense, the president made no comment. But if the man was able to stand perfectly still, as he had undertaken, the president, although again making no comment, would mark him out for promotion.

A similar incident happened at the Battle of Tsushima in 1904. Admiral Togo was on the bridge of his battleship *Mikasa* during a very intense part of the battle. With him was his No. 2. In a critical situation, if one is tense it is said that the testicles seize-up. The No. 2, knowing this, turned to the Admiral and said, 'Sir, may I?' The admiral knew what he meant and just gave a nod. Whereupon the No. 2 took his testicles in

Above: A cartoon from a Japanese business magazine recounting the story of a young executive's plan to outwit the company's president in the share market.

swords for the abacus usually went broke.'

Many of the samurai did fail but, even today, Japanese companies still look to their past to see how they can improve their business both from an economic point of view and in personnel relationships. The *Nikkei* newspaper, the equivalent of the London *Financial Times*, is an example. The paper has frequently carried articles by a leading Japanese historian examining how feudal lords coped as leaders. Here is an abridged account by the historian Yu Tsumoto of the way in which Yoshimune Tokugawa (1716) managed his clan and its finances:

'After 10 years as head of the clan he [Yoshimune] eventually became shogun on the death of his elder brother Yoritomo. When he took over the clan [Kishu-han] they were in the red having borrowed heavily from merchants. But he introduced new, thrifty policies. He encouraged the samurai to look for different merchants and develop more ricefields. After five years they were out of the red. He then wrote a book about his policies, in which he said, "I am afraid of man more than anything else. There are things you cannot trust even to your parents, your brothers or sisters. It is even more dangerous to open your heart to a complete stranger," he said. "People like women, sake and money; and they like people that offer them these. But nobody gives you proper advice. It is just like giving sugar to children." '

Mr Tsumoto says that Yoshimune knowing this, tried to employ more honest people, and one such person was the judge Oka Echizen-no-kami. In order to find out what people were up to, the judge employed special police who used masseurs to gather information as they believed people were more likely to tell them things when they were relaxed. We are told that Yoshimune's observations of people were extraordinary: 'A good master should know how to use his servants. If he is stupid he sends a hawk to catch a fish and a cormorant to catch a bird; the good servants will desert him. If a man is too bright or too physically weak, if he likes sake, women and sex too much, or if he shows off, he should not be employed. The most important thing in being head of a clan is to have patience. A master should not blame his servants for their faults all the time. If a servant works hard you should give him more money or clothes. Treating them well will make everyone work hard. Ignore the servants and they will resort to women, sake, etc.'

Mr Tsumoto concludes that Yoshimune's policy is just like that of Japan's present-day chairmen.

It would be wrong to assume that it is only young businessmen who read these kind of magazines. They are openly read by staff at all levels at the office, whilst commuting or in tea-rooms, and I believe they are popular because they give each person an idea of how to relate and behave to others and this

his hand and was proud to find them hanging down and relaxed.

Even today you find numerous books, magazine and newspapers which analyze and relate the Japanese spirit to both Zen and Bushido, and in particular, Western companies have studied Japanese history to find out why Japan has been so economically successful. In the book *Images of Society* the authors write:

'Misunderstandings of Japan, are, and always have been, legion in the West. A good current example is the craze among Wall Street types for *The Book of Five Rings*, a classical manual on swordsmanship by the seventeenth century samurai, Miyamoto Musashi. Because the book was rumored to be a revelation of the spirit behind Japan's economic muscle, American industrialists have been pouring over the obscurity of its 96 pages in search of the samurai's power of positive thinking. Little do they know that in 1645, when the book was written, samurai were not allowed to engage in business, and those who did give up their is important in a country where the 'clan' feeling is still strong.

Although today one in three Japanese changes company there is still a strong sense of belonging to a group, which gives security and stability, both financial and mental. Until just after the war most people fought and worked for what they called the three Cs: country, company and clan (family). But during the past 40 years or so this order has changed. Now it is: company, clan and country.

A former Australian diplomat to Japan, Gregory Clark wrote a book, *The Japanese Tribe*, in which he said that Japanese turn instinctively to unique aspects of their society such as emperor worship, primitive nationalism, respect for power, and groups, and it is these things that still dominate attitudes of modern Japan.

In his book Clark goes on to explain how national movements (such as consumer groups) fail to forge strong links whilst local interests produce great power.

When I lived in Japan I remember a case in point. A large, well-known electrical manufacturing company found that during a slight recession it did not have enough work to keep all its employees busy. The management suggested that it would be a good idea if these staff went to the local town and helped keep it clean by sweeping the roads and pavements and collecting litter. Each temporarily redundant worker dutifully donned the company uniform and went about the task willingly knowing that what they were doing was not only a help to their community, but a job which could only reflect well on their company. No one thought it beneath him – it was for the good of the 'family.' Japanese company workers sing together, marry together, go on holiday together. Only last year several firms began to provide their employees with corporate mausoleums where their souls can be enshrined after death and rolls of honor can testify to their heroic battles on the company's behalf!

However, Clark says that, 'the Japanese find it difficult to relate to strangers, even in their own society, and the definition of stranger can be amazingly severe. For instance a 30-year successful career in a company does not wipe out the slight stain of 10 months in another company at the beginning of business life. When Japanese energies are directed outside the country, however, the Japanese can expand their awareness to involve the whole nation. It's the concept of the extended clan. Emperor worship appealed to this idea of involving everyone in a parent-child relationship.'

This need to relate can best be summed up by Hideaki Kase, an author and commentator on the monarchy, who spoke at a news conference about the recent death of Emperor Hirohito:

'The emperor is head of the Japanese people as a family. We do not really need a head of state, but we need a head of the family, or chief of the Japanese tribe.'

I do not believe the spirit of the Japanese samurai is extinct. What is more, if you read the Japanese television programme guides you would see that there are at least four samurai dramas a week to choose from. Perhaps therefore there is an appeal to something unconscious in the Japanese who watch them, ostensibly for mere entertainment. In the blood and thunder samurai dramas there are two types of protagonist: the furious, Yang, and the calm called Yin. In the traditional scrolls of the knightly arts it says: 'Before a contest, the Yin fighter is perfectly calm. His expression does not change, he does not defy the enemy, he does not stare at him wide-eyed, or try to intimidate him with feints. He does not come forward with little steps as if he were crossing a plank bridge, but walks as if on a wide road, with a perfectly normal posture. This is an expert who is hardly to be defeated.

'The fighter of Yang on the other hand has an expression which would seem to crush rocks, had an aggressive posture, stares wide-eyed and tries to intimidate the opponent by feints and glaring at him. He advances and retreats awkwardly. Because his heart is agitated he is weak.'

Which of these will be the model for the Japanese of the future?

Left: One of the many Japanese business magazines. Stories are both educational and entertaining.

Index

Figures in *italics* refer to illustrations.